Contributions in Afro-American and African Studies

EBONY KINSHIP

Ebony Kinship

Africa, Africans, and the Afro-American

ROBERT G. WEISBORD

Foreword by FLOYD B. McKISSICK

Contributions in Afro-American and African Studies, Number 14

GREENWOOD PRESS, INC.

Westport, Connecticut • London, England

Library of Congress Cataloging in Publication Data

Weisbord, Robert G
    Ebony kinship.

    (Contributions in Afro-American and African
studies, no. 14)
    Bibliography: p.
    1. Black nationalism—United States. 2.
Negroes—Race identity. 3. Negro race—Race
identity. 4. United States—Relations (general)
with Africa. 5. Africa—Relations (general)
with the United States. I. Title. II. Series.
E185.W436   301.45'19'6   72-847
ISBN 0-8371-6416-8

Library of Congress Catalog Card Number: 72-847
ISBN: 0-8371-6416-8
ISBN: 0-8371-7340-X (paperback)

First published in 1973
Second printing 1974
Paperback edition 1974

Greenwood Press, a division of Williamhouse-Regency Inc.
51 Riverside Avenue, Westport, Connecticut 06880

Manufactured in the United States of America

For Nathan and Dorothy Shamuyarira
and a free Zimbabwe

CONTENTS

FOREWORD

Ebony Kinship: Africa, Africans and the Afro-American is a needed document about a little known side of the Black struggle.

Robert Weisbord, its perceptive author, traces the relationship from the founding of the American Colonization Society in 1816, a hundred years before Garvey flourished, down to the present time. His well-researched chronicle tells the story of the many movements of the American Black to escape a racist society, to find wealth, peace and harmony, and to breathe an air of freedom. Many of these movements ended in deep disappointment for the initiators and participants; many others never even began.

There are chapters on the remarkable Marcus Garvey, among others, and on various African opinions about the Afro-American's yearning to return to his native land. The book ends with a review of the current "African Renaissance" which has taken hold in this country—an enormous interest in the politics, religion, clothing and hairstyles of Africa—partly as a result of the successful drive for independence among the emerging African nations, and partly from an increasing sense of self-pride and awareness.

What is important about Weisbord's book is that he, quite perceptively, views the myriad back-to-Africa movements and their corresponding counter-movements, and the countless arguments and even clashes among Black leaders in this country over the relationship they believe Afro-Americans should have with Africa, as all part of the same on-going struggle of oppressed peoples everywhere for freedom and equality.

There are indeed two kinds of Black power, as Weisbord suggests. One would place the protagonist outside the system, throw-

ing rocks at the mountain. That approach does not change the character of the mountain. The better approach, then, is to climb the mountain — to shape the tactics of the struggle to suit the changing tactics of the oppressors. Thus Weisbord, in describing the long, checkered and continuing history of the back-to-Africa movement, does not label any leader inconsistent or wrong. He simply views each of them as a wager of a fight — the same fight — according to his lights and in response to the nature of his opposition and the opportunities of his time.

I share the author's views in this and commend to you his book. It should be read by a wide audience. It will be particularly useful, however, as a text within our educational system — not limited, though, to "Black Studies" programs. White students desiring to learn to live in a multi-racial America must become aware of the historical aspects of the Black struggle as presented by Weisbord. Young people especially should learn that the struggle for equality did not begin in 1960, but when the first Africans were transported across the ocean on slave ships. Black leaders have been numerous, often unsung, since that time. The names of Frederick Douglass, Booker T. Washington and other early Black leaders are extremely popular names to both Black and white Americans; on the other hand Nationalist leaders, as Weisbord points out, like Garvey have not gained equal popularity. Many, uneducated as they were, displayed wisdom and elegance far surpassing that of their oppressors.

Weisbord sums up very well in his conclusion the potential value of the historical facts of which he writes:

Like Sisyphus, the king of Corinth in Greek mythology, who was punished in Hades by having to push a boulder up a hill only to have it roll back down time after time, the Afro-American has been repeatedly disappointed in his ascent to freedom. In the African he recognizes a fellow Sisyphus. Pushing together they might just reach the hilltop, perhaps even the mountaintop of which Martin Luther King spoke so eloquently.

Floyd B. McKissick
January 1973

ACKNOWLEDGMENTS

In the preparation of this book I have incurred numerous debts. I am especially grateful to Jean Blackwell Huston and Ernest Kaiser of the Schomburg Library in Harlem and to the staffs of the British Museum and the Public Record Office in London. A sizable debt of gratitude is also owed to Abner Gaines and Kathleen Schlenker of The University of Rhode Island Library. For their help I should also like to thank Richard Kazarian and graduate assistants Peter Homen, Edith Beckers, Bob Brunelle, and Sharon Blott. Without the secretarial skills of Julia Hoxsie, Betty Hanke and Barbara Jones, the typescript could never have been completed. The book was finished despite three adorable but frightfully active and demanding children.

EBONY KINSHIP

INTRODUCTION

Largely because of the agonizing Congo crisis which had assumed international dimensions, Africa was much in the news in 1961. In May of that year the prestigious *New Yorker* magazine carried an article about relations between Africans and persons of African descent in the United States. The main thesis of the article which was written by Harold R. Isaacs, a white scholar affiliated with the Massachusetts Institute of Technology, was that there existed "a deep pool of mutual prejudice between Africans and American Negroes."[1] Initially Afro-Americans often received warm welcomes in the land of their forefathers, but soon they discovered that they were strangers to a greater degree than they were brothers.[2] Isaacs contended that the American black was more of an alien in black Africa than he was in white America. Seeking freedom, comfort, and identity, "the Negro pilgrim in Africa finds himself not free at all, more than ever without solace and a sense of identity, fighting new patterns of prejudice and suffering the pangs of a new kind of outsiderness."[3] Without equivocation, Isaacs asserted that black Americans who went to Africa yearning for the acceptance denied them at home did not find it in Africa.

His principal focus was on the tribulations of black Americans who had gone to Africa in various capacities. For example, he dealt with the diverse complaints of black American females who were married to African men who were typically male chauvinists. Afro-Americans were irked by African inefficiency. They were eager not to be mistaken for Africans, Isaacs stated

3

dogmatically. He reported that one American black admitted that he found himself grateful for slavery: "It got me out of this and made me what I am instead."[4] In cataloguing the shortcomings of Africans, Isaacs listed condescension toward servants, feelings of superiority toward mulattoes, and snobbishness on the part of European-trained Africans toward Americans, black and white.[5]

About six weeks after publication of the lengthy Isaacs piece, a much shorter essay with essentially the same theme of African-black American discord appeared in *The Reporter*. Its author was Russell Warren Howe, a white journalist. The average African, according to Howe, perceived the American Negro as a stranger from a different tribe speaking a different tongue and living on a different and obviously higher plane than Africans. Howe also declared categorically that a black American was "more hesitant than a European or white American would be to integrate himself or sympathize with the African way of life."[6] Afro-Americans commonly accused Africans of being arrogant, the author asserted. Given this abundant mutual mistrust, Howe concluded, ". . . on the whole the policy of using a large number of American Negroes in African jobs is dangerous for all concerned—the employer, the usually discontented or disenchanted Negro, the natives, and the United States."[7]

Many of the tendentious points made by Isaacs and Howe were refuted in a trenchant rejoinder penned by Horace Mann Bond, the distinguished black educator and the father of Julian Bond.[8] In particular Dr. Bond faulted Isaacs' anecdotal methodology which relied on a small unrepresentative sample and led to unwarranted generalizations. Mere coincidence could not explain publication of the two articles, each accentuating reciprocal prejudice in African-Negro American encounters, said Professor Bond. He suspected that the editors of *The New Yorker* and *The Reporter* knew that the American reading public would enthusiastically greet elaborations on the stereotypic notion that blacks in America did not like blacks in Africa and vice versa. He suggested that white America's wish was father to its thought in this instance. An underlying belief

was that the United States was a better place than Africa even for blacks.[9] Black Americans in Africa would soon recognize this truth.

In a rebuttal printed in the *Negro History Bulletin,* Howe explicitly denied that there had been any cooperation between the two publications involved.[10] I assume that Messrs. Isaacs and Howe both acted in good faith. Indeed they were correct in claiming that black Americans who go to Africa are frequently disappointed. Many go with unreasonable expectations. Quite understandably others undergo cultural shock and are never able to adjust to their new, exotic milieu. This is not an uncommon experience, but it is not necessarily typical as Howe and Isaacs strongly imply. A substantial number of black Americans—no percentage or absolute figure can be adduced—have found in Africa that freedom of the spirit denied them in this country. This fact seems to be indisputable.

There would appear to be some substance to black suspicions that whites in certain circumstances do incite dissension between diaspora blacks and Africans—perhaps unwittingly out of ignorance, occasionally for political purposes. Take for example the provocative comments made by Vice President Spiro Agnew in July 1971 in the course of an overseas tour which took him to Africa.[11] Mr. Agnew drew invidious distinctions between African leaders he had met and black American spokesmen. The former had impressed him with their understanding and moderation; the latter he found to be complaining, unappreciative, and unreflective of the thinking of ordinary black citizens. Among the Africans the Vice President praised as dedicated, dynamic, and enlightened was Jomo Kenyatta. One can easily imagine how Mr. Agnew would have regarded the Kenyan in the early 1950s when he was interned for his role in the Mau Mau uprising and was characterized by a British colonial official in East Africa as a "leader unto death and darkness."[12]

The Howe-Isaacs-Bond Affair and the Vice President's gratuitous remarks which elicited strong objections from black American leaders should not simply be interpreted as black-

white confrontations. There have been whites who have evinced a sympathetic appreciation of African-black American dealings, recognizing positive facets as well as negative ones. Several white scholars—the names of Melville Herskovits and George Shepperson spring to mind most readily—have done seminal work emphasizing the historical ties between New World blacks and Africans. Moreover the subject, bound up as it is with the questions of identity and self-respect, is not academic for black people and has long produced sharp disagreement and caustic debate within their own ranks.

By the early nineteenth century, free blacks, despite their second-class status, identified with the United States. They were reluctant to refer to themselves as Africans because to do so might have strengthened the cause of those whites who favored their removal to Africa. Cultural arrogance combined with the European's psychological need to rationalize the slave trade had spawned pejorative stereotypes of Africa and Africans. These stereotypes enjoyed wide currency among whites and not infrequently were ingrained in black minds. Africanness was a source of shame to many blacks, but to a highly articulate and vocal minority, African ancestry was unquestionably a source of pride.

Their curiosity piqued by cryptic biblical allusions to Ethiopia, literate blacks in the antebellum period challenged the widespread theory that Africa had no history worth studying before the Europeans' providential appearance on the West African coast in the great age of exploration and commercial revolution. Operating on the premise that absence of evidence is not evidence of absence, blacks diligently and painstakingly sought proof of Africa's cultural leadership in the murky past.

Assertions about Africa's "glorious" history were not rarities in pre-Civil War black writing and oratory. Egyptian, Greek, and Roman achievements in antiquity were credited to African "blood and mind." African accomplishments in arts and sciences were said to have outshone those of Anglo-Saxons. David Nickens, a black orator speaking on Independence Day in 1832 averred that "Africa was the garden and nursery where learning budded and education sprang."[13]

My point is that blacks have never spoken with one voice about Africa's heritage or about their own responsibility to their ancestral homeland. Indeed the Negro American-African connection is a complex and multifaceted conduit. No single volume can do justice to all aspects of the historical and contemporary ebony kinship. This book is definitely not intended to be a comprehensive treatment of links, past and present, between blacks in the United States and their African cousins. It does not pretend to be exhaustive. Except for a glimpse of Jamaica's Rastafarians and the summary of British West Indian reaction to the Italian-Ethiopian war, it deals only tangentially with Caribbean blacks and their bonds with Africa. It does not deal at all with Latin American-African links. Much less attention is paid to African attitudes toward black Americans than Afro-America's outlook on Africa. This work omits consideration of the Atlantic slave trade and the debatable matter of surviving Africanisms. Another conspicuous omission is the saga of the Pan-African congresses, i.e., Pan-Africanism.* The roots of that racial movement are to be found outside the mother continent. Its birth, infancy, and adolescence all occurred in the dispersion. In this respect it has resembled modern political Zionism to which it was once likened by a pioneer Pan-Africanist, Dr. W. E. B. Du Bois.[14]

The first Pan-African conference, convened in London in 1900, was largely the work of H. Sylvester Williams, a lawyer from Trinidad, and Bishop Alexander Walters of the African Methodist Episcopal Zion Church. It was at that conference that Du Bois uttered his oft-quoted prophecy that "the problem of the twentieth century is the problem of the color line."[15] Du

---

*Following the example set by George Shepperson, I shall use the term "Pan-Africanism" employing an upper case "P" when referring specifically to this twentieth century movement. The term "pan-Africanism" written with a small "p" will be used in a generic sense to refer to a general sentiment of international black kinship and numerous short-lived movements with a predominant cultural element. The term "pan-Negroism" is used synonymously with "pan-Africanism." See George Shepperson, "Pan-Africanism and 'Pan-Africanism': Some Historical Notes," *Phylon,* 23, no. 4 (Winter 1962): 346-358.

Bois' pan-Negro outlook was later revealed in *The Crisis,* the journal of the National Association for the Advancement of Colored People, which he edited for two decades.

One of the central themes of negritude or cultural pan-Africanism has been black solidarity or, to use Colin Legum's words, "the wish to create a common identity between all those of Negro stock."[16] On this theme the talented American black poet Langston Hughes once wrote:

> We are related—you and I
> You from the West Indies
> I from Kentucky
> We are related—you and I
> You from Africa
> I from these States
> We are brothers—you and I.[17]

An African theme was also crucial to the literary movement of the 1920s called by some the Harlem Renaissance and by others the Negro Renaissance or the New Negro Movement. Countee Cullen, born in New York, the son of a Methodist minister, voiced his emotional involvement with Africa in the poem, "Heritage."

> What is Africa to me:
> Copper sun or scarlet sea,
> Jungle star or jungle track,
> Strong bronzed men, or regal black
> Women from whose loins I sprang
> When the birds of Eden sang?
> One three centuries removed
> From the scenes his fathers loved,
> Spicy grove, cinnamon tree,
> What is Africa to me?[18]

The central concern but certainly not the only concern of this book is back-to-Africanism in both its physical and spiritual senses. Although the black urge to return to the country of their forefathers is sometimes escapism, pure and simple, the repatriation movement is not infrequently a manifestation of

black nationalism and is treated as such by this writer. Conceived in despair and nourished in adversity, it is an American social phenomenon. That black Americans should have felt the need to find pride and power in an African dream is a serious indictment of the American reality. To ignore that dream is to distort the reality.

Because the book concentrates on the twentieth century, chapter 1 serves mainly as prologue. It sketches sundry back-to-Africa programs and personalities prior to Marcus Garvey. The contributions of Martin R. Delany and Bishop Henry M. Turner (each of whom is a candidate for the honor of being recognized as the father of black nationalism) as well as those of lesser lights, such as Albert Thorne, are limned.

Chapter 2 focuses on Garvey, the formidable Jamaican. Although short in stature, he cast a very long historical shadow. Garvey is treated not just as a repatriationist but as a pan-Negroist or pan-Africanist who thought of the black man's dilemma in universal terms. In this chapter, as in chapter 3 and others, much information has been drawn from English sources, namely, government records and newspapers which have been largely neglected heretofore. It must be remembered that Britain as a great imperial power at the end of the last century and during the early decades of this century wielded enormous influence in African affairs. Consequently, British archives are rich repositories of information about some back-to-Africa enterprises and other black American ventures in Africa.

Centrally, chapter 3 deals with the intense visceral response of blacks in the United States and the British West Indies to Mussolini's designs on Ethiopia in the midst of the Great Depression. In the months before the Italian invasion in October 1935, New World Negroes indicated in many ways their recognition of a black brotherhood with the Ethiopians. The assault in Abyssinia was regarded as an attack on all persons of African descent. Perhaps no event in the twentieth century demonstrated more dramatically the worldwide vulnerability of black peoples than Il Duce's foray into Ethiopia. For that reason the war was highly significant in raising levels of black and African consciousness in Afro-America and the Caribbean.

Chapter 4 portrays back-to-Africa efforts after Garvey's decline. Most of those efforts have been feeble and futile. Nevertheless it is important to note that small repatriation groups have continued to dot the black American landscape from the 1930s to the present. They range from the Negro Nationalist Movement and the Peace Movement of Ethiopia which originated in the dark days of the depression to today's African Nationalist Pioneer Movement and the Philadelphia-based African-American Repatriation Association. These are discussed in chapter 4 as are the Black Israelites who emigrated from the Chicago area to Liberia beginning in 1967. Some re-emigrated to Israel where their troubles with the Israeli government have been given much publicity by the popular media of late. This chapter also contains the generally skeptical statements on the desirability and practicality of back-to-Africanism made by black spokesmen, especially nationalists, in recent years.

Chapter 5 is the obverse side of the coin. Chiefly it addresses itself to the African response to black America, especially to emigrationist plans and projects. The bill introduced in the Kenya legislature in 1968 which if enacted would have granted automatic Kenyan citizenship to diaspora blacks is examined. African images of Afro-Americans and the experiences of Africans as students in the United States are also duly noted.

Chapter 6 entitled "Afro-America's African Renaissance" delves into the black quest for a positive identity, one defined not by whites but by blacks themselves. This quest entailed a reevaluation of African roots and the relationship of black America to contemporary Africa. In the 1960s Afro hair styles and African clothing became de rigeur and the burgeoning interest in Swahili instruction (and black studies curricula in general) led to internal disputes within the black community, not to mention black altercations with public education authorities. Paradoxically, black America's emotional involvement with and intellectual interest in Africa had reached its zenith at the very time when organized physical back-to-Africanism reached its nadir.

NOTES

1. Harold R. Isaacs, "A Reporter At Large—Back to Africa," *The New Yorker*, May 13, 1961, p. 134.
2. Ibid., p. 124.
3. Ibid., p. 105.
4. Ibid., p. 121.
5. Ibid., pp. 112, 126, 134.
6. Russell Warren Howe, "Strangers in Africa," *The Reporter*, June 22, 1961, p. 35.
7. Ibid., p. 34.
8. Horace Mann Bond, "Howe and Isaacs In The Bush: The Ram In The Thicket," *Negro History Bulletin*, December 1961, pp. 72 *ff.*
9. Ibid., p. 70.
10. Russell Howe, "A Reply to Horace Mann Bond," *Negro History Bulletin*, February 1962, pp. 102, 104.
11. *The New York Times*, July 18, 1971.
12. Since independence Kenyatta has been taken to task by some critics for being too pro-Western in his policies. On the other hand, the once-dreaded revolutionary has earned the respect of former colonial enemies. Whites in Kenya are apprehensive about their future after Kenyatta's death but believe they are safe so long as he lives.
13. Benjamin Quarles, "Black History's Early Advocates," *Negro Digest*, February 1970, pp. 4-9.
14. *Crisis*, 17, no. 4 (February 1919): 166.
15. Colin Legum, *Pan-Africanism—A Short Political Guide* (New York: Frederick A. Praeger, 1965), p. 25.
16. Ibid., p. 16.
17. Ibid.
18. Countee Cullen, *Color* (New York: Harper and Brothers, 1925), p. 36. By permission of the publishers.

1

BACK-TO-AFRICANISM BEFORE GARVEY

The idea of returning to Africa is a very old one in New World Negro history, as old as the slave trade itself. Occasionally, captured tribesmen jumped overboard during the infamous Middle Passage and attempted to swim back to Africa, rather than be slaves in the Americas. Slave songs, especially spirituals, gave expression to the blacks' longing for their fatherland, though Africa was not specifically mentioned, lest masters sense dissatisfaction among their bondsmen.[1]

Opportunities for the masses of blacks to realize their African dream were few during the era of slavery. Nevertheless, there were movements that had as their main objective the repatriation of Negroes. Of necessity, before the Civil War, most of these were initiated, organized, financed, and controlled by whites. The launching in 1816 of the American Colonization Society was directly traceable to the growth of a "free" Negro population.[2] Support for colonization was prompted in some persons by compassion for the wretched lot of the free blacks, whose freedom was qualified by political inequality, economic oppression, and social discrimination. In others, and they were the overwhelming majority, the motives were anything but humanitarian. There was fear that the presence of free Negroes could set a dangerous example for those still in bondage. For

some whites the thought of living in the same society with free nonwhites, whom they still regarded as contemptible because of their blackness, was obnoxious. Thus, for reasons both altruistic and more importantly racist, the American Colonization Society worked actively for the settlement of Negroes in Africa; and through its efforts Liberia was founded. Many nationally prominent whites including Abraham Lincoln viewed colonization as an integral part of any formula that would resolve the slavery quandary. In fact the Emancipation Proclamation stipulated that the effort to colonize, with their consent, persons of African extraction on this continent or elsewhere would go forward.

Intermittently since the Civil War, white proposals have been made to transport Negroes to Africa, either on a voluntary or involuntary basis. These have usually originated with outspoken segregationists, for example, Senator John Morgan of Alabama in the 1890s and Senator Theodore Bilbo of Mississippi in the 1930s. In the 1970s the program of the National States Rights party calls for enactment of a law that would strip blacks of their citizenship, reward those willing to repatriate voluntarily with cash bonuses and prefabricated homes in Africa, and forcibly deport those Afro-Americans unwilling to go to Africa. The latter would receive no financial reward.[3]

White-sponsored schemes of repatriation have formed only one kind of African colonization. It is the other kind, the back-to-Africa movements promoted and directed by blacks themselves, that is the focus of this work. Admittedly, at various points the two types of movements overlapped, and there was often cooperation between whites who favored the return of blacks to Africa and Negroes who advocated the same solution to the race problem.

Financial need often compelled black repatriationists to cooperate with white segregationists. In the twentieth century strange bedfellows such as Marcus Garvey and the Ku Klux Klan were produced by their mutual realization that they agreed on the desirability of blacks and whites going their separate ways.

Today a white demonstrator carrying a placard bearing the slogan "Back-to-Africa" would unhesitatingly be labeled a racist even if he advocated voluntary repatriation. A black carrying precisely the same placard would be called a black nationalist. The explanation for this paradox is to be found in the melancholy history of race relations in the United States. The quest for an African Zion by diaspora Africans is a fascinating aspect of that history.

Prior to the American Revolution, Newport, Rhode Island, had the dubious distinction of being America's chief slave-trading port. Two years after the Constitution was drafted in Philadelphia, a contingent of free blacks from Newport made preliminary inquiries about resettlement in West Africa. They were particularly curious about opportunities in Sierra Leone, the newly established sanctuary for blacks whose pitiful lot in England had touched the heart of philanthropist Granville Sharp, who became a leading sponsor of the West African asylum. In 1795 the Newport Afro-Americans dispatched a representative to the new colony to observe conditions firsthand. Land was proferred by Governor Zachary Macaulay but the offer was not accepted.[4]

Sierra Leone also fired the imagination of New Englander Paul Cuffe. A half-Negro, half-Indian convert to the Quaker faith, Cuffe was responsible for a noteworthy attempt to repatriate American blacks in the first quarter of the nineteenth century. Cuffe (sometimes spelled Cuffee) who had been born on Cuttyhunk Island, Massachusetts, in 1759 was to combine stereotypic Yankee business practicality with a genuine humanitarian concern for his fellow blacks. He was no stranger to racial bigotry having personally experienced discrimination both north and south of the Mason-Dixon line. Deeply religious himself, Cuffe professed a desire to enlighten Africans about the blessings of Christianity and on New Year's Day in 1811 he sailed from Philadelphia for Sierra Leone. He found conditions in the British colony "inviting." The soil was fertile and the climate suitable for the cultivation of tropical products.[5] Opportu-

nities for trade between West Africa and the United States excited Cuffe the more so because of his wishful thought that legitimate commerce might supplant the barbarous slave traffic.

The outbreak of the War of 1812 put a damper on Cuffe's ambitious plans but only temporarily. As soon as hostilities ceased, Cuffe again sailed for Sierra Leone. With him were thirty-eight black American repatriates, eighteen adults and twenty children. Upon his return to Massachusetts in 1816, Cuffe received a number of letters from blacks curious about prospects in Sierra Leone. He was also contacted by Robert Finley, a white Presbyterian minister from New Jersey who was instrumental in founding the American Colonization Society.[6] Indeed Cuffe's much publicized journey of repatriation may have provided a fillip to the formation of that body.[7]

Cuffe's untimely death in 1817 abruptly ended his evangelical, mercantile, and back-to-Africa undertakings. Although his may be fairly regarded as the first serious organized repatriation movement, there was nothing of the black nationalist in Cuffe. He was interred in the Society of Friends cemetery in Westport, Massachusetts, segregated from the whites buried in that graveyard.

Following in the footsteps of Cuffe was Daniel Coker, an ordained minister who, with American Colonization Society support, journeyed to Sierra Leone in February 1820. As the ship departed, carrying ninety blacks away from the United States, thousands of persons, blacks and whites, crowded the wharves. Coker and his party anchored in Freetown on March 9 after a pleasant voyage. Nathaniel Peck, a companion of Coker's, undoubtedly spoke for many of the passengers when he thanked God because he was "now treading the soil of my mother country." As was so often the case at least where repatriation *leaders* were concerned, the wish to evangelize the heathen African population provided as strong an impetus as the search for freedom, dignity, and material well-being. Coker urged his black brethren in the United States to "come, and bring ventures, to trade, etc., and you may do much better than you can possibly do in

America, and not work half so hard." But at the same time he wrote of a great and challenging work: "Thousands and thousands of souls here, to be converted from Paganism and Mahometanism [*sic*] to the religion of Jesus." Coker, a man of God, said that he expected to give his own life to "bleeding, groaning, dark, benighted Africa" and he did.[8]

Virginia-born Lott Cary was another colonizing missionary. He went out to West Africa in 1821. Of paramount interest to Cary, a Baptist preacher, was the marvelous opportunity to preach the gospel of Jesus Christ to the "poor Africans." He longed to lead "Africa's sons out of the devil's bush." The dark continent was able to lure Cary away from the land of his birth for another significant reason: his experience with racism in the United States. Cary once wrote: "I am an African; and in this country, however meritorious my conduct and respectable my character, I cannot receive the credit due to either. I wish to go to a country where I shall be estimated by my merits not by my complexion."[9]

As long as they lived, some blacks nurtured the hope of returning to Africa. Newport Gardner who had been wrenched from his native land at the tender age of fourteen did not realize his hope until he was eighty years old. In 1825 Gardner who had achieved freedom in the 1790s had raised enough money to finance a journey to West Africa for himself and a covey of like-minded followers. At the very end of December this platoon of restive Rhode Island blacks sailed out of Boston harbor on board the brig *Vine*. Their destination was Liberia. Gardner, the octogenarian, manifested youthful exuberance. He was emigrating to Africa, he explained, "to set an example to the youth of my race: I go to encourage the young. They can never be elevated here; I have tried it for sixty-years—it is in vain." And so Newport Gardner departed, but his new life in West Africa was ephemeral for he died within half a year of arriving.[10]

A more reluctant back-to-Africanist was John B. Russwurm. Russwurm, a graduate of Bowdoin, was one of the first Afro-Americans to earn a degree from a college in the United States.

By the late 1820s he had made something of a name for himself as a journalist. His vehicle was the *Freedom's Journal* which he founded in 1827. Initially Russwurm took a jaundiced view of colonization but he experienced a dramatic change of heart. His conversion to back-to-Africanism which was complete by 1829 engendered much bitterness on the part of stay-at-homes, his erstwhile allies. Prolonged residence in the United States was destructive of black ambition, Russwurm concluded. He declared that he knew of "no other home for the man of color, of republican principles, than Africa." Russwurm quickly matched word with deed and migrated. During his extended residence in Liberia, Russwurm served as a superintendent of schools and as editor of the *Liberia Herald* which he established. Until his death in 1851, he was governor of the Cape Palmas colony sponsored by the Maryland State Colonization Society.[11]

Despite Paul Cuffe, Daniel Coker, Lott Cary, Newport Gardner, and John Russwurm, there was nothing in the first half of the nineteenth century that could be considered an emigrationist groundswell—not by any stretch of the imagination. Opinion among the quasi-free black population on this sensitive question was sharply divided and there was no love lost between the back-to-Africanists and their opponents, the stay-at-homes. Actually few subjects inflamed northern black passions to the degree that emigrationism did. Discussion was normally acrimonious, exchanges usually acerbic.

Preeminent among the anti-emigrationists was Frederick Douglass, unquestionably one of the most remarkable Americans, black or white, in the last century. Douglass, an exslave who became a leading black abolitionist, was persuaded that the destiny of the black American was tied for better or for worse to that of the white American. "It is idle—worse than idle," he asserted in the pages of his newspaper, *The North Star,* in November 1849, "ever to think of our expatriation, or removal. . . . We are here and here we are likely to be. To imagine that we shall ever be eradicated is absurd and ridiculous . . . this is our country."[12]

To the stay-at-homes, withdrawal to Africa betokened a surrender to bigotry. It signified complicity with the American Colonization Society. Furthermore, the sweat and blood of blacks had built America. Leaving was tantamount to apostasy.

Pittsburgh's Afro-Americans in September 1831 had proclaimed that the United States was their only true and proper home. "Here we were born—here bred—here are our earliest and most pleasant associations—here is all that binds man to earth, and makes life valuable."[13] They pledged their lives, fortunes, and sacred honor not to back an African colony. Any black person who permitted himself to be colonized in Africa or elsewhere was branded a traitor by the Pittsburgh blacks who were explicitly reacting to emigration as the brainchild of the Negrophobe American Colonization Society. Black separatists who wanted to flee the United States were not viewed as nationalists proud of their race but as naive cowardly dupes of the white man.

For decades association with the racist American Colonization Society continued to taint emigrationism even when initiated by blacks themselves. In 1869 a veritable hornet's nest was stirred up at a black national convention by a proposal to confer honorary membership on a former president of Liberia, J. J. Roberts. To great laughter a delegate from Pennsylvania said of Roberts, "He ran away to Liberia in the time of our need, and hid himself in the swamps of Liberia and cried Colonization." A Mr. Downing added that he had a high personal regard for Roberts, "but to admit him as an honorary member, with his connections, and sympathies with the Colonization Society, so prominent, would be accepted by that society and the American people, as an endorsement by the Convention of the American Colonization Society."[14]

Back-to-Africanism had languished in the 1830s and 1840s. However, new vitality was given to the emigrationist concept around mid-century when the goal of full citizenship for free blacks seemed unattainable and the slavocracy won a resounding legislative victory. Ample reason for black pessimism was pro-

vided by passage of the Fugitive Slave Act of 1850. Under the law those persons accused of being fugitives were denied jury trials. Instead, cases were adjudicated at hearings and the alleged fugitive was forbidden to testify in his own behalf. Ex post facto in nature, the statute made possible the apprehension of slaves who had run away years before the measure was enacted into law. The entire enforcement procedure was prejudiced against the black man. Hearings officers were induced to find for slave owners by that section of the law which stipulated that they would receive a five-dollar fee for rendering a verdict in favor of the black defendant but would get a ten-dollar fee in the event they found for the claimant.[15] All that remained was for the judiciary to state that persons of African descent were not citizens of the United States and were incapable of becoming citizens, that they were of an inferior order and had no rights which a white was bound to respect. This was precisely what the Supreme Court was shortly to do in the infamous Dred Scott decision.

Among other things, passage of the Fugitive Slave Act had sharply escalated black emigration to neighboring Canada. This legislative reverse, a stinging rebuke to the anti-slavery cause, coupled with the declaration of independence by Liberia in 1847, caused a number of black leaders to rethink their previously hostile posture on the issue of returning to Africa.

One such leader was Henry Highland Garnet, a militant abolitionist who in 1843 had called upon the slaves to rise up and destroy the slavocracy. In a discourse delivered on February 14, 1848, in Troy, New York, Garnet observed that it was too late to separate the white and black people of the New World. Colonization of a whole race to the shores of Africa was out of the question. "We are planted here," he remarked. America was his home, his only home, Garnet told the assemblage. He loved the good in her institutions but the stain of slavery had to be expunged.[16]

Garnet's opposition to colonization was not nearly as immutable as his Troy listeners might have supposed. In January 1848

he had written to Frederick Douglass, "I would rather see a man free in Liberia than a slave in the United States."[17] As opinion on the slave question became polarized, Garnet came to espouse emigration as the means to economic and political advancement. California, Central America, Mexico, and West Africa were all possible areas for black settlement.

Freedom in a distant asylum was not all that Garnet desired. There was a nationalist strain in his thinking. He yearned for "a grand center of Negro nationality from which shall flow the streams of commercial, intellectual, and political power which shall make colored people respected everywhere."[18] Circumstances required Garnet to accept white assistance which he did in 1858 to establish the African Civilization Society of which he became president. Garnet's society became the whipping boy of a number of black abolitionists who were hostile to colonization.

Shortly before his death, Garnet, the former stay-at-home, expressed a wish to "just reach the land of my forefathers."[19] In 1881 he was designated minister to Liberia, but three months after he arrived to take up his post he passed away.

Garnet's turnabout on the repatriation issue was not unique. Martin R. Delany was another former stay-at-home. Delany was something of a nineteenth century *uomo universale*. During his lifetime he was a physician, a soldier, an explorer, a jurist, an editor, and an author. In 1843 he founded *The Mystery,* an antislavery weekly aimed at the "Moral Elevation of the Africo-American and African race, civilly, politically, religiously. . . . " His racial outlook was truly pan-African. This was reflected in the spectrum of black luminaries for whom he named some of his children: Alexandre Dumas, the French mulatto writer; Toussaint L'Ouverture, the father of Haitian independence; and Faustin Soulouque, a Haitian emperor. He named another Ramses Plácido in honor respectively of the Egyptian pharoah and one of Cuba's outstanding poets, a free mulatto during the slave era. Contemporaries recognized that Delany was black-minded to a high degree. Frederick Douglass,

with whom Delany had worked on *The North Star,* is reported
to have said on one occasion that he was thankful to God simply
for making him a man "but Delany always thanks Him for making him a Black Man."

Delany felt an emotional tie to the United States which he
was loath to sever. In 1852 he wrote

Our common country is the United States. Here were we born, here raised and
educated; here are the scenes of childhood; the pleasant associations of our
school going days; the loved enjoyments of our domestic and fireside relations,
and the sacred graves of our departed fathers and mothers, and from here will
we not be driven by any policy that may be schemed against us.

We are Americans, having a birthright citizenship—natural claims upon the
country—claims common to all others of our fellow citizens—natural rights,
which may, by viture of unjust laws be obstructed, but can never be annulled.[20]

Thus Delany claimed to dearly love America but the feeling
was not reciprocated. America detested blacks. Passage of the
Fugitive Slave law in 1850 was the culmination of that prejudice
and impossible for Delany to accept. It degraded colored people
and rendered free blacks even more insecure than black bondsmen. Their rights as citizens had been declared forfeit. Emigration offered the best remedy, concluded Delany, who had frequently censured the African colonization movement.

In a book which Delany penned in less than one month and
published himself in 1852, he rejected Liberia as an acceptable
destination for black American exiles. Liberia, he asserted, was
not truly an independent country but "a pitiful dependency" of
the American Colonization Society. Delany strongly objected to
Liberia as the product of a slaveholders' conspiracy to purge
the United States of its African population. Liberia was also
unappealing because of its unhealthy geographical position.[21]

Alternatively, Delany favored emigration to certain parts of
the Americas. Canada was becoming a satellite of the United
States and might even be annexed; consequently it would not
do as a refuge for blacks. The future of the Afro-American was
in Central and South America and in the West Indies. Details
were spelled out in Delany's book with the sesquipedalian title,

The Condition, Elevation, Emigration and Destiny of the Colored People of the United States Politically Considered.
In direct contradiction of one of his major theses, Delany in the appendix of his book propounds a project for an expedition to East Africa which he considers the choicest area of the continent. Prior to the completion of the Suez Canal in 1869, East Africa was somewhat inaccessible to Europeans; but England and France, in particular, Delany speculated, would profit from trade with a black settlement there. Using the vocabulary of black nationalism, Delany argued that Afro-Americans constituted a nation within a nation, that they were a distinct nation distinguished by complexion. Blacks had to establish a "National Position" for themselves and eastern Africa was the place for a nation to rise up.[22]

How can one reconcile Delany's preoccupation with an asylum for blacks in the western hemisphere as enunciated in the text and the East African project set forth in the appendix? Theodore Draper attributes the inconsistency to the haste with which the book was written.[23] This is unlikely. Fickleness would be too facile an explanation. Delany's publicly stated aversion to a West African Zion, especially one in Liberia, was probably rooted in the desire to avoid complicity with an African colonization movement under the patronage of white racists. Remote East Africa was not associated with the American Colonization Society. As fate would have it though, Delany's future enterprises in Africa were actually in the west and not in the east.

In 1854 he submitted a "Report on the Political Destiny of the Colored Race on the American Continent" to the national emigration convention of black people which met in Cleveland. At that conclave, from which opponents of emigration were barred, colonization to the eastern hemisphere was explicitly discountenanced. The body was ostensibly determined to narrow the emigration options to the West Indies, Canada, Central and South America.[24] Theoretically no individual who might even raise the subject of emigration to Asia, Africa, or Europe was admitted to the convention. Yet, in the call issued for the con-

vention, it was stated that this restriction was not relevant to "personal preferences or individual enterprise: but to the great question of national claims to come before the Convention." Not only were delegates in actuality "the leading advocates of the regeneration of Africa," but, according to Delany, in their secret sessions they made Africa their "most important point of dependence." In other words, Africa was being held in reserve.[25]

Owing in large measure to the accounts of West Africa provided by explorers in the 1850s, Delany's enthusiasm for the "dark continent" was heightened considerably. Five years after the Cleveland meeting, Delany served as the chief commissioner of an exploring party sent to the Niger valley. During those five years there had been no improvement in a situation described in 1854 as one of "disappointment, discouragement, and degradation." The question was not whether conditions could be bettered by emigration, but whether they could possibly be made worse.

The board of commissioners, established by the Cleveland convention which sponsored the Niger exploring party, saw the primary object of the expedition as scientific. It is obvious that Delany and his companions had a number of long-range goals in mind. One was to promote the cultivation by black American emigrants of cotton and other slave-grown products. Success in that endeavor, it was hoped, would diminish the profits of slavery and encourage the slave owners to manumit their slaves. A second goal was to evangelize and civilize the Africans. As has already been indicated, this motive, this ebony version of Kipling's white man's burden, this *mission civilisatrice* was present in the majority of nineteenth-century back-to-Africa movements. A third objective of the 1858 undertaking was to find a haven for black people where they could develop their faculties. In the document authorizing the journey, the sponsors restated their opposition to emigration to Africa but added that nothing in the instrument was intended to limit the rights of the members of the expedition to negotiate for territory on their

own.[26] Though the privilege of settling was obtained in treaties signed by West African chiefs, no emigration resulted from Delany's labors.

In the years preceding Fort Sumter, black spokesmen were more reluctant to rule out emigration to Africa or elsewhere as a solution. Secession and the ensuing hostilities were a setback to the back-to-Africa movement, but certainly not a deathblow.[27] The Civil War raised the hopes of Negroes in America: the fratricidal conflict would bring them freedom, and freedom would be accompanied by equality. Freedom was achieved, at least under the law; but the hankering for equality was callously disregarded. By the end of the postwar period of Reconstruction (1877), in the ranks of the emancipated, but still impoverished and persecuted, southern Negroes, there was much disillusionment with the American dream. Consequently, the impulse to flee manifested itself from time to time. Almost inevitably the African dream was reborn.

South Carolina in 1877 is a case in point. Deprived of political and civil rights and denied economic opportunities, their insecurity heightened by the violent political campaign of 1876, Negroes looked longingly to Liberia for salvation. Richard H. Cain, a Negro newspaper-publisher and minister, reported that thousands of black people in South Carolina would depart if the means of transportation were furnished them. At a mass meeting held to mark the thirtieth anniversary of Liberia's declaration of independence, the Liberian Exodus Joint Stock Steamship Company was formed. Martin R. Delany, by that time a judge in Charleston, lent his support; and considerable enthusiasm was aroused by wildly exaggerated reports about the benefits of the West African soil and climate. One myth held that Liberia contained not only bacon-producing trees but could boast gigantic potatoes, a single potato being sufficient to meet the food needs for an entire family for a whole day. Given the chronic economic uncertainty of blacks in the South and the typical feeling expressed by one emigrant that "we are no more

than dogs here in South Carolina," it is not surprising that the Liberian fever reached almost epidemic proportions.[28]

With funds accumulated from the sale of stock in the steamship firm, a bark, the *Azor,* was acquired early in 1878. Five thousand Negroes witnessed the consecration of the ship; but only two hundred and six were able to sail for West Africa a month later. Disease, the shortage of food and water, and the absence of a qualified physician resulted in the death of twenty-three emigrants.[29] After a short layover in Sierra Leone, the *Azor* arrived at its destination in June 1878.

It was the only voyage that the soon bankrupt Liberian Exodus Joint Stock Steamship Company ever financed. A number of the emigrants achieved the economic success and true freedom in Liberia that they had so fervently craved. But the deaths that had occurred on the maiden journey and the bad management largely responsible for the fatalities somewhat tempered emigrationist zeal—only temporarily, however. It is perhaps a measure of the despair of the southern Negro at this time that he was prepared to believe the rosiest descriptions of conditions in Africa and to risk a most hazardous journey to change his status quo.

One back-to-Africanist who was exhilarated to learn of the tribulations of the Liberian Exodus Company was Edward Wilmot Blyden. Blyden, a Virgin Islander by birth and a Liberian by choice, had himself emigrated to West Africa in December 1850. Outside of the "mother continent," dignity and respectability were beyond the reach of blacks, he steadfastly maintained. Furthermore Africa required Afro-Americans for its redemption as much as black Americans needed the land of their ancestors for their spiritual salvation. But the *Azor* repatriates had not been properly screened, Blyden thought. He wanted only pure black returnees, not "rubbish," i.e., mulattoes, whose presence in Liberia he feared would be disastrous.[30]

Paradoxically, Blyden placed greater faith in the American Colonization Society because of its apparent willingness to pref-

erentially repatriate very dark Negroes. Indeed his highly com-
petent biographer, Hollis R. Lynch, has written that Blyden regarded the American Colonization Society as the "most important single agency working for the regeneration of Africa."[31]

Africa's regeneration would not redound merely to the benefit
of its inhabitants but to all who were of African extraction.
Thanks to the slave trade, blacks were widely dispersed. Everywhere they lived by the sufferance of other people. Therefore
it was imperative that they develop a racial center, a fount of
physical, financial, and intellectual strength—a generator of
"African power." From such a center Africa could make its
influence felt on behalf of its scattered children. "An African
nationality is our great need," Blyden told black American audiences. "We shall never receive the respect of other races until
we establish a powerful nationality." Liberia was striving to do
just that and needed the skills and wisdom of blacks in exile
in the New World.[32]

But blacks bound for Liberia had to identify their interests
and feelings with Africa and the African race, and Blyden, like
Marcus Garvey, had serious doubts about whether lighter-skinned
Negroes could qualify on this count. Such was the racial philosophy that underlay the back-to-Africanism of Edward Wilmot Blyden.

To be sure, there was no scarcity of Negro saviors or salvation
schemes. One would-be Moses of a Negro exodus was an illiterate former slave, Benjamin "Pap" Singleton. "The whites had
the lands and the sense an' the blacks had nothin' but their freedom," Singleton contended. In his judgment, the remedy was
separation of the races. Initially, he sought Canaan, not in
Africa, but rather in the southwest, in the state of Kansas.

By the end of 1878, Singleton claimed credit for the relocation
of almost seventy-five hundred Negroes from the southern states
to Kansas.[33] In short order, however, Negroes became the ob-
jects of hostility and discrimination in Kansas, which was attracting white immigrants as well as black ones.

Singleton now regarded Canada and Liberia as the new potential Canaans. In an address issued in 1883, he advised his breth-

ren to leave the South, where he saw no chance of economic or political independence. Conditions not being appreciably better in the north, he urged migration to Canada, where he supposed the British government would protect colored interests, or to Liberia, where they could have their own government. When his call went unheeded, Singleton set his sights on Cyprus as the home and haven for oppressed Negroes. His efforts for two years in this direction were similarly fruitless. A chagrined but determined Singleton returned to an African solution, which was also being pressed by others in the lower south.

To accomplish migration to Africa, Singleton formed the United Transatlantic Society at the beginning of 1885. Kansas Negroes were among those who joined the society, believing that manhood could not be achieved in the United States. More than mere relocation was contemplated. Negro nationalism was evidently an integral element in the society's solution to the black man's dilemma. The society passed a number of resolutions favoring Negro "national existence"; and its records refer to a separate nation as a sine qua non of Negro survival. This nation was to be founded in Africa. Despite the society's earnest intentions, it sent out no emigrants in the following years; and Singleton, the father of the stillborn exodus, died impoverished in 1892 at the age of eighty-three.[34]

Southern black fortunes reached their nadir in this post-Reconstruction period. By the 1890s the more-than-occasional lynchings, the disfranchisement, the triumph of Jim Crowism, in short, the consolidation of white supremacy, coupled with an agricultural depression, made the plight of the southern blacks desperate. The moribund American Colonization Society received a torrent of inquiries about repatriating to Africa.

Propaganda about emigration proved appealing to black farmers who were peasants in all but name in that sad era. Symptomatic of the desperation was the trek of a penniless band of Negroes from the hamlet of McCory, Arkansas, to Augusta, Georgia, where they arrived in February 1892 ready to leave for Liberia. When the bottom dropped out of the cotton market,

they had pulled up stakes. The thirty-five men, women, and children carrying their few worldly possessions were led by Judge Thornton, a Baptist preacher. Tall and solemn Thornton carried a lantern which he intended to use to light up "darkest Africa." The Arkansas party had heard beautiful tales about Liberia from a Bishop Turner who passed through their region distributing circulars from the old American Colonization Society[35] of which he was a vice president.

During the 1890s Bishop Henry McNeal Turner of the independent African Methodist Episcopal Church emerged as the principal agitator and leading spirit of the back-to-Africa idea. Turner credited a fellow divine, Alexander Crummell, with his conversion to the back-to-African philosophy at the time of the Civil War. Crummell, an Episcopalian clergyman and black intellectual, although rejecting the notion that black Americans were not at home in the United States, had argued that Africa, lying low and wretched, required fifty-thousand blacks for missionary service and to meet her temporal and material needs. He wanted the children of Africa living in the western hemisphere to avail themselves of Africa's treasures.[36] Liberia, where Crummell spent twenty years, had "a rich and varied soil"; it was well watered and there was proof of its vast mineral resources.[37] Crummell was a member of a three-man commission—Blyden was a second member—appointed by the Liberian legislature to induce West Indians and American blacks to come to West Africa.[38]

Crummell was later to modify significantly his position on emigration. Bishop Turner never did. Although he was denounced by most recognized Negro spokesmen, Turner's appeal for the uneducated, poverty-stricken southern black tenant-farmer was substantial.

Turner could see no tolerable manhood future for the black man in the United States.[39] So great was his disillusionment with the promise of American life that he once observed he wished his country nothing but endless misfortune. Where the black man was concerned, hell was preferable to the United States. Its flag was a "dirty and contemptible rag," its constitution, "a

cheat, a libel" worthy of being spit upon by blacks.[40] He wished to live to see the ruination of the United States and its memory expunged from history. "A man who loves a country that hates him," Turner noted bitterly, "is a human dog and not a man."[41]

In contrast to America, where the black man's freedom was a burlesque and his "citizenship a nullity," Turner wrote that in Liberia the Negro could find the fullest liberty. There he could feel like a lord and act like one. There he could be a man. Thus Turner found the cure for the nightmare of the United States Negro in an African dream. Not only would the manhood of the American Negro be saved, but the African continent would be culturally and religiously redeemed. Emigrating Negroes would transmit both Christianity and the skills to create a prosperous state that would command respect for Africa in the white world. Indeed, Turner maintained this had been God's plan in bringing black men to the New World.

As historian Edwin S. Redkey has pointed out, Turner neither expected nor wanted a mass withdrawal of blacks from the United States. In this he resembled Garvey. Two out of three Afro-Americans he thought were unsuitable for Africa. Would-be whites Turner found particularly repugnant. From West Africa he wrote in 1891 that impecunious black emigrants would be severely handicapped in Liberia: ". . . I would advise no one to come here without a hundred or two dollars. This is not the place for anyone to come with no money."[42] In 1883 he expressed the belief that an annual emigration of between five and ten thousand blacks would be satisfactory. With half a million of the right kind of repatriate, a proud black nation could be built in Africa.[43]

Turner's correspondence during his first trip to West Africa painted an idealized picture of Africans and Africa. The people were fearless, considered themselves equal to any and all human beings on earth, and welcomed a return home by Afro-Americans. As for the land he had seen, it was rich, there was abundant water, and there were "fruits of every beauty." Horses flourished there. Chickens, goats, sheep, and dogs were much in evidence.[44]

Turner's claim that there were two million black people who, given the resources, were prepared to return to Africa was surely extravagant, but it is clear that the "African fever" was widespread. Money was the chief stumbling block for Turner, as it was for all of the black champions of back-to-Africa programs, both those who preceded Turner and those who followed him. Poor black tenant-farmers could not possibly pay for transportation to their ancestral home. Merchant vessels did not ply the Atlantic between West Africa and the United States in the depressed 1890s. Blacks simply lacked the capital to operate a steamship line. Reluctantly, Turner turned to whites for financial assistance. Turner's schemes were endorsed by Senator John Morgan of Alabama who believed blacks incapable of absorbing the white man's culture. Morgan had been an enthusiastic supporter of an African colonization measure introduced in the Senate by Senator Matthew Butler of South Carolina to provide for the emigration of persons of color from the southern states.[45] As quoted in the *Congressional Record,* Senator Morgan told the Senate that there was an "irrepressible conflict" between the races that nothing could cure except their final separation.[46] The federal government was to foot the bill to transport blacks who signified their desire to become citizens of other nations. Butler's bill never even came close to passage. However, with the aid of Morgan and a group of businessmen from Alabama, an International Migration Society was established in 1894.

Guided by Turner's ideas, some of which coincided with those of Negro-baiting white racists, the Society sent two boatloads of emigrants to Liberia: the *Horsa* carrying more than two hundred in 1895, and the *Laurada* a year later with more than three hundred on board. Never again was Turner able to send a batch of blacks to their African Zion. In the estimation of some Turner-sponsored emigrés that was indeed a fortunate happenstance.

In March 1896 a letter from one disgruntled emigrant who had sailed to Liberia the year before aboard the *Horsa* was pub-

lished by the *Savannah Tribune* and other black newspapers. The letter written by one W. R. Haffer of Johnsonville, Liberia, was sent to his mother in Little Rock, Arkansas, with the request that the epistle be distributed to the Negro press.[47] He wanted people to be told to pay no heed to Turner or anyone else who lectured blacks about going to Liberia: "we have suffered enough." Eager to refute Turner's misleading milk and honey depiction of Liberia, Haffer described conditions in the country as he experienced them.

> Something to eat is scarce over here . . . don't have any meal or flour. We eat twice a day, when we can get it, though since I have been over here I have been glad enough to get one meal of dry rice a day, and nothing in it but salt and water. . . . We came over in April 1895 and ever since we have been here we have been in a suffering condition and starving, and me for my part, I have never been in such a fix in my life.

He charged Turner with being untruthful and said that when the bishop visited Liberia earlier in the year he stayed only briefly because he did not want to catch a fever.

Enemies of emigrationist programs lost no opportunity to embarrass Turner and the tales of woe told by returnees and would-be returnees provided many an opportunity. Turner, following the precept that a good offense is the best defense, reiterated his litany of exaggerated praise for the virtues of "mosquito-free" West Africa. In 1903 he still claimed for Liberia the richest soil in the world. Mother Nature's bounty included a bevy of precious mineral resources: " . . . gold dust can be switched up by women and children in marvelous quantities along the shores of rivers and creeks after heavy rains."[48] Land-parcels of twenty-five acres were available free of charge from the government of Liberia. The complaints of emigrants Turner chalked up to indolence. Correspondence from early English settlers in the American colonies, he noted, frequently bemoaned the frightful situation in which they found themselves. Although he continued to be the preeminent apostle of back-to-Africanism until World War I, although he sponsored more repatriates than

any other single back-to-Africanist in black American history, Turner's African dream remained largely a dream. If we subtract the returnees, the total number of Afro-Americans who actually went to Africa between the end of Reconstruction and 1910 may not surpass the two thousand mark. No more than one thousand left the United States during the nightmarish period from 1890 to 1910, hardly a trickle compared to the rural black southern population that inundated the North. It does not even equal the trek to the South of Northern blacks in the first decade of this century. (This latter migration, ordinarily ignored by historians, seems to have involved black professionals, i.e., teachers and doctors in addition to black businessmen seeking better outlets for their energies and talents.)

Why then did so few joyless mobile blacks select Africa as their destination? The financial quandary in which the majority of poor blacks found themselves has already been alluded to. Overland transportation within the United States was much cheaper and easier than an ocean voyage to a faraway place of which they knew very little. Between the American dream and the American reality there was a yawning chasm, seemingly an unbridgeable one. But America was all that most blacks in the late nineteenth and early twentieth centuries had ever known. It was familiar. It was home. Had the handful of repatriates found contentment in Africa, had they sent back word of their material comfort, indigent blacks in the agrarian South might have been more eager to uproot themselves and find a way to return to the land of their forefathers. But stories of food shortages, of disease, and of an unpleasant climate inevitably subverted Turner's back-to-Africanism.

In addition, Professor Melvin Drimmer of Spelman College in a thought-provoking article argues persuasively that Afro-Americans, imbued with the individualistic capitalist ethic, functioned as alien entrepreneurs in Africa where integration into a communal system was necessary for survival. "The same Americanism which kept blacks at home kept those who left from succeeding in Africa." Americo-Liberians and the Creoles

in Sierra Leone never assimilated into African society. They viewed indigenous Africans with condescension and, like European imperialists, had no qualms about exploiting them, Drimmer correctly points out.[49]

Readers who peremptorily dismiss Bishop Turner because his African Zionism was a failure do him a great injustice. Latter-day black nationalists, some of whom might not recognize Turner's name, have unknowingly built upon his philosophical infrastructure. Were Turner alive today his oratory would be most welcome in black nationalist circles. His thesaurus of billingsgate usually reserved for the United States is unequaled even by Cleaver, Carmichael, or H. Rap Brown. Like so many present-day black power advocates, Turner was cynical about realizing equality in his white nation through the electoral process. During the presidential election of 1896 in which currency was the paramount issue he offered this acidulous advice to blacks:

What time has the fool Negro to bother with the gold or silver side either, while he is lynched, burnt, flayed, imprisoned etc., two-thirds of the time for nothing. Vote any way in your power to overthrow, destroy, ruin, blot out, divide, crush, dissolve, wreck, consume, demolish, disorganize, suppress, subvert, smash, shipwreck, crumble, nullify, upset, uproot, expunge, and fragmentize this nation, until it learns to deal justly with the black man. This is all the advice we have to give.[50]

Like his ideological offspring of the 1960s and 1970s, Turner spurned racial integration as a worthwhile goal. From 1900 to 1906 blacks in more than twenty-five southern cities boldly initiated boycotts of newly segregated transit systems. Bishop Turner flouted the boycott and conspicuously rode the Jim-Crow streetcars in Atlanta.[51] Almost certainly today's black nationalists would not commend the gesture itself, but they would doubtlessly appreciate the separatist passion which motivated Turner.

Blackness deserved respect, Turner preached. Blackness in the minds of whites and many blacks had become associated with that which is evil, dirty, and diabolical. Whiteness connoted goodness, cleanliness, and God. Living among whites, Afro-Americans had imbibed harmful notions about their color which

could best be purged by emigration. To envision God as a Caucasian was degrading for black people, according to Turner, who
proclaimed in the pages of his *Voice of Missions* that "God is
a Negro."[52] Christ in human form was also black. At a Congress
on Africa held in Chicago in 1883 Turner had asserted that
Adam, the first of the species, had also been black.[53] Many of
the foregoing concepts have been enunciated in recent years by
Black Christian Nationalists, such as Albert B. Cleage, Jr.,
pastor of the Shrine of the Black Madonna in Detroit.[54]

Turner's philippic against black participation in a war against
Spain reads much like black tirades against Afro-American involvement in the Vietnam war. Even before actual hostilities
commenced, Turner, perhaps actuated by the fear that patriotic
fervor generated by a battle over Cuba might dilute emigrationist ardor among blacks, promised, "If the United States gets
into war with Spain, we shall stump the country against the
black man taking up a gun."[55] Six decades later Stokely Carmichael, in high dudgeon over the disastrous Indochina conflict,
updated Turner's promise with the chant, "Hell no. We won't
go." Of course, blacks did fight in the "splendid little war" in
1898 as they have in all of America's wars including the Southeast Asia conflict.

As a reward for its successful crusade for Cuban independence, the United States seized the Philippine Islands, a Spanish
possession halfway around the world. A bitterly fought insurrection against American occupation was quickly launched by Filipino guerrillas. It lasted for three years. Turner, convalescing
from a stroke, could not contain his anger over American imperialism in the Pacific. Black Americans had no stake in the
American conquest, said the bishop, and he referred to the Fil-
ipinos as fellow blacks. "I boil with disgust when I remember
that colored men from this country that I am personally ac-
quainted with are fighting to subjugate a people of their own
color and bring them to such a degraded state."[56]

Differing with Bishop Turner on the desirability of black soldiers fighting in the Philippines was the most celebrated Negro

of the day, Booker T. Washington. In a book originally published in 1900, the founder of Tuskegee voiced his hope that the colored troops would give a good account of themselves.[57] They had just performed with valor in the Cuban campaign, he averred. Washington was making a futile attempt to demonstrate that Afro-Americans were deserving of first-class citizenship by highlighting the sacrifices they had made for their country.

Washington, the embodiment of "accommodationism," also differed radically with Turner on the issue of emigration to Africa. Writing in 1899, Washington denied that he harbored animosity toward the devotees of back-to-Africanism. For Bishop Turner and his ilk he had great respect, he asserted, but Booker T. could "see no way out of the Negro's present condition in the South by returning to Africa."[58] European nations were carving up the continent and consequently there was no place Afro-Americans could relocate and improve their lot. Migrants to Africa would find themselves in a dependency of some foreign country. Washington preferred a future for blacks in the United States where a satisfactory racial adjustment would have to be worked out. Such counsel must have had a somewhat hollow ring in an age when the racial relationship in America was essentially that of white rider to black horse.

Washington contended that when five hundred blacks had sailed from Savannah with Liberia as their destination, an allusion to the *Horsa* and the *Laurada,* whites mistakenly inferred that blacks were committed to returning to Africa. He denied that a "majority" were so committed but did not hazard a guess as to just how much support for repatriation, latent or active, there was in black America.[59] The black population in 1900 was officially 8,833,994. If only 25 percent were drawn to Turnerism, the number of would-be emigrants would have surpassed the two million figure cited by the bishop. No poll was taken to assess the strength of back-to-Africanism at that juncture in black American history. In the absence of reliable data the question of black Zionist potential remains a subject fit for historical conjecture.

Black Americans were not unique in the 1890s and early 1900s in seeking an asylum in the land of their fathers. East European Jewry was in a comparable situation. Ironically, hundreds and hundreds of thousands found their haven in the same United States that the black emigrationists were trying to flee. Other Jews, those who embraced the Zionist philosophy, concluded that only in a Jewish state would they be truly safe. Palestine was inaccessible and Jewish settlements elsewhere were considered for diplomatic and humanitarian reasons. In 1903 the British government offered the Zionist Congress territory in East Africa for the purpose of establishing a Jewish "colony."[60] Two years later after a heated debate in the Zionist camp, the offer was rejected. Even before official word of the rejection was received from the Zionists, others expressed an interest in the proferred land, the Uasin Gishu plateau in Kenya. One communication received by the Colonial Office came from a man with the improbable and virtually unpronounceable name of Checlzzli—Reverend C.F. Checlzzli, to be precise. His objective was plain: he wanted to induce black Americans to emigrate to East Africa. But the Colonial Office saw no prospect of using his services.[61] Nothing more was ever heard of Checlzzli or of his scheme.

Infinitely more irksome to both British and American governmental authorities was a back-to-Africa movement which involved a self-styled Gold Coast chief, Alfred Charles Sam.[62] It occurred at the beginning of World War I. The way had been paved for Chief Sam by a worsening of conditions in the all-Negro communities of Oklahoma. The widely publicized plans of Edwin P. McCabe, a black man, to transform the Sooner territory into a black state had miscarried primarily because of intensified conflicts among the whites, the Indians, and the blacks.[63] Attempts were made by whites to discourage further Negro immigration which was at flood tide from 1890 to 1910, and to encourage the withdrawal of Afro-Americans who were already occupants of the frontier area. They were discriminated

against in employment and rebuffed by both major political parties. A cotton depression in 1913, causing prices to plummet, was the finishing stroke. The Southwest had proved no more hospitable than the Southeast. Negroes, especially sharecroppers and marginal farmers in Oklahoma and later those in adjacent states, were open to escapist schemes no matter how impractical. Some succumbed to the blandishments of Chief Sam who offered passage to the Gold Coast and free land for twenty-five dollars a head.

To further Sam's plan to carry his wandering black brothers back to Africa, he traveled extensively, selling stock in his emigration company, the Akim Trading Company, and forming clubs to generate enthusiasm for his scheme. Sam concentrated on farming communities where he addressed audiences in schoolhouses, in churches, in barns, even outdoors. In common with his predecessors, Sam magnified the virtues of the Utopia to which he proposed to transport his gullible followers. Diamonds were to be found in profusion in ravines and gullies following rain. Moreover, there were bread-bearing trees and cotton bushes that grew as high as trees. Opposition to Chief Sam came from various quarters. The British consul-general in New York City and the British ambassador in Washington, D.C., closely monitored Chief Sam's activities. In February 1914 when Chief Sam's ship, the *Curityba,* was about to depart for the Promised Land, the consul-general announced that Chief Sam had confessed that he was not a chief after all. Furthermore he was wanted on the Gold Coast for procuring funds under false pretenses.[64]

The Negro press heaped additional criticism upon the man who immodestly compared himself to Moses and promised to lead his people to a land of milk and honey. The *Crisis,* the journal of the middle-class National Association for the Advancement of Colored People, warned against the poorly conceived Oklahoma movement. Calling for an end to the emigration idea, the *Crisis* exhorted its readers to fight the battle in

Oklahoma and to protect the masses against mountebanks. Chief Sam was "nothing but a common cheat who belongs in jail."[65]

Nevertheless, the colonists-to-be could not be deterred. They gave various reasons for leaving America, all of which were succinctly summed up by one emigrationist who observed: "We had no rights." In August 1914 with Negroes thronging the beribboned waterfront of Galveston, Texas, Chief Sam's *S.S. Liberia* set sail for the Gold Coast with sixty passengers. Shortly after the Negroes arrived in West Africa, at the beginning of 1915, they learned that their new home was not the Garden of Eden they had been led to expect. Tropical maladies, nettlesome British restrictions, and the discovery that most land was held in common caused the bulk of the settlers to return to the United States.[66] Sam himself remained in West Africa until his death.

Whether Chief Sam was a confidence man is still a moot question. Critics pictured him as a kind of Reverend Deke O'Malley, the back-to-Africa swindler in Chester Himes' novel, *Cotton Comes to Harlem*.[67] To each black family, regardless of size, the fictional O'Malley offered free transportation, five acres of rich African land, a mule, a plough, and an unlimited supply of seed for $1,000. More fruitful than speculating about the integrity of Chief Sam and other real-life back-to-Africanists, the reader should reconsider the disgraceful conditions prevailing in America which all but compelled myriad blacks to believe that emigration was a panacea.

Just prior to the outbreak of the Boer War, Bishop Turner had visited South Africa on behalf of the African Methodist Episcopal Church of which he was senior bishop by 1898. As was his habit in the United States, Turner blended his clerical duties in South Africa with racial propagandizing. He traced the descent of the Xhosa peoples back to Kush, extolled African civilization, and confidently predicted that the future belonged to the black man. One day blacks would throw off the yoke of the whites.[68] Turner's message was incendiary, alarmed the authorities, and heightened suspicions about the real motives of

Negro American evangelists. Not coincidentally, Bantu dissidents were involved in riots in the Transkei in 1902.

Also through the efforts of Turner and other missionaries, young Africans were sent to the United States to study at Negro universities. There they often imbibed radical doctrines which they subsequently transferred to the African continent. A case in point is John Chilembwe, leader of the highly significant although abortive, Nyasaland uprising of 1915.[69]

There were several causes of the Nyasaland rebellion. Pervasive racism, increased taxes, forced labor, and famine aggravated by drought were but a few. Conscription of Africans to fight in World War I, an "imperialist" fray, provided the immediate spark. Chilembwe had no illusions about destroying settler hegemony in the Nyasaland Protectorate. In his instructions to his army, those whom he called patriots, he said: "This very night you are to go and strike the blow and then die."[70] It was the only way to dramatically show the Europeans their deep-seated discontent over the bad treatment meted out to Africans.

One might say that the philosophical roots of the explosion stretched beyond the boundaries of Africa to other continents. Chilembwe compared himself with John Brown and seemed to view the frustrating conditions confronting the "natives" of Nyasaland in 1915 as analogous to those which prompted Brown's ill-fated raid on Harpers Ferry in 1859. Inspiration for Chilembwe had also come, perhaps ironically, from Joseph Booth, an English missionary, who had made his way to Central Africa in 1892. At the time, according to Shepperson and Price, Booth had a "predisposition towards religious pacifism,"[71] an odd bent for a man later to be directly linked to the Chilembwe rebellion. But Booth was something of a maverick. He soon developed a sympathy for the Africans and published a book whose title, *Africa for the Africans,* became a widely used slogan in the Garvey era.

In 1897 Booth and Chilembwe, whose association had begun when the latter applied for a menial job as a cook boy and was actually retained as a servant, went to the United States togeth-

er. The journey was a watershed in Chilembwe's life. While in America Chilembwe was exposed to a motley array of pan-African, black chauvinist, and back-to-Africa concepts as well as the accommodationism of Booker T. Washington. For two years Chilembwe was a student at the Virginia Theological Seminary and College, a black Baptist institution located in Lynchburg, Virginia. It is instructive to note that political notions absorbed by Chilembwe at Lynchburg were cited by the official commission of inquiry in its explanation of the rebellion. Inflammatory black American literature imported by Chilembwe also was allegedly connected to the uprising.[72]

Among Chilembwe's extracurricular activities at college was his involvement with the Lynchburg African Development Society founded circa 1899. Its general solicitor was none other than "Che. John Chilembwe of East Central Africa." The society's prospectus implied that he had been sent to Afro-Americans by certain Christian natives to solicit "their cooperation and direction in the development of the rich resources of their country." A portion of profits earned by the society would be earmarked for the creation of Afro-American settlements in Africa seemingly along lines set forth by Chilembwe's mentor, Joseph Booth, in his *Africa for the Africans.*

The society's plans never reached fruition. Chilembwe returned home in 1900 to establish his Providence Industrial Mission. For a while he was aided by black American missionaries and financed by black American Baptists. The presence of Afro-Americans was disturbing to some Britons in Nyasaland but there was nothing to suggest that Chilembwe would one day lead a revolt for African dignity and forfeit his life in the ill-starred adventure. The commission of inquiry was probably at least partially right in suggesting that the seeds of that revolt had been sown by black Americans. A renegade insofar as the British Empire was concerned, Chilembwe is a patriotic and heroic figure in independent Malawi. A commemorative stamp has been issued in his honor.

Malawi, or Nyasaland as it was known in pre-independence

days, figured prominently in the project of a Barbadian, J. Albert Thorne. James Weldon Johnson, writing in the *New York Age* in 1922, called the history of African colonization schemes for American blacks a "colossal failure."[73] Arguing that political conditions in Africa were less conducive to the founding of black colonies than they had been a hundred years earlier, Johnson cited two back-to-Africanists, J. Albert Thorne and Marcus Garvey, who were then advancing repatriation schemes. Thorne, he thought, was the less impractical of the two.

Thorne's name is familiar to just a handful of scholars. As has been the case with other black advocates of repatriation, Thorne has been eclipsed by the charismatic Garvey. Both as a precursor and a contemporary of Garvey, he deserves better.

Thorne was born in Barbados in 1860, the son of a highly respected and resourceful small-landed proprietor.[74] Finding government work closed to blacks and commerce dominated by Europeans, he became a public school teacher before sailing to Britain to further his education. He earned a degree in medicine from the University of Edinburgh.

Although Thorne had long contemplated African colonization as a solution to the Negro dilemma, it was not until 1896 that he set forth the details of his plan. This was done in a pamphlet dedicated to the memory of William Wilberforce, the noted abolitionist, and David Livingstone, the famous explorer and missionary.[75] Thorne was deeply distressed by the plight of people of African descent in the West Indies and in the United States. These blacks were "shrewd, sober, thrifty"; not a few were educated and skilled. All were nominal Christians. If some of these Afro-Americans and Afro-West Indians could be assisted to resettle in their motherland, they would effectively open up the "Dark Continent," Thorne reasoned. Moreover, the scheme "would also prove a true, complete and perfectly feasible solution of the race problem as it is now understood in European Countries."[76] His instrument was to be the African Colonial Enterprise which he organized.

Unlike most back-to-Africanists who focused their attention

on West Africa whence New World Negroes had originally
come, Thorne hoped to secure a tract of land in British Central
Africa or British East Africa. Nyasaland was the site he eventually selected.

As stated in his pamphlet, Thorne's plan called for an initial
free grant of ten thousand acres situated close to a civilized center to enable the colonists to obtain a market to which produce
could be easily transported. One hundred carefully selected
families were to be located on each such tract of land. The land
would be divided into ten parcels of one thousand acres each
on which ten families representing a variety of complementary
occupations would be settled. For ten years, heads of families
would receive food and clothing. At the end of that period the
land would become the property of those who developed it. Net
earnings from the third to the tenth year would be utilized to
uplift the native and to assist other eligible blacks to return to
Africa on the same terms.[77] Thus the scheme's chief recommendation according to its author was its "self-supporting and self-
propagating basis."

Clearly, however, the assistance of the British government
would be crucial to Thorne's success. The Barbadian fervently
believed that Britain had an obligation to aid him. He averred
that slavery had been at the root of the black man's troubles.
True, the Emancipation Act of 1833 had eliminated that curse.
Still, it was unfair because it indemnified the slaveowners while
it abandoned the displaced African whose earnings had been appropriated for more than two centuries. Over sixty years after
the act, Thorne steadfastly maintained that "the wrong has not
yet been righted." Proper reparation to the descendants of the
liberated slaves could be made in two ways. Those who foolishly
opted to stay in the New World could be given the wherewithal
to make a fresh start in life. Thorne, of course, based on his
experience, believed colonization a preferable course to "wasting
time and energy in endeavoring to overcome prejudices that are
so hard to die." He felt that Britain should finance the restoration of the would-be colonists. Without doubt Africa was the

only region of the world where blacks would be permanently respected as a race.[78]

In common with other black Zionists, Thorne seemed to subscribe to the notion that the Africans' enslavement in the New World had been part of a divine design, the ultimate objective of which was to Christianize Africa.[79] Thus, repatriated blacks from the United States and the Caribbean were to be God's agents. Indeed they were physiologically suited to this work in African climes so hazardous for whites. Thorne was persuaded that Negroes in the Americas were immune to the more virulent fevers while Europeans were not; and whereas the blacks' period of seasoning was short, Europeans never really became acclimatized.[80]

To test his philanthropic, religious, and medical theories, Thorne sought the support of a variety of eminent Britons familiar with Africa. He claimed that he had secured the backing of Henry M. Stanley, the African explorer, for one.[81] Captain Lugard (later Lord Lugard) was quoted by Thorne as observing, "if undertaken by thoroughly capable men, and if the families consist of capable and industrious artisans, the scheme should have in it the promise of success."[82]

Because of Thorne's particular interest in Nyasaland, the opinion of Sir Harry Johnston, who had been the first British commissioner and consul-general in that protectorate, would carry considerable weight. His help was solicited by Thorne in 1896. Sir Harry informed Thorne that British Central Africa already possessed a fairly large indigenous population. Frankly "we are not particularly anxious to have American or West Indian negroes." The proconsul didn't feel justified in assisting such persons in any special way to settle themselves. Interesting to note in view of Dr. Thorne's claims of immunity and rapid acclimatization for exiled sons of Africa is Johnston's contention that "men of this type do not stand the climate much better than Europeans or Indians." Furthermore, they were more disposed to be troublesome and to quarrel with the natives. Nevertheless, he stated, if the Negro immigrants were of good reputa-

tion, they might receive small free grants (thirty acres each) on the condition that the land be occupied and cultivated for at least two consecutive years.[83]

Thorne took this to be an unqualified endorsement of his scheme. He promised Johnston that his settlers would not merely be of good reputation, but honest, industrious, enterprising, and efficient. Thorne's disillusionment with life in the white man's world was reflected in his assertion that all these settlers expected was to be treated with humane consideration as men.[84]

In any event the Nyasaland project made no progress. In fact almost nothing was heard of it again until 1922 when Thorne attempted to raise funds to start operations in Central Africa. Then residing in Harlem, he predicted that "within the year" there would be a mass exodus of Negroes to Africa. The *New York World* in reporting this story commented that Thorne had actually obtained a concession of ten thousand acres on the Zambezi river "on terms which indicate the cooperation of the British Foreign Office." Allegedly, in every hundred acres, thirty would be donated gratis and the remaining seventy would be purchased for sixty cents an acre. Although the details of the scheme had been altered somewhat, its twin objectives were still "repatriation of the exiles" and "the civilization of the natives."[85] However, $10,000 was needed to implement the plan. Money, to be sure, was not easy to come by, particularly when Thorne had to compete with Garvey's Universal Negro Improvement Association. The frustrated Barbadian actually told a reporter from the *World* that Garvey plagiarized his back-to-Africa scheme from the African Colonial Enterprise.[86]

Money was not Thorne's only problem. His statements quoted by New York and London newspapers about a concession in Nyasaland and a promise of support from the British government were wishful thinking. Thorne probably believed that land was his for the asking. In an interview with the British consul-general in New York he mentioned the concession he had received from Sir Harry Johnston and produced the 1896 correspondence.[87] On the other hand, George Smith, the governor of Nyasaland, stated unequivocally in September 1922 that

there was no record of any land having been transferred to any person named Thorne and added that he did not suppose for a moment that any such project would receive the support of the colonial secretary.[88] He supposed correctly.

Little was heard from or about Thorne again. Curiously, in 1933 one Arden Bryan, a former Garveyite and president of the Nationalist-Negro Movement and African Colonization Association, proposed to the League of Nations and the British government that Negro colonization be undertaken in the Cameroons. As a precedent he noted that "thirty-eight years ago the British government granted a concession in the Nyasaland Protectorate to one John Albert Thorne."[89] Needless to say Bryan was no more successful than his fellow Barbadian.

The two men had appeared together at a mass meeting in July 1932. Significantly, the subject discussed on that occasion was "The Way Out." Thorne was then seventy-two. He died in total obscurity. Precisely when and where is not known. Lacking Garvey's flamboyance and organizing ability, he had only a dream which never even approached realization. That dream, born of racial oppression, often caused him to exaggerate his achievements and prospects. But that he was a fake, as some in the British government thought him, is almost certainly untrue.

NOTES

1. Miles Mark Fisher, *Negro Slave Songs in the United States* (New York: Citadel Press, 1963).

2. See P.J. Staudenraus, *The African Colonization Movement, 1816-1865* (New York: Columbia University Press, 1961).

3. This information about a back-to-Africa law was provided by the National States Rights party with headquarters in Marietta, Georgia.

4. Christopher Fyfe, *A History of Sierra Leone* (London: Oxford University Press, 1962), p. 112.

5. Paul Cuffe, *A Brief Account of the Settlement and Present Situation of the Colony of Sierra Leone in Africa* (New York: Printed by Samuel Wood, 1812), p. 4. For additional information about Cuffe see George Salvador, *Paul Cuffe, The Black Yankee* (New Bedford: Reynolds-DeWalt Printing, Inc., 1969); Henry Noble Sherwood, "Paul Cuffe," *Journal of Negro History, 8* (April 1923). 153-229; Henry Noble Sherwood, "Paul Cuffe and His Contribution to the American Colonization Society," *Proceedings of the Mississippi Valley Historical Association for the Year 1912-1913, 6* (1913): 371-402.

6. Cuffe Manuscripts, New Bedford Public Library, New Bedford, Mass.: Robert Finley to Paul Cuffe, December 5, 1816.

7. Under the aegis of the American Colonization Society, eighty-eight settlers went to Sierra Leone in 1820. Another group set sail for Freetown from Virginia the following year. A third platoon left from Charleston in 1822.

8. Daniel Coker, *Journal of Daniel Coker, a Descendant of Africa* (Baltimore: Edward J. Coale, 1820), pp. 42, 44.

9. Archibald Alexander, *A History of Colonization on the Western Coast of Africa* (Philadelphia: William S. Martien, 1846), pp. 243-244, 248. Cary's life was tragically ended by an accident in 1828.

10. George Mason, *Reminiscences of Newport* (Newport, 1884), pp.154-159.

11. William M. Brewer, "John B. Russwurm," *Journal of Negro History,* 13 (October, 1928): 413-422.

12. *The North Star,* November 16, 1849. Yet Douglass toyed with the idea of black American colonization in Haiti in 1860 and his newspaper carried advertisements paid for by the Haitian government, advertisements aimed at luring black Americans to the former French colony. In 1893 toward the end of his life, Douglass drew a distinction between individual black emigration and a wholesale exodus. The latter he still adamantly rejected, the former he had come to countenance.

13. Quoted in William Lloyd Garrison, *Thoughts on African Colonization* (New York: Arno Press and *The New York Times,* 1969), Part II, p. 35. This work was originally published in 1832. Anticolonization was a recurring theme of the so-called Negro Convention Movement, especially before the Compromise of 1850. See William H. Pease and Jane H. Pease, "The Negro Convention Movement," *Key Issues in the Afro-American Experience,* vol. 1, eds. Nathan I. Huggins, Martin Kilson, Daniel M. Fox (New York: Harcourt Brace Jovanovich Inc., 1971), pp. 191-205; Howard H. Bell, ed., *Minutes of the Proceedings of the National Negro Convention 1830-1864* (New York: Arno Press and *The New York Times,* 1969).

14. *Proceedings of the National Convention of the Colored Men of America,* held in Washington, D.C., January 13, 14, 15, and 16, 1869 (Washington, D.C., 1869).

15. John D. Hicks, George E. Mowry, Robert E. Burke, *The Federal Union—A History of the United States to 1877* (Boston: Houghton Mifflin Company, 1964), p. 572.

16. Henry Highland Garnet, *The Past and the Present Condition, and the Destiny of the Colored Race: A Discourse Delivered at the Fifteenth Anniversary of the Female Benevolent Society of Troy, February 14, 1848* (Troy: J.C. Kneeland and Co., 1848), pp. 25, 29.

17. Quoted in Benjamin Quarles, *Black Abolitionists* (London: Oxford University Press, 1970), p. 216.

18. Quoted in Hollis R. Lynch, "Pan-Negro Nationalism in the New World before 1862." *Boston University Papers on Africa,* Vol. II, *African History,* ed. Jeffrey Butler (Boston: Boston University Press, 1966), pp. 167-168.

19. William M. Brewer, "Henry Highland Garnet," *Journal of Negro History,* 13, no. 1 (January 1828): 50-51.

20. Martin R. Delany, *The Condition, Elevation, Emigration, and Destiny of the Colored People of the United States Politically Considered* (Philadelphia: Published by the Author, 1852), pp. 48-49.

21. Ibid., p. 169.

22. Ibid., pp. 209-215.

23. Theodore Draper, *The Rediscovery of Black Nationalism* (New York: Viking Press, 1970), p. 25.

24. At the Cleveland convention James Theodore Holly emerged as the major proponent of emigration to Haiti which some regarded as a natural mecca for black Americans because it was the first independent black nation in the New World. Holly, a shoemaker and an ordained Episcopal cleric, visited Haiti in 1855 and emigrated there six years later. See James Theodore Holly and J. Dennis Harris, *Black Separatism and the Caribbean 1860,* ed. Howard H. Bell (Ann Arbor: University of Michigan Press, 1970).

25. Martin R. Delany and Robert Campbell, *Search for a Place—Black Separatism and Africa, 1860* (Ann Arbor: University of Michigan Press, 1969), pp. 28, 33.

26. Ibid., p. 39.

27. In 1862 some black Californians petitioned the United States Congress to appropriate funds to make possible their colonization to any unspecified country where their blackness would not be a stigma of degradation. First choice for many was a territory in Africa. For additional information about repatriation programs in the postwar period, see Willis Dolmond Boyd, "Negro Colonization in the Reconstruction Era 1865-1870," *Georgia Historical Quarterly,* 40 (December 1956): 370-382.

28. The story of this South Carolinian exodus to Liberia is contained in George Brown Tindall, *South Carolina Negroes 1877-1900* (Baton Rouge: Louisiana State University Press, 1966), pp. 153-168.

29. Ibid., pp. 160-162.

30. Hollis R. Lynch, *Edward Wilmot Blyden—Pan-Negro Patriot 1832-1912* (London: Oxford University Press, 1970), p. 108.

31. Ibid., p. 109, and Hollis R. Lynch, ed. *Black Spokesman—Selected Published Writings of Edward Wilmot Blyden* (New York: Humanities Press, 1971) p. 51.

32. Lynch, *Black Spokesman,* pp. 28-29.

33. For the story of the great exodus westward, see Roy Garvin, "Benjamin or 'Pap' Singleton and His Followers," *Journal of Negro History,* 33, no. 1

(1948): 7-23; John G. Van Deusen, "The Exodus of 1879," *Journal of Negro History*, 21, no. 2 (1936): 111-129; J. K. Obatala, "Exodus: Black Zionism," *Liberator*, October 1969, pp. 14-17.

34. Walter L. Fleming, "'Pap' Singleton, the Moses of the Colored Exodus," *American Journal of Sociology*, 15 (July 1909): 61-82.

35. *The New York Times*, February 23, 1892.

36. Alexander Crummell, *The Future of Africa* (New York: Charles Scribner, 1862), pp. 217, 219, 233, 255.

37. Ibid., p. 251.

38. Alexander Crummell, *Africa and America—Addresses and Discourses* (Springfield, Massachusetts: Willey and Co., 1891), p. 423.

39. J. W. E. Bowen, ed., *Addresses and Proceedings of the Congress on Africa—December 13-15, 1895* (Atlanta: Gammon Theological Seminary, 1896), p. 195.

40. Edwin S. Redkey, "Bishop Turner's African Dream," *Journal of American History*, 54, no. 2 (September 1967): 283.

41. Quoted in August Meier, *Negro Thought in America 1880—1915—Racial Ideologies in the Age of Booker T. Washington* (Ann Arbor: University of Michigan Press, 1966), p. 66.

42. Edwin S. Redkey, ed., *Respect Black: The Writings and Speeches of Henry McNeal Turner* (New York; Arno Press, 1971), p. 131.

43. Edwin S. Redkey, *Black Exodus—Black Nationalist and Back-to-Africa Movements, 1890-1910* (New Haven and London: Yale University Press, 1969), p. 37.

44. Redkey, *Respect Black*, pp. 113, 131.

45. Senate 1121. For Butler's comments in support of his bill see the *Congressional Record*, January 16, 1890, pp. 622-630.

46. *Congressional Record*, January 7, 1890, p. 420.

47. *Savannah Tribune*, March 21, 1896.

48. Redkey, *Respect Black*, pp. 192-193.

49. Melvin Drimmer, "Review Article—Black Exodus," *Journal of American Studies* 4,2 (1970): 249-256.

50. Redkey, *Respect Black*, p. 175.

51. August Meier and Elliot Rudwick, "The Boycott Movement Against Jim Crow Streetcars in the South 1900-1906," *Journal of American History* 55, no. 4 (March 1969): 769.

52. Redkey, *Respect Black*, pp. 176-177.

53. Redkey, *Black Exodus*, p. 182.

54. Albert B. Cleage, Jr., *The Black Messiah* (New York: Sheed and Ward, 1968).

55. Redkey, *Black Exodus*, p. 245. For a good picture of the scope of black opposition to the Spanish-American war and the Filipino insurrection, see George P. Marks III, *The Black Press Views American Imperialism* (New

York: Arno Press, 1971). Especially useful is William Loren Katz's preface to the volume.

56. Redkey, *Respect Black,* pp. 186-187.

57. Booker T. Washington, *A New Negro for a New Century* (Miami, Florida: Mnemosyne Publishing Co., 1969), pp. 33-34.

58. Booker T. Washington, *The Future of the American Negro* (New York: Negro Universities Press, 1969), p. 159. For an interesting survey of Washington's involvement with Africa, see Louis Harlan, "Booker T. Washington and the White Man's Burden," *American Historical Review,* 71, no. 2 (January 1966): 441-467. Harlan argues persuasively that Washington's "African experience illuminates his essential conservatism."

59. Ibid., pp. 163-164.

60. Robert G. Weisbord, *African Zion: The Attempt to Establish a Jewish Colony in the East Africa Protectorate 1903-1905* (Philadelphia: Jewish Publication Society, 1968).

61. No copies of the Checlzzli letter or the Colonial Office reply exist. However, they have been referred to and abstracted in Colonial Office Ind. 17849 and 17850, respectively.

62. The chief source of information about Chief Sam is William E. Bittle and Gilbert Geis, *The Longest Way Home—Chief Alfred C. Sam's Back-to-Africa Movement* (Detroit: Wayne State University Press, 1964).

63. See Mozell C. Hill. "The All-Negro Communities of Oklahoma: The Natural History of a Social Movement," *Journal of Negro History,* 31, no. 3 (July 1946): 254-268.

64. *The New York Times;* February 26, 1914.

65. *Crisis,* February 1914, p. 190.

66. Bittle and Geis, *The Longest Way Home,* pp. 188-198.

67. Chester Himes, *Cotton Comes to Harlem* (London: Frederick Muller Ltd., 1965).

68. Daniel Thwaite, *The Seething African Pot—A Study of Black Nationalism 1882-1935* (London: Constable and Co. Ltd., 1956), pp. 36-37.

69. The fascinating Chilembwe story is told in vivid detail in George Shepperson and Thomas Price, *Independent African: John Chilembwe and the Origins, Setting and Significance of the Nyasaland Native Rising of 1915* (Edinburgh: University Press, 1958).

70. George Simeon Mwase, *Strike A Blow and Die—A Narrative of Race Relations in Colonial Africa,* ed., Robert I. Rotberg (Cambridge, Massachusetts: Harvard University Press, 1967), p. 48.

71. Shepperson and Price, *Independent African,* p. 18.

72. Ibid., pp. 93-94.

73. *New York Age,* August 12, 1922.

74. *Illustrated Missionary News,* May 15, 1897.

75. J. Albert Thorne, *An Appeal Addressed to the Friends of the African Race—The African Colonial Enterprise,* 1896.

76. Ibid., p. 10.

77. Ibid., p. 11.

78. Ibid., pp. 18-19.

79. James Aggrey, the African educator, once observed: "God sent the black man to America. Was this all a matter of chance? You who are philosophers know there is no such thing as chance; God always has a programme. He meant America to play a special part in the history of Africa." Quoted in Kenneth King, "James E. K. Aggrey: Collaborator, Nationalist, Pan-African," *Canadian Journal of African Studies*, 3, no. 3 (Fall 1970): 511-530. Blyden and Turner expressed similar sentiments as did a host of nineteenth-century black personalities.

80. Thorne, *An Appeal Addressed to the Friends of the African Race*, p. 23.

81. Ibid., p. 13.

82. Ibid., p. 35.

83. Public Record Office, Foreign Office 371/7316: Johnston to Thorne, November 12, 1896.

84. Ibid., Thorne to Johnston, November 16, 1896.

85. *New York World*, July 29, 1922. In the same year there was some talk about using the former German colonies in Africa as outlets for America's "surplus" black population. Such a scheme was advanced by the former governor of German East Africa (Tanganyika), Dr. Heinrich Schnee. See *The New York Times*, April 17, 1922.

86. *New York World*, July 29, 1922.

87. P.R.O., F.O. 371/7316: British Consul-General to British Ambassador to the United States, November 22, 1922.

88. Ibid., George Smith to Colonial Secretary, September 15, 1922.

89. P.R.O., F.O. 371/16618: Arden Bryan to Sir Ronald Lindsay, British Ambassador to the United States, September 18, 1933.

2

MARCUS GARVEY, PAN-NEGROIST NONPAREIL

It was in March 1916 that Marcus Garvey first set foot in the United States. He was a short, portly, very black man who had been born nearly twenty-nine years earlier in St. Ann's Bay, Jamaica. No fanfare attended his arrival in 1916, but for the next stormy eleven years which he spent mostly in this country he was to claim infinitely more than his share of the limelight. His success in building what one historian called "the first and only really mass movement among Negroes in the United States"[1] was attributable to many factors—to Garvey's charisma, his showmanship and flair for public relations, to the pageantry he offered, and to a philosophy designed to invigorate the sagging self-esteem of the black masses. Then too the times were propitious for a black nationalist crusade. Garvey's organizational activities coincided with the so-called Great Migration, the demographic watershed in black American history. Before it occurred Afro-Americans were overwhelmingly rural Southern agriculturists. As a result of this population shift blacks entered a new age, an urban age. Unlike Bishop Turner who recruited primarily among widely scattered farming folk working out in the country, Garvey had the distinct advantage of proselytizing among people heavily concentrated in the new but already intolerable ghettos. (West Indian urbanites, particularly

in New York City, formed the nucleus of Garvey's following.)
World War I sharply accelerated the pace of migration from
Dixie to the North and West. Explicitly encouraging the massive
move were elements of the black press, e.g., the *Christian Re-
corder* and, notably, the *Chicago Defender*. Wishful thinking
compounded by despair had led economically exploited and racially oppressed blacks to expect or at least to hope that beyond
the Mason-Dixon line life would be appreciably better for themselves and their families. Those expectations and hopes were exploded in short order. Overcrowded slum dwellings and job discrimination greeted the uprooted black when he entered what
he had been led to believe was the long-awaited promised land.
To his sorrow the migrant discovered that racism was not confined to just one region of the United States. It was a national
phenomenon.

World War I and its aftermath, the era of Garvey's greatest
popularity, was also a period of almost unparalleled black unrest
and interracial strife. Very shortly after Garvey came to Harlem,
Joseph Black was lynched in Kingston, North Carolina. Black's
son had been accused of attacking a white youngster. When the
boy was apprehended and taken out of harm's way, a frustrated
mob, bent on doing violence to the son, hanged the father
instead.[2] Lynchings were nothing new of course. Between 1889
and 1919 there were 3,224 authenticated and recorded lynchings.
Of the victims 2,522 were black. In 1917, the year in which the
United States entered World War I, forty-eight blacks forfeited
their lives to lynch mobs. A Memphis newspaper described the
lynching in May 1917 of a black man, Eu Person, who had been
indicted for murder. He was burned to death before a screaming,
cheering crowd of fifteen thousand spectators—including women
and small children.[3] Despite a plea from President Wilson to
end this "disgraceful evil," the following year lynchings continued with undiminished fury, taking, in fact, a still larger toll
of black victims—sixty-three in all.[4]

Returning black soldiers who had fought "to make the world
safe for democracy," saw not only an increase in the incidence

of lynching but a revival of the Ku Klux Klan and a series of bloody race riots.[5] The latter were not Watts-style urban convulsions but indiscriminate attacks by whites on black communities. Between June and the end of 1919 no fewer than twenty-five racial pogroms took place, the goriest in July in Chicago where the black population had mushroomed. So bloody was the summer of 1919 that James Weldon Johnson dubbed it the "Red Summer." John Hope Franklin has written that it "ushered in the greatest period of interracial strife the nation had ever witnessed."[6] Against this background of carnage and amid the ensuing climate of disillusionment and hopelessness, Garvey was able to find followers by the hundreds of thousands, perhaps by the millions. Recent history had rendered them psychologically ripe for the new prophet and his black nationalist tidings.

Garvey, eloquently preaching race pride, fully exploited his opportunity. Directing his appeal to the darker Negroes in particular, he rhapsodized about things black. He disparaged the history of the white man and glorified the history of the African.

. . . our race gave the first great civilization to the world; and, for centuries Africa, our ancestral home, was the seat of learning; and when blackmen, who were only fit then for the company of the gods, were philosophers, artists, scientists and men of vision and leadership, the people of other races were groping in savagery, darkness and continental barbarism.[7]

On another occasion he asserted dogmatically that "honest students of history can recall the day when Egypt, Ethiopia and Timbuctu towered in their civilizations, towered above Europe, towered above Asia." Blacks had been indoctrinated with the humiliating notion that they were a people without a past, a race devoid of a culture. Garvey taught them that the opposite was true. They had once been great. They would be great again.[8] For the benefit of American blacks, an African nobility was created including the appropriately titled dukes of the Niger and Uganda, knights of the Nile, and knights of the Distinguished Service Order of Ethiopia. In 1921 Garvey formally called into existence the Empire of Africa with himself as provisional president.

Garvey taught that a black skin was not a badge of inferiority; on the contrary, it represented beauty and power. Negroid features should be a source of pride, not shame. To instill such pride Garvey promoted the manufacture and sale of black dolls to Negro children and his widely read newspaper, the *Negro World,* was loath to take advertisements for skin lightening or hair straightening products. Such advertisements were very lucrative. It must not be forgotten that one of Harlem's earliest black fortunes was made in cosmetics by an ex-laundress, Madame Walker. She invented the Walker system of hair straightening and produced Tan-Off, a preparation which promised to "bleach out the blemishes in your skin." Emulating whites was not only futile, Garvey argued—it was repugnant.[9]

Garveyism also propagated a black nationalist theology. In this, Garvey was aided and abetted by a fellow West Indian, George Alexander McGuire.[10] McGuire, who had been born in March 1866 on the island of Antigua, became chaplain general of Garvey's Universal Negro Improvement Association (UNIA). Angered by the discrimination he had encountered in the Episcopal Church, McGuire in 1921 became the founder, first bishop, and patriarch of the African Orthodox Church. One writer has speculated that McGuire's ultimate objective was a single church encompassing all black Americans and, eventually, African and Caribbean peoples too.[11] Garvey, whom McGuire once compared with John the Baptist, St. Paul, and Moses,[12] would almost certainly have shared such a lofty pan-Negro ideal.

A black religion required black symbols. For black nationalists to worship a Caucasian deity was not merely foolish—it was self-deprecating. Consequently, during the parade which opened the fourth annual UNIA convention in August 1924 paintings of an ebony Madonna and child were carried aloft.[13] At one evening meeting held in Garvey's Liberty Hall headquarters, McGuire urged a wildly enthusiastic audience to designate a date when blacks throughout the world would burn their pictures of white Christs and white Madonnas. Large gold-framed paintings of a black Virgin Mary and a black Jesus stood in front

of the platform from which the bishop declared that if Christ were to journey to New York City he would be excluded from living on Riverside Drive because of his skin pigmentation. He would have to reside in Harlem "because all the darker peoples live here in Harlem."[14]

Psychological and religious independence from the white man were essential to Garveyism. Even more crucial was economic self-determination by blacks. So long as blacks lived in houses owned by whites, so long as they worked for whites, they were not masters of their own fate. For this reason Garvey promoted black businesses. For this reason he admonished his followers to build and operate their own factories and banks. For this reason he established the Black Star Steamship Line, a commercial enterprise which quickly captured the imagination of the black masses who rallied to Garvey's standard but which also hastened his downfall. In 1925 he was imprisoned, having been convicted of fraudulently using the United States mails to raise funds for the Black Star Line.

Much of Garvey's sulfurous rhetoric was directed at the need for African redemption. Until Africa was freed from the vise of European colonialism there would be no compromise, he promised a Liberty Hall audience. To prolonged cheers, he declaimed: "Modern Germany fell and England is about to fall, as she must fall, and after the fall of Europe a new power shall rise up. Tonight I say unto scattered Ethiopia: Acquit yourselves like men and women and prepare for that day."[15]

Garvey unremittingly advocated the cause of Africa for the Africans, both those at home and abroad. If the black man was to have a government of his own of any importance, then there was no better place for it than in Africa. Africa was to be built up as a "Negro Empire, where every black man, whether he was born in Africa or in the Western world, will have the opportunity to develop on his own lines under the protection of the most favorable democratic institutions."[16]

Garvey was exceedingly pessimistic about the future of the heavily outnumbered black man in the western hemisphere. Be-

yond the boundaries of the mother continent, he could see only "ruin and disaster" for his people. Consequently, he asked that Africa's scattered and abused children be restored to her. Garvey claimed that the "legitimate, moral and righteous home of all Negroes" was Africa,[17] but he did not favor an immediate wholesale exodus from the New World. Even if the necessary assistance were available, he said in March 1924, it would take half a century to "largely depopulate a country of people who have been its residents for centuries."[18] Not all blacks were wanted in Africa anyway. "Some are no good here and naturally will be no good there." Unwanted were the indolent and dependent. Much needed were the adventurous and industrious, such as members of the UNIA, "six million strong," whose objective was an independent nationality.

Even stay-at-homes would profit from the redemption of Africa, Garvey maintained. As his widow, Amy Jacques Garvey, phrased it recently, "Garvey saw Africa as a *nation* to which the African peoples of the world could look for help and support, moral and physical, when ill-treated or abused for being black."[19] In 1960 she said that there had never been a Garveyite back-to-Africa movement "except in a spiritual sense." If her husband had not died, she believed, "he would have studied the conditions in Africa even more than in the New World and he would have realized that the return to Africa had taken place and that the black man in the New World could make a greater contribution to Africa by remaining in America, rather than migrating."[20] While it is superficial to treat Garvey simply as an advocate of repatriation as is often done especially by the popular media, it is still true that in his writings and his speeches the spellbinding Jamaican frequently invoked the prospect of a physical relocation by New World blacks. Regardless of Garvey's repatriation plans—and his ideas on the subject apparently varied from time to time and from place to place—a large percentage of his rank-and-file disciples, perhaps the bulk of them, must have thought that their physical return to Africa would be effected sooner or later.

Although he reached the zenith of his fantastic career while residing in the United States, Garvey was born in a British colony, remained a British subject during his entire lifetime, spent his declining years in Britain, and died in relative obscurity in London in 1940. Whitehall's view of Garvey adds another chapter to the extraordinary saga of this twentieth-century black titan. During his era Great Britain could still boast of an empire containing a sizable number of the four hundred million colored people for whom Garvey was the self-proclaimed leader. Therefore, Whitehall's concern with Garvey, especially in his heyday, is not at all surprising. The depth and scope of that concern have not been fully understood. Fortunately, pertinent Foreign Office and Colonial Office documents, until recently inaccessible to scholars, are now open for examination at the Public Record Office in London. Dispatches from embassies, legations, and consulates on at least three continents repeatedly touched on the threat posed by Garvey and his local followers during the years of his American period (1916-1927).

A document recently discovered in America's National Archives reveals that in 1919 unrest among Negroes in the United States and elsewhere was being closely watched by the British government.[21] In that year a strictly confidential report was sent to the American State Department listing groups important to radical Negro movements and providing notes on individual black agitators and propagandists. Garvey and his Universal Negro Improvement Association were prominently mentioned in the report. "Marcus Garvey is a strong force among negroes [*sic*] throughout the East, and perhaps he is strongest in Chicago. . . ." The British government was alarmed by the possibility that Garvey's organization would awaken race-consciousness in Africa and the Caribbean and thereby threaten British interests.

In 1920, two years after the armistice, the much older German menace still absorbed a good portion of Whitehall's attention and energy. As late as May 1920 the Garveyite and German problems were linked in a secret dispatch from Eyre Hutson,

British governor in Honduras, who believed it possible that Garvey's Universal Negro Improvement Association was "originated by German propaganda and money, and probably supported by German Americans."[22] No evidence was cited for this unfounded accusation.

The governor's uneasiness was justified since a riot in Belize the previous year was largely ascribable to the race question. White merchants charging increased prices had generated resentment among people who felt that British Honduras was properly a black man's country in which the whites were interlopers. In the midst of the 1919 outburst, rioters were heard to cry out: "This is our country and we want to get the white man out. The white man has no right here."[23] Hence, in 1920 Governor Hutson was understandably upset by the Garveyite forces in Honduras. He had no doubt that their movement was seditious. Meetings had been held in Belize, separate ones for men and women, at which black people were urged to join branches of the UNIA and to become independent of Europeans. Garvey's following in British Honduras was very substantial. A weekly newspaper there ran a column signed by "The Garvey Eye."[24] Hutson had been sent a copy of the "Constitution and Book of Laws" by the local general secretary of the UNIA, one S. A. Haynes, and he was characteristically inclined to think that the documents emanated "from some enemy propaganda source—probably aimed in the main against the United States Government in fomenting racial troubles in that country; and indirectly against British possessions in the West Indies." Although aware of the danger, even paranoid about it, Hutson in 1920 was opposed to banning Garvey's paper, the *Negro World,* which had been withheld from distribution in the colony early the previous year. The ban had proved unsuccessful since copies had been smuggled in from Guatemala and Mexico. Consequently, Governor Hutson decided to subscribe to the paper and study its policies rather than advertise the movement by officially prohibiting its journal.[25]

One factor militating against great support for Garvey in

Belize, according to Hutson, was the high percentage of mulattoes or Creoles in the nonwhite population. Garvey's appeal was explicitly to the "pure black." When the stocky Jamaican visited British Honduras in July 1921 he received a warm welcome, but when he exhorted his listeners at a meeting to invest all they could in his Black Star Line stock, a police observer noted sarcastically, "The rush for shares was not so great that I deemed it necessary to detail Police to preserve order." Although Garvey's speeches contained "strong racial antagonism," references to British royalty were made in deference and the police heard no remarks that could be construed as seditious. Garvey spoke forcefully about the Negro's unrewarded contributions to the war effort. What black people wanted was Africa, their ancestral home. Liberia was just the beginning. From there they would spread until they dominated the whole continent.[26]

Before his departure Garvey requested and was granted an interview at Government House. On that occasion Governor Hutson asked Garvey to explain a statement in the *Negro World* of December 18, 1920, reporting on a speech he delivered in Philadelphia:

England's doom is at hand . . . and as the Czar lost his throne some years ago, so I fear George of England may have to run for his life, and that will be the chance for the Negro . . . let us pray for the "downfall of England." Why do I want the downfall of England? Because I want the freedom of Africa.

Garvey categorically denied that he had made any such statement and steadfastly proclaimed his loyalty as a British subject.[27] The Governor did not record his own sentiments about Garvey's loyalty, but it may be surmised that he remained rather skeptical.

Hutson was not alone in his skepticism and concern. A few months earlier Garvey had visited Costa Rica where he gave a series of lectures to the West Indian population of that Central American nation. He spoke about the bright future of the Negro race and collected funds to establish factories in Liberia, a country of which he was the *soi-disant* president-elect. Garveyites in Costa Rica were promised that one of the Black Star Line's

largest vessels would soon call for them.[28] No derogatory statements were made about the "white man." In reporting on the
visit of this "negro-agitator," His Majesty's consul in Limón observed that the West Indians had been shown that "his wild-
cat schemes and teachings are impossible."[29] A vastly different
assessment was given by the general manager of the United
Fruit Company, who was deeply impressed by the sizable contributions made to Garvey, even after the promotional odyssey
ended.[30]

From Costa Rica, Garvey had traveled to Panama. The large
West Indian community on the isthmus had played a vital part
in constructing the canal. More importantly, from Garvey's
point of view, the community was a restive one. There was considerable friction with the government of Panama and with the
American government of the Canal Zone. West Indian dissatisfaction was fed by the Panamanians' dislike for them which appears to have been general. Equally significant was the contempt
of the American Canal Zone employees for Negroes.

Garvey advised his devotees in Panama to "prepare for the
pilgrimage in Africa."[31] Constantine Graham of the British legation thought that much that Garvey said in Panama was "crude
and even ludicrous," but interesting because of the determination shown "to escape from race subjection and
eventually . . . place negroes [*sic*] on a footing of at least
equality with other races as an independent force."[32] In the
wake of Garvey's visit, local UNIA members in Bocas Del Toro
stepped up their activities among the West Indians employed by
United Fruit. Precautionary measures had to be taken by the
Panamanian government. Public meetings were prohibited, and
the bearing of arms on the property of United Fruit was forbidden.[33] In the annual report on Panama and the Canal Zone
for 1924 the consequences of his brief stay were summarized as
follows: "Garvey succeeded in creating a good deal of mischief
amongst his countrymen when he visited the isthmus . . . . By
extravagant promises, futile talk and thinly veiled anti-white sentiments, the poison he left behind has not yet died away."[34]

Garvey's crusade was conducted primarily on behalf of Africans, those blacks in the diaspora as well as those still in the motherland. However, on some occasions he championed the cause of other nonwhites who were subject peoples. For example, in March 1922 Garvey in his capacity as provisional president of Africa pledged the support of four hundred million Negroes to Mahatma Gandhi, "one of the noblest characters of the day," in the cause of a free India. Speaking to a massive audience at his Liberty Hall headquarters in New York, Garvey commented that it was customary for the British to suppress liberty and typical of them to imprison and execute the leaders of libertarian causes everywhere. In a cable to Lloyd George, then prime minister, Garvey asserted: "We are for the freedom of India and the complete liberation of African colonies, including the Nigerias, Sierra Leone, Gold Coast and Southwest and East Africa. We wish your nation all that is good, but not at the expense of the darker and weaker peoples of the earth."[35]

Of course, many of the darker and weaker peoples Garvey had in mind were under British rule in Africa. Also in March of 1922 a mammoth Garveyite assemblage unanimously and enthusiastically protested the "brutal manner" in which the British government had treated the indigenous population of Kenya. "You have shot down a defenseless people in their own native land for exercising their rights as men." The same protest contained an undisguised warning that: "Such a policy will only tend to aggravate the many historic injustices heaped upon a race that will one day be placed in a position to truly defend itself, not with mere sticks, clubs and stones, but with modern implements of science. Again we ask you and your government to be just to our race, for surely we shall not forget you."[36]

The event in Kenya that had precipitated the Garveyite protest was a bloody disturbance which followed the arrest of Harry Thuku, secretary of the Young Kikuyu Association. Thuku, a telephone operator in the employ of the government, had been waging a strenuous campaign against the increased hut and poll taxes and in opposition to the iniquitous *kipande* labor system

which required all males sixteen years of age and older to register and carry identification cards showing their finger prints. Thuku's progress among the Kikuyu alarmed the authorities who decided to banish him. As many as eight thousand persons protested shortly after he was taken into custody. When violence erupted outside the police station where Thuku was being held, more than a score of Africans were killed.[37]

Sir Edward Northey, British governor of Kenya Colony in 1922, had ascertained that Thuku was in communication with the UNIA. In a letter to a Mr. Kamulegeya, a Muganda employed by the office of the provincial commissions in Kampala, Uganda, Thuku mentioned the fact that he had asked the "Negro Association" for advice and help.[38] A copy of this letter fell into the hands of the British. Publications of UNIA had also been sent into Kenya. It did not appear that the Garveyites had propagandized extensively in the colony and, as a matter of fact, exceedingly little was known about local UNIA activities, but Sir Edward sent a confidential dispatch on the subject to the colonial secretary, Winston Churchill.[39] When Garvey applied for travel documents to go to East Africa in 1923 his application was flatly rejected.

We now know in retrospect that a number of East Africans fell under Garvey's spell in the early 1920s. Daudi Basudde, a Muganda who chafed under colonial rule, had visited England in 1921 and returned deeply impressed by Garvey and the UNIA.

He . . . is the head of the wonderful group which exists today, which has a membership of close on five millions. . . . It's convinced that the four hundred million Blacks in the world will undoubtedly acquire a Kingdom in their land of Africa. This man Garvey, the work which he has done cause all people to be afraid and the fame of him will spread to all lands.[40]

Another Ugandan inspired by Garveyism was Reuben Spartas Mukasa who had performed military service during World War I. Spartas became curious about the movement after reading the *Negro World*. In 1925 he corresponded with McGuire informing the patriarch that he had established the African Progressive As-

sociation and explaining that he was willing to "go to hell, jail or die for the redemption of Africa."[41] A few years later Spartas founded the African Orthodox Church in Uganda "for all right-thinking Africans, men who wish to be free in their own home, not always thought of as boys." The political implications of Spartas' assertion of denominational independence were obvious. In 1949 his involvement in anti-colonial political activities led to Spartas' imprisonment for eight years.

In 1922 there was some apprehension in the Colonial Office owing to the connections being forged gradually between East Africans and blacks in the United States. Robert Coryndon, governor of the Uganda Protectorate, informed the colonial secretary in May of that year that applications for passports were being received from some of the more prominent and wealthy natives who wanted to study abroad—in England, in America, and elsewhere. Although he rated such bodies as the UNIA "scarcely . . . formidable political organizations," Governor Coryndon considered it "advisable to avoid as far as possible anything that may facilitate communication between the leaders of such movements and young natives of this Protectorate."[42] He wished to refuse to issue passports to the southern states of the United States. The Colonial Office agreed. Henceforth, passports for Ugandans to study in America became extremely difficult to come by.[43]

Garvey's voice was heard in southern Africa as well as eastern Africa. Amy Jacques Garvey was told by the king of Swaziland (Swaziland was at that time a British High Commission territory) that the monarch knew of only two blacks in the western hemisphere: Jack Johnson who in 1908 incensed white America by becoming the first black heavyweight champion and Marcus Garvey.[44]

From the white-supremacist Union of South Africa there were also indications that Garvey had struck a responsive chord among black Africans. Mary Benson has written that "even in remote corners of the Ciskei, illiterate peasants suddenly became wildly excited over the anticipated advent of Garvey to liberate

them."[45] Garveyism had a particularly powerful impact on two individuals: T. D. Mweli Skota and Dr. James Thaeli. Skota was active in the African National Congress, the principal agent of Bantu resistance to *baaskaap,* but his concerns were not confined to South Africa. Pan-Africanism was evident in Skota's call for a "monster conclave" of representatives from various parts of the African continent.[46] Of mixed Basuto and Cape Coloured parentage, Dr. Thaeli studied for fifteen years in the United States. Allegedly motivated by Garvey he returned to South Africa and became president of the Cape Western branch of the African National Congress.[47] Despite the many reverses Garvey suffered, the bubble of hope that the Jamaican had inspired was not punctured. Almost five years after Garvey's deportation, James Stehazu, a Bantu, wrote of the "lion-hearted M. Garvey . . . a great African leader."[48] If the African motherland were to be redeemed for the black race, he believed, the only way was that illuminated by the gospel of the UNIA.

Garvey's influence was even greater in West Africa than in East Africa or South Africa. The *Negro World* was eagerly read in many parts of both British- and French-controlled West Africa. One resident of Ibadan, Nigeria, became "greatly infused with the spirit of Garveyism" and thought Garvey "a great champion of the race."[49] A vocal UNIA branch was established in Lagos, Nigeria. Membership reached approximately three hundred but only one-tenth of those were dues-payers. Nevertheless the group stimulated much discussion of Garvey and Garveyism. Some middle-class Nigerian critics associated with the newly formed National Congress of West Africa thought Garvey's pan-Negro schemes grandiose and irreconcilable with their goals of independence and nationalism. But still they appreciated the black economic self-determination exemplified by the Black Star Line. "The idea of establishing a line of steamers owned and controlled by Africans is a great and even sublime conception for which everybody of African origin will bless the name of Marcus Garvey . . ." editorialized the *Times of Nigeria.*[50] To give every member of the black race the "golden opportunity" to

participate in the Black Star corporation, one hundred thousand shares were offered for sale in Nigeria for five dollars or thirty shillings each. The offering was publicized in newspapers such as the *Lagos Weekly Record* in 1921.

The Colonial Office secretly solicited opinions from its personnel in Nigeria about Garveyite operations, especially the Black Star Line. Some Nigerians, it was reported to Whitehall in 1922, had indeed purchased stock in Garvey's shipping enterprise. Behind Garvey's activities in West Africa, it was assumed, was a dishonest desire to raise money from the Africans "for which it is not proposed to make any very adequate return."[51] Colonial officials in Nigeria concluded that, in general, the "natives" were not responding favorably to Garveyism. Reeking of the smugness and self-deception that formed so vital a part of the mentality of colonialism, the report asserted that, "They [the Africans] recognize they are much better off under British Rule and have no desire to change . . . for American Negro rule."[52]

In 1923 there were rumors that the Black Moses was planning a sojourn to the land of his forefathers. The acting governor of Nigeria was of the opinion that Garvey should be refused a passport to visit that colony, and the majority of the Executive Council in Sierra Leone strongly believed that he should not be permitted to land in Freetown. In a letter to the new colonial secretary, the Duke of Devonshire, on May 28, 1923, the acting governor of Sierra Leone stated that Garvey appeared to "advocate an open repudiation of obedience to the established European Governments in Africa accompanied with violent abuse of them." He described Garvey's views as mischievous and seditious. The *Negro World,* though not absolutely prohibited in Sierra Leone, had been carefully regulated. To support his description, the acting governor cited an ominous article in that newspaper.

When it comes to Africa we feel that the Negro has no obligation to anyone but himself. Whatsoever kind of Government we have in Africa . . . has been imposed on us by stealth and deception; therefore we are not compelled to recog-

nize them . . . . If it takes a thousand years we shall work for and probably
fight for, the freedom of our Fatherland.[53]

It is interesting to note that UNIA adherents from Sierra
Leone had been active not only in their native land, but also
in neighboring Senegal. They were instrumental in setting up
branches in Dakar, Rufisque, and Thiès, in widely disseminating
information about Garvey's programs, and in collecting subscriptions for his schemes. After nervously scrutinizing the
UNIA's activities for some months, the French authorities had
in 1922 deported some of the Sierra Leonians in question. To
the British consul-general in Dakar, the French move presented
a curious spectacle of the UNIA, presumably an anti-European
movement originating in the United States, indulgently tolerated
in four British colonies and sternly repressed in eleven French
dependencies.[54]

Liberia, Sierra Leone's neighbor to the southeast, was envisioned by Garvey to be the nucleus of his African liberation
movement. As is well known, the republic was founded by
American Negroes in the first half of the nineteenth century
and has been ruled by Americo-Liberians ever since. Mayor
Gabriel Johnson of Monrovia, born of American parents, was appointed the local UNIA representative with the exalted title of
"potentate" at an extremely generous salary. Although the British legation felt that the ruling elite in the main had displayed
no enthusiasm for Garveyism, it was fearful that the nearly
bankrupt Liberian government, annoyed by its inability to justify
its pretensions to equality with white nations, might turn to the
UNIA for assistance. And because Liberia was regarded as the
jumping-off point for a black-dominated African empire, Garveyite actions were closely examined.

In 1920 Garvey dispatched one Elie Garcia to consult the
Liberian government about colonization possibilities for New
World Negroes. The UNIA proposed to transfer its headquarters from New York City to Monrovia. Moreover, it promised
to do everything possible to help Liberia liquidate its debt to
foreign governments. On June 14 Edwin Barclay, Liberian secre-

tary of state, writing to Garcia at the behest of President Charles D. B. King stated that his government "appreciating as they do the aims of your organization as outlined by you, have no hesitancy in assuring you that they will afford the association every facility legally possible in effectuating in Liberia its industrial, agricultural and business projects."[55] In March of the same year he had been even more specific when he told UNIA officials that his government would "be glad to have your Association occupy . . . certain settlements already laid out."[56]

On the strength of these commitments and others made by Mayor Johnson, early in 1924 three representatives of the UNIA, reportedly well-financed, arrived in Liberia to propose a settlement scheme involving three thousand blacks. The plan allegedly was to establish six communities, two on the British border and four on the French frontier. According to the British chargé d'affaires, Francis O'Meara, President King did actually offer a trial concession of five hundred acres, but not in the areas desired by the UNIA.

The delegation had been successful in having a committee formed to receive the repatriated Negroes due to arrive later in 1924. That committee consisted of influential Liberians. The initial settlement was to be established near Cape Palmas on the Cavallah river in Maryland County. Although not satisfied on a number of points, the UNIA nevertheless instituted a campaign to raise two million dollars to construct the first colony.

But in mid-year when it was bruited about in Liberia that three thousand disciples of Garvey would be departing for Monrovia in November, the government abruptly reversed itself. Barclay in a letter to Messrs. Elder Dempster and Company, Ltd., shipping agents, stated categorically that no member of the Garvey movement would be allowed to enter the country.[57] Steamship companies received the same notification. British officials were delighted, to say the least.

When three representatives of Garvey did actually disembark on July 25 they were immediately placed under police guard and deported in short order. Later in the year, after the deportation

of Reginald C. Hurley, a Barbadian with Garveyite leanings, the British chargé became alarmed over the possibility of other British subjects entering Sierra Leone as a result of expulsion from Liberia.[58] In October O'Meara was instructed by cipher telegram to forewarn the governor of any British colony to which deportation of UNIA personnel might be contemplated.

President King, in his message to the legislature of Liberia delivered on December 9, 1924, dealt with the Garveyite problem in extremely strong terms. He stated that the apparent intention of the UNIA was "to use Liberia as its base for the dissemination of its propaganda of racial hatred and ill will." The president was particularly disturbed by the "loud and continued boasts of numbers of that association, in America, to the effect that they had obtained a firm foothold in Liberia, and that the Republic would be used as a point'd'appui whence the grandiose schemes of their leader . . . would be launched." Therefore it was necessary for the government to take such steps as "would show to our friendly territorial neighbours and the world at large, that Liberia was not in any way associated or in sympathy with any movement . . . which tends to intensify racial feelings of hatred and ill-will." President King proceeded to denounce political incendiarism, whether Negro or not, and asserted that the objective of his country was not racialism, but nationalism. Negroes in the United States who desired to settle in the Republic and were willing to take an oath of exclusive allegiance to Liberia would be heartily welcomed. However, and there can be no doubt that King was talking about Garvey here, Liberia's doors would be securely closed to a movement which planned to launch "a race war against friendly states in Africa."[59]

Early in January 1925 when the Liberian president visited Sierra Leone, the governor of that colony applauded his "statesmanship."

Your Excellency by slamming the door on spurious patriots from across the Atlantic, men who sought to make Liberia a focus for racial animosity on this Continent, deservedly earned the gratitude not only of every West African Government but all who have the true welfare of the African at heart.[60]

Edmund Cronon in his *Black Moses* explained Liberia's volte-face by alluding to *The Liberian News* which averred that both Britain and France coveted the country and Garveyism would provide a convenient excuse for partition.[61] Cronon also commented that the contents of the Garcia report, so disparaging about the Americo-Liberians, "the most despicable element in Liberia," Garcia had called them, had become known to the government.[62]

Garcia's report, theretofore secret, had been stolen along with other valuable documents from the UNIA vault. The purloined papers were recovered by a private detective agency but the contents were made public. Garcia had been candid about actual conditions in Liberia. He found the country rich in natural resources, but paradoxically "the poorest place on the face of the earth and the people are actually starving." Liberia's ruling elite, he concluded, objected to any element that might end "their political tyranny, their habits of graft and their polygamic freedom." In his report Garcia recommended that representatives of Garvey going to Liberia deny firmly any intention of entering politics. "This attitude will remove any possible idea of opposition and will not prevent us after having a strong foothold in the country to act as we see best for their own betterment and that of the race at large." These remarks were probably construed by the Liberian authorities to mean that once the Garveyites had entrenched themselves they would attempt to take over the government.[63] Disclosure of the UNIA's "revolutionary purposes" in Liberia had solidified governmental opposition to Garvey according to *The Liberian News*. Former president Arthur Barclay, at one time a champion of the UNIA, publicly reversed his position in August 1924, charging the Jamaican whom he considered a security risk with "stirring up a race war."[64] It is also noteworthy that shortly after Liberia unequivocally disavowed the Garveyite program, an agreement was concluded with the Firestone Rubber Company. Some of the same territory earmarked for development by the UNIA was leased to Firestone for rubber exploitation.[65]

At the time he carried out his research, Cronon could not determine the extent to which England had instigated the Liberian rejection of Garvey. Relevant British official records were closed to him under the old fifty-year rule. Now open for inspection, they do *not* indicate that Britain played any active role. It should be noted, however, that some of the correspondence dealing with Garvey was officially destroyed many years ago. One can only guess if documents implicating Whitehall were among those destroyed.

Garvey himself suspected that his critic, W. E. B. Du Bois, of the "National Association for the Advancement of Colored, Light People," as representative of the United States at President King's second inauguration, had also played a sinister role in the Liberian affair.[66] One can only speculate about Dr. Du Bois' standing in Monrovia. He had certainly done his share to portray Garvey as a subversive force in Liberian affairs.

In an assessment of Garvey published in the *Crisis,* Du Bois asked rhetorically if his Jamaican bête noir presumed to seize power in Liberia, a land which had successfully resisted France, England, and the United States. "How long," Du Bois inquired, "does Mr. Garvey think that President King would permit his anti-English propaganda on Liberian soil, when the government is straining every nerve to escape the Lion's Paw?"[67] A few years after Du Bois launched his attack on Garvey, he was appointed by President Coolidge to be his special representative at the inauguration of President King. To a large degree the appointment was politically motivated. Coolidge was persuaded to placate the Negro vote, long taken for granted by the Republican party, by giving the editor of the *Crisis* the rather pretentious but unsalaried post of Envoy Extraordinary and Minister Plenipotentiary. Du Bois found his brief stay in Liberia exhilarating. He returned to the United States, his fertile brain filled with plans for Liberia's economic development to be accomplished with American aid, private and governmental.[68]

Du Bois did not intend to use Liberia or any other African land as a sanctuary for persecuted American blacks. In 1922

he had written that opportunities for emigration to Africa were very circumscribed indeed.[69] However, at times he was loath to completely rule out the possibility of a significant portion of the black population eventually migrating from the United States. This might take place, he conjectured, if "they could find a chance for free and favorable development unmolested and unthreatened, and in case the race prejudice in America persisted to such an extent that it would not permit the full development of the capacities and aspirations of the Negro race."[70] Du Bois' ultimate objective remained the achievement of full equality for blacks within the borders of the United States. Bad as conditions were, as late as 1940 he felt that Afro-Americans could not find a place where subjugation by white imperialism was less severe. Yet in 1961 Du Bois, then an embittered nonagenarian alienated from the land of his birth, decided to take up residence in Ghana. Before his death there in 1963 he had become a Ghanaian citizen.

That Du Bois was no stranger to the British in the 1920s is certain. In June 1921 he had written to Sir Auckland Geddes, His Majesty's ambassador to Washington, about his plans to hold a Pan-African congress in Europe. Some sessions were scheduled for London. Du Bois was especially eager to secure British cooperation. He wanted a spokesman to attend for the Colonial Office to clarify its policy regarding Africa. Significantly, Du Bois reminded Geddes that the Pan-African congress had nothing to do with the Garvey movement.[71] Pan-African congresses were often confused with UNIA activities. Whitehall, although it associated Du Bois with the more moderate American Negroes, declined to send a representative. Du Bois continued to differentiate between his own activities and those of the UNIA. Before sailing he told reporters that the Pan-African movement was not a scheme of migration either to Africa or anywhere else, nor was it based on race hatred or revolution. In Paris Du Bois stated bluntly: "The colored American cannot withstand the African climate. We cannot oust the Europeans and do not desire to do so."[72] Lord Hardinge,

who reported to the Foreign Office on the Paris Pan-African meetings, informed Lord Curzon that Du Bois, later an admitted Marxist, had accused Garvey of having "relations with the Reds, with whom the negroes did not wish to have anything to do."[73]

Over the years Garvey and Du Bois frequently traded epithets and launched *ad hominem* attacks and counterattacks against one another.[74] Du Bois described his West Indian rival as a "little, fat, black man; ugly, but with intelligent eyes and a big head."[75] He called Garvey "vain, egotistical . . . a poor judge of human nature." On another occasion he spoke about Garvey's "monumental and persistent lying." In 1924 Du Bois asserted unequivocally that the leader of the UNIA was "the most dangerous enemy of the Negro race in America and in the world," adding gratuitously that he was "either a lunatic or a traitor."[76]

In a piece in the *Negro World* of February 13, 1923, subsequently reprinted in *Philosophy and Opinions*, Garvey fired his own volley of invectives. He excoriated Du Bois as "a hater of dark people," "the Negro misleader," "this lazy dependent mulatto," and "a liar."[77] Even during his twilight period, Garvey's enmity toward Du Bois and the NAACP as lackeys of the white man did not wane. In 1935 Garvey's *Black Man* carried an article about the "Barefaced Coloured Leader," calling him "the most brazen fellow that one knows in Negro leadership." No attempt whatsoever was made by Garvey to mask his hostility toward Du Bois who, by that juncture in the lean years of the Great Depression, had had his own disagreements with the NAACP. He was simply "a white man's nigger." He was "a man of prejudice," "imbecilic," and devoid of vision. Garvey was steadfast in his belief that Du Bois had been responsible in part for his imprisonment and deportation. It was he, Garvey maintained to the end, who had sabotaged the Liberian colonization scheme in the 1920s.[78] How tragic that these two extraordinary men—each a giant in his own right, each a pan-Negroist in outlook, each sincere in his determination to build a brighter future for the black race—should have been rabid opponents instead of allies in those troubled times.[79]

Du Bois was hardly the only black man to cast himself as a counterpoise to Garvey. Not all Africans were pleased with the attention shown Africa by Garvey. To some he was an unwelcome intruder, a pretentious upstart, an outlander, and a subversive. Blaise Diagne, a Senegalese black who served as a deputy in Paris, spoke for those "French natives" who wished to remain "French." Writing to Garvey in 1922, Diagne was clearly guilty of hyperbole when he commented, "France has given us every liberty and . . . has unreservedly accepted us on the same basis as her European children." France alone, he said, was capable of "working generously for the advancement of the black race." Diagne expressed his concern to Garvey about "the revolutionary theories of separation and emancipation, to which you have given your name." He feared trouble and disorder from the Garveyites.[80]

Occasionally an African opponent would do verbal battle with Garvey in the United States. One who was prepared to consult American officials about Garveyite schemes was Prince Madarikan Deniyi. The prince was colorfully described by the *Chicago Defender*[81] as a former pharmacist and embalmer from Lagos, Nigeria. He wrote a series of articles in 1921 purporting to show that the UNIA and earlier like-minded movements were about as substantial as "tissue paper." Back-to-Africanism was a farce predicated on the false notion that Africa was peopled by savages who would meekly acquiesce to the rule of repatriated New World blacks. Prince Deniyi contended that African kings, chiefs, and presidents were not eager to share, much less relinquish, their power. His indictment of Garvey included the charge that Liberia had not endorsed UNIA plans in which it figured prominently; the charge that Garvey had spent excessive sums of money to advertise himself and to keep out of prison; the declaration that the Black Star Line was bankrupt and that the UNIA lacked the money to purchase a good seaworthy ship. Garvey and Bruce Gritt [*sic*][82] were also accused of misrepresenting Africa as a means of fomenting revolution.

One M. Mokete Manoedi of Basutoland also took up the cudgels against the Garvey movement and requested British as-

sistance. Manoedi, the son of a headman in the Leribe district, wrote to the colonial secretary, Winston Churchill, in September 1922 to enlist his cooperation.[83] Manoedi was then conducting a vigorous campaign to discredit Garvey and his movement. He claimed that the Jamaican, preaching "the most dangerous and vicious kind of doctrines" had had some influence on the unthinking black masses in the United States, the West Indies, Central and South America, and Africa. The influence had to be destroyed. Manoedi's ambitious plans included writing to both the Negro and white press in the United States, issuing pamphlets and traveling throughout the country lecturing on the menace of Garveyism.[84] The financial burden of the campaign was too much for Manoedi to bear alone.

Additional information about Manoedi and his request was sought from South Africa. Officials there were well aware of UNIA propaganda work carried out with little apparent success in Johannesburg and Cape Town. No trouble in the immediate future was anticipated.[85] Therefore, Arthur Frederick, British High Commissioner in Pretoria, advised the Colonial Office that he did not think a contribution "from Basutoland's funds towards the expenses of a 'campaign' in America would be justified." Money could be expended to a greater advantage in South Africa.[86]

Denied British governmental support, Manoedi doggedly continued his attack on the Garvey movement, publishing a pamphlet entitled *Garvey and Africa* for the benefit of the non-African world. He contemptuously called Garvey a "magolomaniac [*sic*]," "this mythical Moses," "a sort of Black Billy Sunday," and a "demagogue not a great leader."[87] He charged that Garveyism was synonymous with the overthrow of white rule, and, furthermore, it was causing increased oppression of natives by whites.[88]

Not infrequently blacks who were estranged from the black nationalist cause informed the British about the doings of Garvey and of eminent lieutenants such as Bishop McGuire. In Sep-

tember 1924 Edwin Urban Lewis, formerly a priest in the African Orthodox Church, wrote to the British consul in New York City. Of the African Orthodox Church, Lewis declared that it was "nothing more than a political unit of a seditious association," meaning the UNIA. As to McGuire, Lewis was very much afraid that he would be a "menace to the good and well being of our people in the West Indies were he or his gang of religeous [sic] fanatics allowed to organize in any of the West Indian Islands." In effect he accused McGuire of conspiring to subvert British rule throughout the Caribbean. Therefore Lewis hoped that the British would not allow the African Orthodox Church to function in that region.[89]

On November 1, 1924, Lewis informed the British authorities that a few days earlier Bishop McGuire had held a secret conference at UNIA headquarters in Manhattan. On that occasion the Antiguan-born prelate supposedly read a letter from the "Archdeacon of Pretoria" in South Africa applying on behalf of himself and five-hundred congregants for admittance to the African Orthodox Church. As Lewis quoted it, the bishop's reply was as follows: "Yourself and congregation coming over to us will be welcome, and as Lord Primate of the African Orthodox Church, should you make it possible for Sir Marcus Garvey to get in to that country I am sure the day will not be far off when by virtue of my high office, I will consecrete you as bishop of South Africa."[90] Lewis beseeched the British consular officials in New York to communicate these schemes to Pretoria for they were a threat to "our Government" and to the welfare of Christian churches in South Africa.[91] Exactly what the British consul-general chose to do with this information cannot be ascertained. In any event, Garvey, unlike Bishop Turner, never entered South Africa's white *laager*.

To offset UNIA propaganda, representatives of the British government in the United States did help to finance a new magazine called *The British West Indian Review.* It was hoped that the publication would affect the interests of West Indians resid-

ing in New York, a group which was drawn to the Garvey crusade. The British consul-general even assisted in the preparation of the first number of the magazine which appeared in April 1923.[92]

Generally, it may be said that as apprehensive as the British were about the destructive impact that Garvey might have on the empire, they felt that the United States government was chiefly responsible for him within its borders. UNIA activities in British colonies or in countries where British interests were vitally involved were another matter. Garvey's *Negro World* was banned in many dependencies; and members of the UNIA were denied entry to others. Just days after Garvey was convicted in June 1923 for using the mails to defraud investors in the Black Star Line, the Foreign Office began to predict his moves after imprisonment. If, after the expiration of his term, Garvey applied for a passport to travel to any British West African colonies, facilities were not to be granted. Ironically, Garvey, the passionate apostle of "back-to-Africanism," never did set foot on African soil.[93]

Garvey would doubtlessly have been amused by the way in which British officials impugned his motives. One wrote in 1923 that "it is more than suspected that Garvey's efforts . . . .are not without considerable financial profit to himself and his immediate associates."[94] As previously mentioned the governor of British Honduras saw Germany as the evil force behind Garveyism. Others claimed that the UNIA was linked with the Wobblies, the International Workers of the World.[95] In the judgment of one observer, Garvey's paper attacked Britain "with a malignity reminiscent of the 'Irish World.'"[96] Clearly, *Negro World* malignity was no greater than that of an official who lamented in 1924 about Garvey: "It's a pity the cannibals do not get hold of this man."[97] Die-hard champions of the erstwhile British empire might share those intemperate sentiments for the reverberations of Garveyism are still being felt.

In 1953 the *Chicago Defender,* which had strenuously opposed Garvey, observed that his ideas were turning Africa topsy-turvy.

An article on turmoil in Africa asserted that wherever the indigenous population was attempting to overthrow European rule Garvey's name was revered. Referring specifically to the emergency in Kenya which had been declared the previous year, the *Defender* stated that "every serious student of the black nationalism that has developed in Kenya especially among the Kikuyu, attributes it to the influence of Marcus Garvey."[98] This was an exaggeration of course. But it was not the last time Garveyism and the Mau Mau were linked. For example, the British command paper on the origins and growth of Mau Mau accuses the African Orthodox Church of anticolonial activism in East Africa in the 1930s. Bishop McGuire is mentioned by name in the report on Mau Mau, as is William Daniel Alexander, who had been consecrated primate of the African province of the African Orthodox Church and who established branches of the sect in Kenya and Uganda in the 1930s. In Kenya the church became Kikuyu-dominated and "by the time the emergency was declared Jomo Kenyatta had become its deity."[99]

Mzee Jomo Kenyatta, putative leader of the Mau Mau and today president of an independent Kenya, once related to C. L. R. James

how in 1921 Kenya nationalists, unable to read, would gather around a reader of Garvey's newspaper, the Negro World, and listen to an article two or three times. Then they would run various ways through the forest, carefully to repeat the whole, which they had memorized, to Africans hungry for some doctrine which lifted them from the servile consciousness in which Africans lived.[100]

On the eve of independence Kwame Nkrumah acknowledged Ghana's debt to Marcus Garvey.[101] And in his autobiography Nkrumah stated that Garvey's *Philosophy and Opinions* did more to fire his enthusiasm than any other book.[102] James Coleman, in his book *Nigeria: Background to Nationalism,* has written, "Many themes in latter-day Nigerian nationalism have been cast in the spirit if not in the exact words of Garvey." Garveyite ideas deeply impressed Nigerians who were involved in proto-nationalistic organizations such as the Nigerian Youth

Movement and the National Congress of British West Africa. Nnamdi Azikiwe, later Nigeria's first chief of state, called Garvey "one of the most farsighted persons of African descent to walk upon God's earth."[103]

As early as 1920 a weekly published in Lagos editorialized about Garveyism: "The way has been boldly and clearly marked out for us by our brothers across the sea; all we have to do is fall in line; follow the examples they have given us of oneness of purpose and aim. The present time is the most opportune and favorable for the initiation of any great movement for the betterment of our race. . . ."[104]

Almost three decades later, Osita Egbuniwe eulogized Garvey in these words published in the *Daily Comet:*

> Nigeria, oh my Nigeria
> . . . .
> For thy redemption brave Garvey fell,
> But yet in the gang of the immortals,
> Thy sons shall fight unseen by mortals,
> And ere long regain thy pride, oh Nigeria.[105]

In June 1940 when Marcus Garvey breathed his last in a modest house in West Kensington, London, his death aroused no great excitement. Only a handful of blacks were at his bedside when death came at the age of fifty-two. One, a black clergyman sadly bid farewell: "Well done, good and faithful servant."[106]

Ten years after his death, the *Kingston Gleaner* stated, ". . . it would be true to say of Jamaica, and to a lesser extent of the other British West Indies that national consciousness received its main inpetus, if it was not actually born, from the racial movement associated with the still revered Marcus Garvey."[107]

In November 1956 in Kingston, an estimated fifteen thousand people, including many dignitaries, paid tribute to his memory.[108] Fittingly, a bust of Garvey now graces King George VI Memorial Park in Kingston and a thoroughfare is named in his honor. He has been enshrined as the first national hero of his

native land. His countenance appears on Jamaican currency. A Marcus Garvey Prize for Human Rights is annually awarded by the Jamaican government. His remains were disinterred and brought to Jamaica in 1964.[109] Significantly, on that occasion when Garvey's remains were laid to rest, Jamaica's minister of development and welfare observed that "Garvey's stage was not Jamaica; it was the continents of colored peoples."[110] In 1965 at the celebration of Ghana Republican Day held at the Garvey shrine in Kingston, Chief Nana Kobina Nketsia of Ghana called Garvey "my international leader."[111]

Today, in England itself, Garvey is lauded, even deified, by black power advocates from the West Indies and Africa. In a very real sense, as far as the British empire is concerned, Garveyism has triumphed. Whitehall had had good reason to be worried.

Back in the United States, where he had once made such a forceful impression, memories of Garvey had faded by the time of his death. Among the multitudes who had shared his ideology and dreams, his passing doubtlessly conjured up once cherished hopes and visions. In 1940 the name of Garvey was probably an unfamiliar one to younger blacks. When Cronon began work on his story of Garvey in the 1940s, he was "struck by how nearly complete Garvey's obscurity was among younger black Americans, most of whom seemed to have scant knowledge of and little interest in his career and ideas."[112]

Even with the Jamaican out of the United States without the slightest hope of ever returning, his mystique was not wholly dissipated. There were still some Garveyites on the black American scene. Not all had lost faith in their Black Moses.

On July 18, 1937, a leaflet announcing a rally to the Harlem community reminded blacks that the UNIA was not dead. "Since Marcus Garvey left these shores we have been Father Divinists, Communists, Bayenists and heaven knows what. Why? Because men and women have strayed from the truth." The truth in question was the truth as told by Marcus Garvey, gone but far from forgotten by some zealous apostles.

May 1, 1938, was the occasion for a march of Garvey's Royal African Legions through the crowded streets of Harlem. Conspicuous in the procession amid the black nationalist "aristocracy," i.e., members of the Supreme Order of the Nile and the Distinguished Order of Ethiopia, was an automobile carrying a life-size picture of the exiled Garvey.[113]

At the end of World War II, five years after the Jamaican's untimely death, Garvey clubs were still operating as they are today. A Garveyite tabloid, the *Voice of Freedom,* was published monthly in New York. Pan-Negro in outlook, it was devoted to the interests of black peoples not merely in the United States but throughout the world.

In August 1945 an international convention was convoked in New York by the so-called Garvey clubs. There was a birthday eulogy to Garvey, a message from his widow, speeches by Afro-Americans, one-time officials of the UNIA, and by Africans, including the secretary of state of Liberia. Yet it provided only a faint echo of the once-thunderous Garveyite conclaves. Active Garveyites in 1945 constituted an infinitesimal fraction of the huge UNIA following in Garvey's prime.

Before the 1960s both college-level and secondary school history textbooks gave Garvey and Garveyism short shrift. Most ignored the movement altogether. Needless to say, the situation has changed dramatically in recent years. Books and articles about Garvey fairly tumble off the presses. A second edition of Cronon's book was published in 1969. Discovery in 1970 of a sizable cache of Garvey papers, some ten thousand documents in all, virtually guarantees a spate of monographs in the near future. The resurgence of reverence for Garvey by a new generation of youthful, militant blacks and the corresponding increase in scholarly interest about the West Indian has nothing to do with Garvey's back-to-Africanism. Rather it is because of Garvey's accentuation of race pride, his call for black autonomy, and his pan-Negro contemplations—all of which have come to be viewed in the light of the decolonization of Africa and the black revolution in the United States.

In 1958 when a Marcus Garvey Day celebration was held in Harlem, black nationalists were not the only participants in the festivities. It is a truism that politicians are and must be political animals; their attendance on that occasion reflected the black public's steadily growing appreciation of Garvey's contribution to the freedom struggle. Adam Clayton Powell, Councilman Earl Brown, a rival of Powell's, and Manhattan Borough President Hulan Jack, a political opponent of Powell's, were all present. In fact all apparently reached agreement on one point—that Garvey richly deserved the tribute they paid him. Brown said that Garvey's spirit lived on in Ghana which had attained independence the previous year. Rarely timorous about employing superlatives, Congressman Powell declared categorically that Garvey was "the greatest black man to live in this century—bar none—living or dead."[114]

Gestures of appreciation of the Jamaican by Afro-Americans were frequently made in the next decade or so. A fifty-block area, earmarked to become New York's first Model Cities renewal site, was named after him. That was in Brooklyn's Brownsville section. In the same community blacks successfully agitated to have the city rename a playground the Marcus Garvey Park.[115]

In view of Garvey's separatist ideology, it may be surprising that he was saluted by Dr. Martin Luther King in 1965.[116] Of course it is no surprise that Garvey has won the plaudits of Eldridge Cleaver,[117] Floyd McKissick,[118] and Stokely Carmichael.[119] It is no wonder Garvey was all but canonized by Malcolm X whose own father had been an organizer for the UNIA. In his autobiography Malcolm fondly remembered his father's "crusading and militant campaigning with the words of Marcus Garvey." As a youth Malcolm was taken to UNIA meetings where slogans such as "Africa for the Africans," "Ethiopians Awake," and "Up, you mighty race," were indelibly inscribed on his consciousness. Malcolm never did forget the shiny photographs of the Jamaican black nationalist that were circulated at those meetings.[120] In 1964 Malcolm attributed

the African and West Indian liberation struggle to Garvey's inspiration and added: "All of the freedom movement that is taking place right here in America was initiated by the work and teachings of Marcus Garvey. The entire Black Muslim philosophy here in America is feeding upon the seeds that were planted by Marcus Garvey."[121]

Elijah Muhammad, titular leader of the Black Muslims, has also lauded Garvey's work and courage. He has hailed Garvey, has coupled him with Noble Drew Ali,[122] and has called both "fine Muslims."[123] It was no coincidence that Essien-Udom found written in bold letters on a bulletin board at the University of Islam, the Garveyite exhortation: "Up, you mighty race. You can accomplish what you will!"[124]

Thus, today Garvey is lionized by blacks in the United States, in his native Jamaica, in Africa, his ancestral homeland, in Britain—in short wherever there are race-conscious persons of African extraction. Future historians may well view him as the central figure in twentieth-century black history. Already he is widely regarded as the patron saint of black nationalism and the progenitor of black power. More than any other black leader, Garvey, through his worldwide activities, underlined the international character of the color problem. He was a pan-Negroist without equal.

NOTES

1. John Hope Franklin, *From Slavery to Freedom: A History of Negro Americans* (New York: Vintage Books, 1969), p. 492.

2. *Thirty Years of Lynching in the United States—1889-1918* (New York: NAACP, 1919), p. 23.

3. Ibid., p. 25.

4. Ibid., pp. 5, 29. Wilson's own record as president on race relations was abysmal. For example, he was responsible for greatly expanding segregation in federal departments.

5. In July 1917 an especially tragic riot occurred in East St. Louis, Illinois. Thirty-nine blacks and nine whites lost their lives. A few months later a riot erupted in Houston. Black soldiers and white civilians were involved. In what can best be described as a "legal lynching," thirteen of the former were summarily tried, convicted, and hanged. Forty-one others were sentenced to life terms. Black Americans were deeply shocked by this outrage.

6. Franklin, *From Slavery to Freedom*, p. 480.

7. Marcus Garvey, *Philosophy and Opinions of Marcus Garvey or Africa for the Africans*, ed. Amy Jacques Garvey (London: Frank Cass & Co., Ltd., 1967), p. 82.

8. Ibid., p. 57.

9. The Garveyites were not wholly consistent on this point. The *Negro World* did carry bleaching cream ads but only for the Walker Company. After the death of the founder of that concern, her daughter became a backer of the UNIA.

10. The best article on this remarkable figure is Gavin White, "Patriarch McGuire and The Episcopal Church," *Historical Magazine of The Protestant Episcopal Church*, 38, no. 2 (June 1969): 109-141.

11. Ibid., p. 119. White has shown that the African Orthodox Church was not an auxiliary of the UNIA as is commonly supposed. Many members of the AOC were not disciples of Garvey who never actually joined McGuire's church himself (p. 120). Most Garveyites had nothing to do with the AOC.

12. See McGuire's Preface to Marcus Garvey, *Philosophy and Opinions of Marcus Garvey*, Part II, pp. XI-XII.

13. *Opportunity*, 2, no. 21 (September 1924), p. 284.

14. *The New York Times*, August 6, 1924. Garvey himself often spoke of Christ as black. Paradoxically, he also observed that "our God has no color." That God he felt had to be seen through the "spectacles of Ethiopia" and not through white spectacles. See Marcus Garvey, *Philosophy and Opinions*, pp. 33-34. The AOC has *not* emphasized a black Christ.

15. Public Record Office, Foreign Office 371/4567: Report. No. 232(5) on *Negro Agitation*, January 7, 1920.

16. Marcus Garvey, *Philosophy and Opinions*, p. 53.

17. Ibid., p. 122.

18. Ibid.

19. Beverley Reed, "Amy Jacques Garvey: Black, Beautiful and Free," *Ebony*, June 1971, p. 48.

20. Quoted in Lerone Bennett, Jr., "The Ghost of Marcus Garvey: Interviews with Crusader's Two Wives," *Ebony*, March 1960, p. 59. Mrs. Garvey said that she did not feel that the "back-to-Africa movement would be valid for American Negroes today." Bishop McGuire has written that Garvey neither advocated nor planned a wholesale back-to-Africa pilgrimage. See his Preface to *Philosophy and Opinions*, Part II, pp. XII-XIII.

21. The entire report can be found in W. F. Elkins, "'Unrest Among the Negroes': A British Document of 1919," *Science and Society*, 32, no. 1 (Winter 1968): 66-79.

22. Public Record Office, Foreign Office 371/4567: Eyre Hutson to Colonial Secretary, May 10, 1920.

23. Ibid., Colonial Office 884/13: Confidential Report on Riot in Belize, July 1919.

24. One writer contends that the UNIA in British Honduras "earned a respectability unmatched in any other colonized country in the 1920's." The government actually accorded it the status of a "friendly society," a term usually reserved for charitable, fraternal, and civic groups. Theodore G. Vincent, *Black Power and the Garvey Movement* (Berkeley, California: Ramparts Press, 1971), p. 175.

25. P.R.O., F.O. 371/4567: Eyre Hutson to Colonial Secretary, May 10, 1920.

26. Ibid., F.O. 371/5684: Reports of Police Superintendent, July 3 and 4, 1921.

27. Ibid.: Memo of Interview with Marcus Garvey at Government House, Belize, July 5, 1921.

28. Vincent, *Black Power and the Garvey Movement*, p. 174.

29. P.R.O., F.O. 371/5684: F. Gordon to A. R. Bennett, British Minister in San Jose, Costa Rica, May 9, 1921.

30. Edmund Cronon, *Black Moses: The Story of Marcus Garvey and the Universal Negro Improvement Association* (Madison: University of Wisconsin Press, 1962), p. 88.

31. Vincent, *Black Power and the Garvey Movement*, p. 174.

32. P.R.O., F.O. 371/5684: Graham to Lord Curzon, May 27, 1921.

33. Ibid., F.O. 371/7236: Graham to Lord Curzon, September 8, 1922.

34. Ibid., F.O. 371/10632: Annual Report for 1924 for Panama and Canal Zone submitted by Braithwaite Wallis.

35. Ibid., F.O. 371/7286: Copy of Press Release from UNIA, March 13, 1922.

36. Ibid., Copy of Press Release from UNIA, March 20, 1922.

37. George Bennett, *Kenya, A Political History: The Colonial Period* (London: Oxford University Press, 1963), pp. 45-46; Carl G. Rosberg, Jr., and John Nottingham, *The Myth of Mau Mau: Nationalism in Kenya* (New York: Frederic A. Praeger, 1966), pp. 50-52. One eyewitness said there were fifty-six African fatalities.

38. P.R.O., C.O. 536/277: H. Thuku to Kamulegeya, September 9, 1921.

39. Ibid.: Northey to Churchill, May 4, 1922.

40. Quoted in Kenneth King, "Early Pan-African Politicians in East Africa," *Mawazo*, 2, no. 1 (1968); 8.

41. F. B. Welbourn, *East African Rebels—A Study of Some Independent Churches* (London: SCM Press Ltd., 1961), p. 81.

42. P.R.O., C.O. 536/119: Coryndon to Colonial Secretary, May 30, 1922.

43. King, "Early Pan-African Politicians in East Africa," p. 5.

44. See John Henrik Charke's Introduction to Amy Jacques Garvey, *Garvey and Garveyism* (London and New York: Collier-Macmillan Ltd., 1970), p. xiv.

45. Mary Benson, *The African Patriots—The Story of the African National*

Congress of South Africa (New York: Encyclopaedia Brittanica Press, 1964), p. 57.

46. Ibid., pp. 56-57.

47. Ibid., pp. 70-71.

48. Jabez Ayodele Langley, "Garveyism and African Nationalism," *Race,* 11, 2 (1969): 158.

49. J. B. Webster, A. A. Boahen, with H. O. Idowu, *History of West Africa—The Revolutionary Years—1815 to Today* (New York and Washington: Praeger Publishers, 1967), p. 282. The individual in question did think that Garvey's plans were somewhat impractical.

50. Quoted in Langley, "Garveyism and African Nationalism," p. 159.

51. Ibid., p. 162, quoting from Sir Hugh Clifford, Report on UNIA Activities in Nigeria, February 27, 1922.

52. Ibid.

53. P.R.O., C.O. 267/600: Acting Governor of Sierra Leone to Duke of Devonshire, May 28, 1923.

54. Ibid., F.O. 371/7286: Consul-General, Dakar to Foreign Secretary, August 17, 1922.

55. Barclay to Garcia, June 14, 1920, in Marcus Garvey, *Philosophy and Opinions of Marcus Garvey* (London: Frank Cass & Co., Ltd.), p. 365.

56. Cronon, *Black Moses,* p. 125. According to the Garcia report he denounced the editor of a Liberian newspaper who was opposed to the UNIA, asserting, "Any Negro who fails to see the benefit to be derived from the Association was a consummate fool." *Amsterdam News,* September 10, 1924.

57. P.R.O., F.O. 371/9553: Barclay to Messrs. Elder Dempster and Co., June 30, 1924.

58. Ibid., O'Meara to Foreign Secretary, August 23, 1924. The Garveyites arrested and deported in July 1924 were engineers who had been assigned the task of erecting housing.

59. Ibid., C.O. 267/607: Message of President King to the Liberian legislature, December 9, 1924.

60. Ibid., Speech by Governor of Sierra Leone, January 22, 1925.

61. Cronon, *Black Moses,* p. 130. After consultation with Ernest Lyon, the Liberian consul general in Baltimore, William Castle of the State Department reported that the Liberian government feared seizure by the French and British.

62. Ibid., pp. 124, 130.

63. *Amsterdam News,* September 10, 1924.

64. Frank Chalk, "Du Bois and Garvey Confront Liberia: Two Incidents of the Coolidge Years." Paper delivered at the 52nd annual meeting of the Association for the Study of Negro Life and History, October 13-17, 1967, Greensboro, N.C.

65. Garvey, *Philosophy & Opinions,* p. 384. Speaking at the Royal Albert Hall in London in June 1928, Garvey stated that Firestone's agent had influ-

enced President King to reverse himself. He also blamed his imprisonment on the fact that Firestone, backed by Herbert Hoover, then secretary of commerce, knew that he could prevent President King's reelection.

66. Garvey, *Philosophy and Opinions*, p. 379.

67. *Crisis*, Vols. 20-21 (January 1921).

68. Chalk, "Du Bois and Garvey Confront Liberia," pp. 5-7.

69. *Crisis*, 23, 4 (February 1922).

70. W. E. B. Du Bois, *Dusk of Dawn: An Essay Toward an Autobiography of a Race Concept* (New York: Schocken Books, 1968), p. 199.

71. P.R.O., F.O. 371/5708: Du Bois to Geddes, June 16, 1921.

72. *New York Tribune*, September 6, 1921..

73. P.R.O., F.O. 371/5708: Hardinge to Curzon, September 6, 1921.

74. The first two *Crisis* articles about Garvey (March 1920 and January 1921) were actually quite positive in many respects.

75. W. E. B. Du Bois, "Back to Africa," *The Century Magazine*, 105, no. 4 (February 1923): 539.

76. *Crisis*, 28 (May 1924).

77. Garvey, *Philosophy and Opinions*, pp. 310, 312, 318.

78. Marcus Garvey, "Barefaced Coloured Leader" *Black Man*, 1, no. 8 (Late 1935): 8.

79. For a comparison of the two men and their policies, see Elliott M. Rudwick, "Du Bois versus Garvey: Race Propagandists at War," *Journal of Negro Education*, 28 (Fall 1959): 421-429.

80. Raymond Leslie Buell, *The Native Problem in Africa* (Hamden, Connecticut: Archon Books, 1965), II, p. 81. James E. K. Aggrey, the Gold Coast-born educator was a frequent critic of Garvey. He implored South African students: "If you love your race, tell it around that Marcus Garvey is their greatest enemy." Quoted in Kenneth King, "James E. K. Aggrey: Collaborator, Nationalist, Pan African," *Canadian Journal of African Studies*, 3, no. 3 (Fall 1970): 519.

81. *Chicago Defender*, May 14, 1921. Garvey called the *Defender* his "arch enemy in the newspaper field." He scored the *Defender* for printing hair-straightening and skin-bleaching advertisements. See Garvey, *Philosophy and Opinions*, pp. 78-79.

82. John "Grit" Bruce was a Garveyite journalist who wrote a regular column for the *Negro World*.

83. P.R.O., F.O. 371/8153: Manoedi to Churchill, September 30, 1922.

84. Once when Manoedi apprised his street-corner listeners that black Africans found Garvey presumptuous in designating himself provisional president of Africa, a melee ensued. Cronon, *Black Moses*, pp. 106-107.

85. P.R.O., F.O. 371/8153. J. C. Smuts minute, February 28, 1923.

86. Ibid.: High Commissioner Frederick to Devonshire, March 23, 1923.

87. M. Mokete Manoedi, *Garvey and Africa* (New York: The New York Age Press, 192?), pp. 3, 9, 14.

88. Ibid., pp. 14, 20.

89. P.R.O., F.O. 371/9633: Edwin Urban Lewis to His Majesty's Counsul General, September 24, 1924.

90. Ibid.: Edwin Urban Lewis to Pro-Consul James, November 1, 1924. Lewis thought that the man in question was named "Alexander." Daniel William Alexander who had been born in the Cape Province in 1883 did join the African Orthodox Church in 1924. He subsequently became archbishop and primate of the African Province of the AOC.

91. Ibid.

92. P.R.O., F.O. 371/8513: Armstrong, Consul-General to His Majesty's Ambassador in Washington, D. C., April 18, 1923.

93. In 1927 Mary White Ovington wrote that "it would be easier for the proverbial camel to go through the eye of the needle than for a professed Garveyite to enter Negro Africa today." Mary White Ovington, *Portrait In Color* (New York: Viking Press, 1927), p. 29.

94. P.R.O., F.O. 371/8513: Maurice Peterson minute on Garvey press release, February 9, 1923.

95. Ibid., F.O. 371/5684: R. H. Hadow minute (February 21, 23, 1921, on Gov. Willcocks of Bermuda to Churchill, January 16, 1921). The same claim was made by the secret report of 1919, "Unrest Among the Negroes."

96. Ibid., F.O. 395/389: Angus Fletcher report, June 12, 1923.

97. Ibid., F.O. 371/9633: Minute of June 20, 1924 (Author not identified) on British Embassy, Washington, D. C., to MacDonald, June 6, 1924.

98. *Chicago Defender*, June 6, 1953. There is no evidence whatever to support the *Defender's* claim that Jomo Kenyatta, Kwame Nkrumah, and Garvey "met and talked and dreamed and planned together" in London, "for a period roughly covering 10 years." Garvey himself was only residing in London from 1935-40.

99. *Historical Survey of the Origins and Growth of the Mau Mau*, Cmnd. 1030 (London: H.M.S.O., 1960), p. 45.

100. C.L.R. James, *The Black Jacobins* (New York: Vintage Books, 1963), p. 397.

101. Kwame Nkrumah, *I Speak of Freedom* (New York: Frederick A. Praeger, 1962), p. 107.

102. Kwame Nkrumah, *Ghana: The Autobiography of Kwame Nkrumah* (New York: Thomas Nelson and Sons, 1957), p. 45.

103. James Coleman, *Nigeria: Background to Nationalism* (Berkeley and Los Angeles: University of California Press, 1965), p. 190; Nnamdi Azikiwe, *Renascent Africa* (Accra: Published by the author, 1937), p. 98.

104. *Lagos Weekly Record*, February 7, 1920. Quoted by E. U. Essien-Udom in his Introduction of Marcus Garvey, *Philosophy and Opinions*, p. 25.

105. Ibid., pp. 26-27.

106. Len S. Nembhard, *Trials and Triumphs of Marcus Garvey* (Kingston: The Gleaner Co., Ltd., 1940), p. 237.

107. Quoted in Cronon, *Black Moses*, p. 217.

108. *Jamaica Times*, November 10, 1956.

109. Adolph Edwards, *Marcus Garvey 1887-1940* (London and Port-of-Spain: Beacon Publications, 1967), pp. 33, 35.

110. *Amsterdam News,* November 28, 1964.

111. *Jamaica Star,* July 9, 1965.

112. Cronon, *Black Moses,* p. 12.

113. Arna Bontemps and Jack Conroy, *Anyplace but Here* (New York: Hill and Wang, 1966), p. 212.

114. *New York Post,* August 3, 1958.

115. *The New York Times,* July 13, 1968 and August 17, 1968. The trend is continuing in the 1970s. In 1971 the Robert Treat School in Newark, named for the seventeenth century Puritan founder of the city, was renamed the Marcus Garvey School.

116. See Essien-Udom's Introduction to *Philosophy and Opinions,* p. 26. Dr. King, an exponent of integration, was impressed by the fact that Garvey had given "millions of Negroes a sense of dignity and destiny" and had made "the Negro feel he was somebody."

117. Eldridge Cleaver, *Post-Prison Writings and Speeches,* ed. Robert Scheer (New York: Random House, Vintage Books, 1969), pp. 66-67.

118. McKissick has written that Garvey was "one of the most outspoken, dynamic, and dedicated Black Nationalists in America." See Floyd McKissick, *Three-Fifths of a Man* (London: Macmillan & Co., 1969), pp. 124-126.

119. Stokely Carmichael, *Stokely Speaks—Black Power Back to Pan-Africanism* (New York: Vintage Books, 1971), p. 198.

120. Malcolm X and Alex Haley, *Autobiography of Malcolm X* (New York: Grove Press, Inc., 1966), pp 6-7.

121. Interview in the *Jamaica Gleaner,* July 12, 1964.

122. Born Timothy Drew in North Carolina, Noble Drew Ali established a Moorish American Science Temple in Newark, New Jersey, in 1913. He taught that the provenance of American Negro slaves had been Morocco.

123. E. U. Essien-Udom, *Black Nationalism* (New York: Dell Publishing Co., 1964), p. 76.

124. Ibid., 160.

3

BLACK AMERICA
AND THE ITALIAN-ETHIOPIAN CRISIS:

An Episode in Pan-Negroism

Perhaps no single event in the twentieth century more clearly illuminated the nexus between diaspora blacks and continental blacks than the Italian-Ethiopian war. It is not at all surprising that Benito Mussolini's invasion of Ethiopia in October 1935 stoked passions deep in black Americans. Ethiopia has long held a special place in the hearts and minds of many Afro-Americans. In large measure this has been due to two factors: an impressive cultural tradition traceable to ancient Axum and a uniquely successful resistance to the European intrusion in Africa in the latter part of the nineteenth century.

Black writing is replete with references to Ethiopia's legacy. The brilliant pan-Africanist Edward Wilmot Blyden (1832-1912) called the Ethiopians of antiquity "the most creditable of ancient peoples" and claimed that they had achieved "the highest rank of knowledge and civilization."[1] J. A. Rogers, the lecturer, columnist, traveler, and chronicler of Negro achievements, asserted categorically that the Ethiopian royal family was the "most ancient lineage in the world." He maintained further that at least eighteen rulers of ancient Egypt were "unmixed" Negroes or Ethiopians.[2] And W. E. B. Du Bois wrote of Ethiopia as the "sunrise of human culture" and the "cradle of Egyptian civilization."[3]

In the final decade of the nineteenth century, the same decade which saw the humiliating defeat of the Italians at Aduwa by the Ethiopians,[4] a phenomenon occurred which both reflected and enhanced Ethiopia's extraordinary status in the eyes of American blacks. Black churches were established in the United States (and in South Africa) with names such as Abyssinian, Ethiopian, and Kush. Confronted by a deteriorating rural economy and a hardening of white racism, some American Negroes seized upon the theory that their ancestry could be traced to the once-glorious Ethiopian kingdom. The theory had no basis whatsoever in historical fact, but quite understandably it had great appeal for a downtrodden people who had been culturally castrated. They wanted to tie themselves ethnically to Africans who have successfully preserved an independent nation and an independent Christian church in the face of the European scramble. Additional impetus and rationalization for "Ethiopianism" was provided by the Scriptural prophecy: "Princes shall come out of Egypt; Ethiopia shall stretch out her hands to God."[5]

It was not by mere coincidence that the official anthem of Marcus Garvey's Universal Negro Improvement Association was entitled "Ethiopia, Thou Land of Our Fathers." On a number of occasions Garvey rhetorically used Ethiopia as a synonym for the whole African continent. "Scattered Ethiopia" was a phrase he used to describe Africans in the diaspora.[6] "Wake up Ethiopia! Wake up Africa!" he wrote fervently, "Let us work towards the one glorious end of a free, redeemed and mighty nation. Let Africa be a bright star among the constellation of nations."[7] Despite this rhetoric, the empire of Ethiopia in northeast Africa was not the target of Garvey's back-to-Africanism.

Only rarely did any of the advocates of black repatriation set their sights on Abyssinia.[8] In 1903 one W. H. Ellis, a black multilingual businessman from San Antonio who had previously attempted to create a Negro settlement in Mexico, had tried to set up a refuge for Afro-Americans there.[9] To that end he had visited Emperor Menelik, grand uncle to Haile Selassie and vic-

tor over the Italians in the historic battle at Aduwa. Nothing came of the repatriation scheme although Ellis appears to have won the confidence of the Negus.[10]

In December 1935 the *Chicago Defender,* eager to strengthen Afro-America's bonds with Ethiopia reprinted excerpts from a letter allegedly written by Crown Prince Johannes in 1909 for his father, the ailing Emperor Menelik. Addressed to a Negro newspaperman, it demonstrated, in the judgment of the *Defender,* that Menelik died expressing love for black Americans. The letter promised that six million acres would be reserved in the land of Judah for all "colored people" who were willing to return home. There they would find gold and diamonds in plentiful supply. In fact, Ethiopia was "too rich."[11]

After World War I, Chicago was the headquarters of Abyssinianism, a movement blending religion and black nationalism. Adherents referred to themselves as Ethiopians or Abyssinians, but disdained the terms Negro and colored. The authorities in Chicago had become concerned when in June 1920 one Abyssinian leader burned an American flag to symbolize the surrender of allegiance to the United States and the assumption of allegiance to Ethiopia.[12]

One of the principal goals of the movement was the emigration of black Americans to Africa, particularly to Ethiopia. Grover Cleveland Redding, a cofounder of the movement who claimed birth in Ethiopia, traveled to several black ghettos throughout the country recruiting for the Star Order of Ethiopia. A recruit could become an "Ethiopian Missionary to Abyssinia" and in theory indicate his willingness to return to the African homeland in one of forty-four useful capacities. Redding's guiding thesis was that "the Ethiopians do not belong here and should be taken back to their own country."[13] A picture of the "Prince of the Abyssinians," an Ethiopian flag, a copy of an American-Ethiopian treaty, and a statement prophesying the return of black-skinned people to Africa were available to members—all for a dollar.[14]

Awareness of Ethiopia had been heightened considerably by

a visit to New York in 1919 by a party of Ethiopian officials. In Harlem the group was warmly welcomed on behalf of black Americans. Belanghetta Herouy, mayor of Addis Ababa and a future foreign secretary, took the opportunity to express satisfaction at the "wonderful progress Africans have made in this country" and went on to say, "We want you to remember us after we have returned to the native country."[15] In 1927 the Ethiopian ambassador to the Court of St. James, Dr. Azaz Wahrnek Martin, was dispatched to America to encourage blacks to settle in the ancient kingdom. To lure physicians, dentists, engineers, mechanics—in short, those with badly needed professional and technical skills—attractive salaries and free land were proferred. The publicity generated by the coronation of Haile Selassie in 1930 again focused Afro-America's attention on the "Last of Free Africa."

During the next two or three years a small community of Afro-American expatriates developed in Ethiopia. There are no precise census data on this New World Negro contingent. Roi Ottley estimated that several hundred resettled in Ethiopia.[16] An article published in 1933 stated that the black American community consisted of about one hundred and fifty souls.[17] A present-day scholar's retrospective enumeration puts the Afro-American population at around the one hundred mark.[18]

Dean of the black American community was Daniel R. Alexander, a Missouri-born missionary, who had settled in Ethiopia three decades earlier. Reputed to have been a favorite of Emperor Menelik's, he had become quite affluent over the years. Periodically, adventurous Afro-Americans would arrive with proposals for all manner of whimsical enterprises. Among these were a scheme to shoot monkeys and sell their skins, a project to open hair-straightening parlors, and a quixotic one to establish Menelik as leader of the world's black population.[19]

Not all of the expatriates were so fanciful. Some made solid, meaningful contributions. It is noteworthy that a West Indian Negro, Menelik's own doctor, was responsible for establishing Ethiopia's first hospital. In the 1930s there was a carpenter, a

cabinet maker, and a teacher. There was a skilled auto mechanic, James Hart, and there were social workers as well. Of course many others were unschooled and unskilled.

Undeniably, the post-coronation migration contained a number of bizarre characters. Richly deserving of commentary is Rabbi Arnold Josiah Ford who appeared in Ethiopia in 1930. Ford, a native Barbadian, had for a time in the 1920s ministered to the spiritual needs of Harlem's black Jews. He had also served as musical director for Garvey's UNIA. The circumstances surrounding his migration to Ethiopia are still murky. According to a recent explanation, Ford's decision to go to Ethiopia was prompted by a meeting with a Falasha who was touring America in 1928 or 1929. In 1930 Ford's congregation sent him to Ethiopia for the dual purpose of officially representing them at Haile Selassie's coronation and doing the spade work necessary to establish a settlement near Lake Tana.[20]

According to an unsympathetic contemporary source, Ford claimed that Negro organizations in New York had instructed him to take up residence in Africa in response to requests from the Ethiopian government. One organization was the Urieloth Club which had been formed by Ford himself to encourage a movement of colored peoples to Ethiopia. Prior to his departure from New York, Ford collected donations and subscriptions, some sizable. Supposedly he promised to negotiate with the government of Ethiopia for 125 acres per family of immigrants.[21]

Ford was viewed as something of a radical and his objectives were seen as rather sinister by both English and American diplomatic personnel in Addis Ababa. One distressed American official asked the State Department to investigate the matter and to discourage American blacks from going to Ethiopia.[22]

It turned out that the Ethiopian government was not interested in Ford's project. Subscriptions began to decline. His treasury became depleted and by the end of 1934 almost half of his sixty disillusioned followers had returned to the United States. As the war with Italy became imminent, the American government repatriated most of the others. An impoverished Ford ended his days playing

banjo with a dance band in Addis Ababa—or so a British diplomat in Ethiopia reported with condescending glee.[23]

Without question, the most flamboyant New World Negro to involve himself in Ethiopian affairs in this era was Colonel Hubert Fauntleroy Julian, the "Black Eagle" of Harlem. One black contemporary described him as "tall, tan, terrific."[24] His critics were less kind. Born in Trinidad in 1897, Julian was to become a well-known parachutist and the most celebrated black pilot of his day. In the 1920s he was associated with the Garvey movement and apparently shared Garvey's concern for the well-being of Africa. His particular esteem for Ethiopia was reflected by the fact that the two planes he hoped to use for flights to Africa were named Ethiopia I and Ethiopia II.[25] Julian's first widely publicized attempt at a solo flight to Africa in 1924 proved to be a fiasco. His destination was Liberia but the flight ended in the mud flats of Long Island's Flushing Bay a few minutes after takeoff. In 1930 he managed to get to Africa but by ship not plane. His reputation had won him an invitation to become Haile Selassie's personal pilot and to organize His Majesty's air force. Julian's thoughts as the ship neared the African coast were set down in an autobiography published almost thirty-five years later.

This was one of the most emotion-packed moments of my life. . . . . I had a very strong sense of race, of the generations which had gone before and, as a result, this green coastline seemed to me to be the threshhold of my ancestral home. . . . I felt I was coming home, and I looked on all the dark-skinned people on the shore as part of my family. So overcome was I that as soon as the ship docked I ran down the gangway and knelt and kissed that first dirty, dusty piece of Africa on which I had set foot.[26]

Little time passed before the Lion of Judah decorated Julian with the Order of Menelik and commissioned him a colonel. Later interviewed about his meteoric rise to fame, Julian, attired in a pith helmet, a pink polo shirt, and white breeches with green stripes, modestly observed: "Brother, once I got there it was just will power and personality—that's the Alpha and axis."[27] How-

ever, Julian's prestige plummeted when the nine-lived adventurer crashed his plane during a flying display for the emperor. This occurred just prior to the coronation. Julian called it "a clear case of sabotage." Nevertheless, he ignominiously left Ethiopia.

A few years later as war clouds gathered over Abyssinia and Mussolini bombastically spoke of regaining the glory of ancient imperial Rome, Julian returned. Sartorially splendid as usual, the monocled Julian was given a somewhat cool reception upon his arrival in Addis Ababa in April 1935. He was there "to help my country if hostilities should come." A few months passed before his request to fly and fight for Ethiopia was granted by the emperor who also bestowed Ethiopian citizenship upon the "Black Eagle" and made him the nation's chief of aviation. Shortly thereafter, during a military review, Julian characteristically rode a white charger through the streets of the capital city. But once again he alienated His Majesty, this time by becoming embroiled in a fist fight with a former Chicago aviator, John C. Robinson. A Tuskegee graduate, Robinson dubbed himself the "Brown Condor." In the wake of the altercation, Robinson became commander of the Emperor's Royal Air Forces, a pitifully small fighting unit. Julian, having fallen from favor, was temporarily given the rather demeaning job of training infantry recruits in a remote region four hundred miles from Addis Ababa. Subsequently he became a military governor in Ambo. A week after the Italian invasion, Julian rode into Addis, this time less majestically on a mule. Upon learning that Aduwa had been lost, the Black Eagle declared his intention to recapture it. He then sent his trainees into battle and commented confidently: "I put fire and the devil into them. Now under my special training anyone of them can stand up against six Italians. I know just how to fight these Fascists, because I knocked out a lot of them in Harlem with only my fists."[28]

For reasons still nebulous, Julian never did see combat. News dispatches out of Ethiopia in November 1935 disclosed that the Black Eagle had asked to be relieved of duties because his authority was not being respected. In his autobiography Julian says

he made the decision to leave Ethiopia because the military situation was hopeless. The Ethiopians were desperately short of ammunition and weapons while the well-trained Italians were heavily armed. "I thought of the old proverb—'He who fights and runs away . . . .' "[29]

Back in the United States Colonel Julian made some remarks highly critical of Ethiopia, remarks which he retrospectively explains as part of a scheme to assassinate Benito Mussolini. As Julian relates the story, his calculated and well-publicized volte-face on the Ethiopian controversy led to the hoped for invitation to Rome where he was to meet with Il Duce. Only at the last moment did Count Ciano, the foreign minister, become suspicious of Julian's intentions and cancel the interview. Even for the Colonel, it was a "fantastic episode."[30]

The imperialistic adventure of fascist Italy came at a critical juncture in the history of black America. The Great Depression was ravaging people long frustrated and anguished by economic privation and racial discrimination. No wonder Mussolini's wanton aggression triggered an outpouring of cold fury. In 1943 a black writer was able to observe: "I know of no event in recent times that stirred the rank and file of Negroes more than the Italo-Ethiopian War."[31]

Even before the Italian invasion actually began in early October 1935, as tensions mounted in the horn of Africa, anti-Italian sentiment bubbled to the surface in black ghettos. In June 1935 heavyweights Joe Louis and Primo Carnera became the personification of the Ethiopian and Italian causes. When Louis, the "Brown Bomber," pulverized the gargantuan Carnera, the victory was treated as an event of enormous import. The *Chicago Defender's* front-page banner headline reported Louis' spectacular knockout with great relish. Clearly, it was much more than a ring victory for a black fighter. It was a triumph for the entire race. One *Defender* story was entitled "Ethiopia Stretched Forth A Hand And Italy Hit The Canvas." Other *Defender* pieces pointedly referred to Carnera as "Italy's Favorite Son" and "Mussolini's pride and joy."[32]

Ad hoc groups were formed to rally support for Ethiopia in several of America's black communities. Dr. Willis N. Huggins, a historian, led the International Council of Friends of Ethiopia. Haile Selassie's son-in-law on a visit to New York in 1933 implored him to "Keep Ethiopia alive in the hearts of American blacks."[33] Two years later in Geneva, Huggins represented his organization and defended Ethiopian interests before the League of Nations.

Funds were raised and medical supplies were purchased for embattled Ethiopia by countless Afro-American sympathizers. Boycotts of Italian-made goods were organized. Many wished to join the fighting but recruitment of blacks for service in Ethiopia was discouraged because of the cost. In an interview, one Ethiopian diplomat, Tecie N. Hawariat, said that technical, flying, and medical units would be useful. Generally, however, those sympathetic to the emperor's cause could be most helpful by acquiring arms and ammunition for Ethiopia.[34]

As John Hope Franklin, the distinguished Negro historian, has observed, the defeat of Ethiopia was dreaded as the symbol of the Caucasians' final triumph. Consequently, "almost overnight even the most provincial among the American Negroes became international-minded."[35]

Editorial opinion in the Negro press was unanimous in voicing indignation over Mussolini's foul deed and in urging the League to succor Ethiopia. The *Afro-American* in October 1935 admonished the League "to hasten its economic penalties upon Italy and, even though late, approve the sale of modern arms to Ethiopia, so that this ancient nation may put up a real defense against the cut-throat brigands now invading its firesides."[36] Harlem's *Amsterdam News* bristled with anger and editorialized: ". . .that his [Mussolini's] invasion of Ethiopia is a barefaced defiance of every moral law goes without saying. . . . He is like a mad dog running through a town."[37]

The *Pittsburgh Courier,* perhaps the most influential Negro weekly in that era, added to the chorus of black voices protesting the rape of Ethiopia. The *Courier* suspected a conspiracy on the

part of the major European powers to advance their own interests at the expense of that African nation and the black man.
White imperialism was seen as the real enemy because it was
presenting a united front against the colored people.[38] Also
blameworthy was the Roman Catholic church, the target of a
blistering *Courier* editorial entitled "The Church Blesses Murder." An Italian cardinal was singled out and taken to task for
praying that the Italian armies be protected when they were
murdering Ethiopians.[39]

The editors of and contributors to the *Crisis,* the journal of
the NAACP, were also deeply nettled by the incursion of the
blackshirted legions. "Civilization Is Taken to Ethiopia" was the
sarcastic title of one *Crisis* editorial published toward the end
of 1935.

Coverage of the Ethiopian crisis was extensive, passionate,
and even occasionally fraudulent in Robert S. Abbott's *Chicago
Defender.* Its wrath was not directed solely at Italy, "The Beast
of Prey." It was extended to an Ethiopian general, Ras Gugsa,
who defected to the Italians. Gugsa was called "Ethiopia's modern Judas" and the *Defender* invented the term "Gugsacrat"
meaning one who betrays his country. The term never caught
on as did its Norwegian counterpart, "Quisling." Abbott's biographer says that a crusading journalist even fabricated a report
about how the Ethiopians averted the capture of Aduwa at one
point. The spurious *Defender* story, which was republished in
several other newspapers, told of a Coptic priest who had fashioned clay containers into which he had put tsetse flies. At the
appropriate moment the flies were released and the Italians
foiled![40]

The Ethiopian monarch was all but deified in much of the
black press. J. A. Rogers who had been dispatched to the war
zone by the *Courier* described Haile Selassie as a "wise and
peerless leader" and the "foremost living statesman."[41] Upon his
return to the United States Rogers wrote a pamphlet called *The
Real Facts About Ethiopia.* On the cover was a picture of
Menelik II, "Liberator of Ethiopia from Italy in 1896." Rogers

advocated close ties between blacks and Ethiopia, a land which offered a vast outlet for the skills and energies of Afro-Americans. He also proposed that Amharic, the official Ethiopian tongue, be taught in black schools.

Negro leaders, separatists and integrationists alike, angrily excoriated Il Duce for his infamous act. A London-based Marcus Garvey, then in the twilight of his career, poetically predicted:

> We'll march to crush the Italian dog
> And at the points of gleaming, shining swords
> We'll lay low the violent, Roman hog[42]

He characterized Mussolini variously as "the beast of Rome," "the arch-barbarian of our present age," and "madman Mussolini."[43] For Garvey writing in October 1935 nothing less than the black man's heritage was at stake in the Italian-Ethiopian conflict.

It is significant that Walter White, executive secretary of the NAACP, an organization so often at loggerheads with Garvey, was moved to speak of events in Abyssinia in very strong terms, racial terms at that. "Italy, brazenly, has set fire under the powder keg of white arrogance and greed which seems destined to become an act of suicide for the so-called white world."[44]

There were other manifestations of black American solidarity with the Ethiopians. Special religious services were held to enable Afro-Americans to offer their prayerful support for Ethiopia in its hour of need. One Negro church in Indianapolis remained open all night. Pedestrians entered, kneeled, and prayed for the safety of Ethiopia.[45] A Garveyite organization, the Nationalist-Negro Movement, distributed the following prayer to many black houses of worship in the United States and the West Indies with a request that it be made a regular part of the service: "Great God grant no Ethiopian soldier misses when he fires and that every Italian bullet go astray. Amen."

In some cases black hostility was difficult to control. Street-corner orators lambasted Mussolini from their stepladder platforms. The *Amsterdam News* reported on a black mob being

whipped into a frenzy. Protest demonstrations took place. And there were clashes between Italian-Americans and Afro-Americans on Harlem's Lenox Avenue and elsewhere.[46]

Detracting only slightly from black enthusiasm for the Ethiopian cause was the dispute over whether the Ethiopians were truly racial brothers. The matter was raised in both black and white circles. Some Ethiopians had balked at being called Negroes, a designation which they associated with enslaved Africans. Abyssinian, derived from the Arabic and meaning slave, was also frowned upon. White anthropologists usually differentiated Hamitic Ethiopians from most sub-Saharan peoples and acknowledged that Hamites had more impressive cultural credentials. Not a few Ethiopians were pleased by this distinction which conferred greater prestige upon them in European eyes. Though the Ethiopians possessed kinky hair, a flat nose, and thick lips, according to a *National Geographic* magazine generalization, he was not Negroid. "If he is not colored, then neither is Paul Robeson, Kelly Miller or any of the rest of us," retorted the *Afro-American.*[47] The retort was accompanied by a picture of a "typical" Ethiopian who undoubtedly would have qualified for the back of the bus in strictly segregated Dixie. In an editorial, "Are Ethiopians Colored," the same newspaper admitted considerable miscegenation in the history of Ethiopia but concluded, "despite all this mixing, Ethiopia at base, is predominantly African and black."[48]

In this connection it is noteworthy that when Dr. Malaku Bayen, Haile Selassie's personal representative, arrived in New York in 1936 with his American Negro wife, he was unable to find suitable accommodations downtown because of racial discrimination. Instead he stayed in Harlem which gave him a warm welcome.[49] Dr. Bayen, who was unmistakably Negroid, took great pains to explain that Ethiopians merely objected to the word "Negro" and not to being classified with their blood brothers in America with whom they shared a common ancestry.[50] Furthermore, Dr. Huggins, after consulting Ethiopian legations abroad, commented that the emperor was well aware

of the fact that he was "the only Black Sovereign in the world, and he considers himself as the natural leader of the (black) Negro race." The emperor, Huggins was quoted as saying, liked the phrase, "Ethiopia is the trustee for the future of the black races."[51]

On the other hand it has been alleged that the exiled Lion of Judah when in London purposely avoided contact with Negroes. This reportedly infuriated Garvey who had previously championed the emperor's cause. "Haile Selassie is the ruler of a country where black men are chained and flogged," wrote Garvey.[52]

In the summer of 1936 Garvey further asserted that if the "negro Abyssinian" was ashamed to be a Negro, he would be deserted by those Negroes of the world who were unashamed of their race. Referring to the tradition that holds that Ethiopian sovereigns are lineal descendants of Solomon and Sheba, Garvey said: "The new Negro doesn't give two pence about the line of Solomon. Solomon has been long dead. Solomon was a Jew The Negro is no Jew. The Negro has a racial origin running from Sheba to the present, of which he is proud. He is proud of Sheba but he is not proud of Solomon."[53] Selassie was taken to task for "playing white" and depending on white governments and white advisers. At the same time Garvey contended that in 1920 Ethiopia, along with other black countries, had been invited to send delegates to the International Convention of Negro Peoples. Others replied. Many sent representatives. The Abyssinians had returned their invitation unopened.[54]

Doubts about Ethiopia's commitment to the concept of black brotherhood notwithstanding, the pan-Negro implications of the Italo-Ethiopian struggle were obvious and were repeatedly alluded to. Terms such as "Ethiopian brothers" and "fatherland" or "motherland" meaning Ethiopia recurred in Negro periodicals with great frequency. The white author of an article in the *Crisis* stated bluntly: "The rape of Ethiopia is the rape of the Negro race."[55] He feared that Abyssinia might well be the fulcrum upon which the fate of the entire black liberation

movement would turn. A letter to the editor of the *Afro-American* articulated the feeling that "every colored person throughout the world should do his utmost to maintain the independence of the fatherland."[56]

Langston Hughes, the multitalented Afro-American writer, addressed himself in verse to the challenge posed to pan-Negroism by Mussolini's imperialistic land-grab. His "Ballad of Ethiopia" included these thoughts.

> Where the mighty Nile's
> Great headwaters rise
> And the black man's flag
> In bright freedom flies
>
> All you colored peoples
> No matter where you be
> Take for your slogan
> Africa Be Free
>
> All you colored peoples
> Be a man at last
> Say to Mussolini
> No! You shall not pass[57]

Blacks in the West Indies thought along the same lines. Caribbean interest in Ethiopia had not been widespread previous to the Italian onslaught, but the war created large-scale concern.[58] Colony after colony reacted, sometimes violently, to what was seen as an attack on all black people.

On the island of Barbados a series of mass prayer meetings was held for all who were sympathetic to Ethiopia and money was collected for the benefit of the Ethiopian Red Cross. The *Barbados Advocate,* which strongly supported League sanctions, regularly carried front-page news of the war. Local interest in the fray was even exploited by enterprising businessmen. An *Advocate* advertisement pointed out: "The Ethiopians' lack of modern war equipment has been a handicap to them. Why be

handicapped by Old-Fashioned Cooking Appliances? See the Modern Gas Appliances at the Gas Showrooms."[59]

In early October 1935 various organizations met in Georgetown, Guyana, and petitioned King George V to be allowed to fight on behalf of Ethiopia. "Twenty years ago Negroes fought to save white civilization," declared the president of one organization, "surely they cannot now be refused permission to fight for what they regard as the symbol of their own civilization."[60] So much concern over the Ethiopian tragedy was manifested in Guyana that the censors banned a Paul Robeson film, *Emperor Jones,* fearing that it would precipitate racial strife.[61] When a rumor was spread that Italian spies had distributed poisoned candy to Georgetown school children, it actually led to a panic. Several schools were closed. Frantic mothers kept their youngsters indoors and a white school inspector was almost killed by an enraged mob which took him for an Italian.[62]

In the 1930s a particular kinship with Ethiopia was felt by certain segments of the population of Jamaica: the Rastafaris who revered Haile Selassie as the living God,[63] and the disciples of Marcus Garvey. The Garveyites were in the forefront of the Jamaican response to Italian aggression. At a rally held in Liberty Hall, the headquarters of the Kingston division of Garvey's Universal Negro Improvement Association, Mrs. Amy Jacques Garvey argued that events in Abyssinia proved her husband was right. To her, Mussolini was God's instrument to bring black people to a greater realization of their real position in the world and the critical need for unity. Therefore the Italian invasion was a blessing in disguise.[64]

A petition signed by no fewer than fourteen hundred persons was drafted asking the king to allow Jamaicans to enlist in the Ethiopian army "to fight to preserve the glories of our ancient and beloved Empire." The petitioners thought of themselves as "Africans in the true sense of their being." They believed that some day they would return to "our Native Land to assist in the up-building of our Country." They subscribed to the theory that Africa was given to the sons of Ham by Divine Providence. As the descendants of the sons of Ham, they felt every right

to have "free parts of our country at our disposal whenever it
is our desire to go there."[65]

The petition was duly submitted to the governor of Jamaica
who then transmitted it to the colonial secretary. Not surpris-
ingly, the Colonial Office was unfavorably disposed to the idea
of permitting black Jamaicans to join the Ethiopian armed
forces. In fact, one official, sensing the pan-African implications
of the petition, wrote contemptuously of the "bellicose sons of
Ham in Jamaica, so anxious to serve two masters."[66]

Lest it be thought that only repatriation-oriented Jamaicans
were concerned with Ethiopia's fate, mention should be made
of a public meeting which was held in Kingston on October 13,
1935, under the auspices of a number of local organizations. One
speaker told the audience which had packed the Ward Theatre
to overflowing that they were there not merely as Jamaicans but
as a race of people. Another denounced the "political
drunkenness of Mussolini." Resolutions were adopted sympa-
thizing with the Ethiopian emperor, deprecating the action of
the fascist leader, and strongly supporting the League. In Mon-
tego Bay, on the northern coast, two thousand persons staged
a demonstration against Italian aggression.[67]

Trinidad responded to the Italian invasion with as much indignation as any of the islands. Longshoremen resolved to boycott
Italian ships and adamantly refused to help unload them. Black
anger was so widespread that a large department store whose
owner was the agent for the Italian Line, was forced to take
down its shipping agency sign because it was materially affecting
his business.[68] On October 10, a demonstration was held in Port-
of-Spain in connection with the Italian-Abyssinian affair. The
crowd marched to the Italian consulate shouting "Down with
Mussolini" and handed the consul a protest resolution.

The Trinidadian mentality was well illustrated by an incident
which occurred in Port-of-Spain. A Portuguese man was
celebrating the twenty-fifth anniversary of the Portuguese republic and two of his nation's flags were pulled off his premises
by persons who mistakenly thought they were Italian flags.

In early November more than twenty-five hundred people attended an open-air service commemorating the coronation of Haile Selassie. Life-size photographs of the emperor and empress and a large colored map of Ethiopia were shown to the assemblage.

In December the most bizarre stories, arousing a great deal of comment, were widely circulated that Yoruba incantations, the singing of weird hymns, grand feasting, tom-tom beating, and bloody sacrificial ceremonies were being indulged in on a daily basis at a village near Port-of-Spain. Cows, goats, sheep, pigeons, and turtles were slain. All of these strange rituals were carried out in the hope of invoking divine assistance for Ethiopia. It was believed that not one of the Trinidadians involved had ever seen Africa,[69] but apparently the probability that the last remaining independent kingdom in Africa was to be destroyed struck a highly sensitive emotional chord.

Of course, racial sentiment alone cannot explain the attitudes of West Indians to the war. The depression had hurt industry in the Caribbean rather badly in the 1930s. Unemployment was commonplace both in the towns and countryside. Distress was widespread and the workers' grievances were many. It is not coincidental that labor parties and unions frequently spearheaded the anti-Italian agitation. Thus the Italian aggression and the unemployment problem were merged in Trinidad and elsewhere.

In August there had been demonstrations by the unemployed which led to a ban on all such meetings and processions in Port-of-Spain. It is significant that on October 10, two resolutions which were unanimously passed by a "citizens' committee" (a) condemned the "shooting and bombing of thousands of defenseless men, women, and children for the purpose of glorifying Italian Fascist Imperialism" and (b) criticized the prohibition of meetings and marches as a direct attack upon the political rights of the working class by a government incompetent to solve the unemployment crisis.[70] The inspector general of the local constabulary reported that the individuals involved in the October disturbance were "identical with those who organized unem-

ployed and unemployable demonstrations early in August last."[71] Rioting which occurred on the island of St. Vincent was also attributable not only to the spirit of racial antagonism engendered by the conflict in Abyssinia but by unjustifiable increases in the prices of essential commodities. St. Kitts was also volatile in 1935 and the sugar workers there went on strike for higher wages.

West Indian restiveness was reflected in the many resolutions that were passed throughout the islands and transmitted to London. In St. Lucia, the International Friends of Ethiopia, at a mass meeting held in November 1935, passed a series of resolutions. One made the fairly common request that St. Lucians who desired to do so be permitted to volunteer for service in Ethiopia. Another protested against the mother country's embargo on arms and munitions to Ethiopia.[72] In April 1936 the same committee was urging the British government to adopt a more energetic policy to protect the sovereignty of Ethiopia in the Geneva peace talks than had been pursued in the first place to avert the war or to stop hostilities.[73] A resolution with almost the exact wording was adopted by the Trinidadian Friends of Ethiopia Committee.[74] That there was some inter-island communication on this issue seems very likely.

On the occasion of West India Day, two resolutions were passed by the St. Kitts Workers League, expressing "its deepest sympathy with the ancient Kingdom of Ethiopia" in its conflict with Italy. Resentment was expressed at the unjustifiable aggression committed against Ethiopia. It was further resolved that a copy of the resolutions be forwarded to the colonial secretary for transmission to the Ethiopian minister to the Court of St. James.[75] This service was not performed however. One official minuted that he did not feel that the Foreign Office should be used for "nonsense of this kind."

To be sure, resolutions on the Italo-Ethiopian war and Britain's role in it were not regarded as nonsensical by the Colonial Office. So concerned was Colonial Secretary Malcolm MacDonald that he forwarded dispatches to all of the British repre-

sentatives in East and West Africa. MacDonald was well aware of the charge that Britain had failed to make it clear to Italy at an early stage of the dispute that an Italian attack would be viewed in the gravest light. Due notice was taken of the fact that in the West Indies "a very considerable degree of interest, amounting at times to undesirable excitement" had been evoked by the conflict.[76] The colonial secretary was therefore understandably worried about "native opinion" in the African dependencies.

In that worry he was not alone. Moved by reports of the St. Vincent riots which had resulted in the killing and wounding of several people and the need for special protection of the whites, Hesketh Bell, a former governor of Uganda, wrote

The fact that the coloured inhabitants of a distant West Indian island, remembering their African ancestry, should appear to feel so deeply this attack by a white power on the only remaining negro nation shows how widely spread and vigorous can be the influences of race and colour. While the rise of feelings of racial antagonism in the West Indies is unfortunate the development of such an attitude among the teeming population of our vast African territories would be a misfortune of the first magnitude.[77]

West Indians living in the United States were no less interested in developments in Ethiopia than were their kinsmen back in the islands. They formed an organization called United Aid for Ethiopia which represented black people from British Guiana, Antigua, Trinidad, Barbados, Jamaica, Nassau, and many other colonies. In a letter of May 27, 1936, to Gerald Campbell, British consul-general in New York, the group asked Great Britain to insist upon severer sanctions, to refuse to recognize Italian sovereignty in any part of Ethiopia, and to deny the Italian government any loans that might be requested. They also pointed out that Britain's "implied indifference to the needs of our blood brothers" was keenly felt by West Indians at home and abroad.[78]

A few days later, without any prior notice, between twenty-five and thirty members of the West Indian organization visited Campbell and complained that nothing was being done to save the "Father of the coloured people" from destruction at the

hands of Italians.[79] Still not satisfied, they sent a letter to
Foreign Secretary Anthony Eden on June 5, 1936, expressing
great alarm over the rumored possibility that sanctions would
be revoked and British loans utilized to develop Ethiopian
territory.[80]

Considerable distrust of the British had been generated by the
Hoare-Laval plan to end hostilities which would have required
Ethiopia to cede two-thirds of its territory to Mussolini. Although never implemented, the plan revealed His Majesty's government to be a weak reed as far as Ethiopia and her sympathizers were concerned.

By May 1936 it had become increasingly clear that Britain
had retreated from a solution based on effective sanctions, one
perhaps necessitating force. A settlement, however unjust, based
on negotiations between Ethiopia and Italy was preferred. By
May, the Italians fighting with the advantage of modern weap-
onry including poison gas, had won militarily. Mussolini had
avenged the humiliating defeat suffered at Aduwa in 1896. At
long last the Italians had an empire and Haile Selassie began
a five-year exile in Britain. The worst fears of the West Indians
had been realized.

Those fears, indeed the intensity of West Indian feeling for
Ethiopia, were principally rooted in a sense of racial consanguin-
ity. Local economic problems were an aggravating factor which
rendered Negro inhabitants of the islands particularly sensitive
about their subjugation, economic or political, by whites in the
Caribbean or in Africa. Loyalty to the empire, frequently fragile
even before the crisis, was replaced during the war by identification with a kindred, although distant, African people.

The full meaning of the Italian-Ethiopian war for pan-Africanism was summed up by the Trinidadian, George Padmore,
one of the movement's most articulate spokesmen. For him the
conflict was simply a reflection of world politics. The West had
ignored Haile Selassie's appeal. Worse still it "actually connived
at Mussolini's gassing of defenceless Ethiopians by selling oil
to the dictator."[81] Writing in the *Crisis* in May 1935, Padmore

stated that it was "the duty of every black man and woman to render the maximum moral and material support to the Ethiopian people in their singlehanded struggle against Italian fascism and a not too friendly world,"[82] Padmore who had settled in London in 1935 was a member of the executive committee of the International African Friends of Abyssinia (IAFA) whose chief objective was to generate support and sympathy for Ethiopia. Chairman of the organization was another Trinidadian dedicated to the twin ideals of African independence and pan-Africanism — C. L. R. James. A few years later, James, using a pseudonym, wrote a phamplet entitled *Why Negroes Should Oppose the War*. Regarding Mussolini's invasion he observed, "Ethiopia was the last piece of Africa left free. . . . Every Negro with a spark of pride knows what happened, and remembers it with justified bitterness."[83] Others prominent in the IAFA were Jomo Kenyatta, honorary secretary; Mrs. Amy Ashwood Garvey, Marcus Garvey's ex-wife who served as honorary treasurer; and Dr. Joseph Danquah, a barrister and one of the founders of the Gold Coast Youth Conference. Closely associated with Padmore and James but not a member of the IAFA was Eric Williams, then a young student and today a distinguished historian and prime minister of Trinidad and Tobago.[84]

Padmore in his classic work, *Pan-Africanism or Communism,* succinctly explained the cooperation of Africans and West Indians in an hour of great danger.

The brutal rape of Ethiopia combined with the cynical attitude of the Great Powers convinced Africans and peoples of African descent everywhere that black men had no rights which white men felt bound to respect if they stood in the way of their imperialist interests. . . . With the realization of their utter defencelessness against the new aggression from Europeans in Africa, the blacks felt it necessary to look to themselves.[85]

Responding to the provocation of Il Duce, Padmore was reiterating a *raison d'être* for pan-Africanism. In doing so he gave voice to the thoughts and emotions of many British West Indians in 1935 and 1936, and afterwards.

From the foregoing evidence it is abundantly clear that New World Negroes at a critical moment made a strong racial identification with their beleaguered brothers in Ethiopia. Their enthusiasm for the African cause reached new heights. Regrettably, the black world had the will but not the power to stem the tide of fascist aggression. Perhaps the greater tragedy is that the white world which had the power lacked the will.

NOTES

1. Hollis R. Lynch, *Edward Wilmot Blyden: Pan-Negro Patriot, 1832-1912* (London: Oxford University Press, 1967), p. 57.

2. J. A. Rogers, *One Hundred Amazing Facts About The Negro With Complete Proof* (New York: J. A. Rogers, 1957), p. 4. On the cover of this book was a picture of Zaiditu, empress of Ethiopia and daughter of Menelik II.

3. W. E. B. Du Bois, *The World and Africa: Inquiry into the Part Which Africa Has Played in World History* (New York: International Publishers, 1968), p. 117.

4. Black Americans insofar as they were aware of events in Africa in 1896 almost certainly shared the sentiments of the *Savannah Tribune*, a Negro publication, which editorialized as follows: "The Abyssinians are defending their homes and native land; they are perfectly right in expelling foreign aggressions. This overbearing spirit exercised by European nations over African nations should be stopped. It is cruel, unworthy of Christian nations and unjust." *Savannah Tribune*, March 21, 1896, p. 2.

5. Psalm 68:31. See George Shepperson. "Ethiopianism and African Nationalism," *Phylon*, 14 (1953): 9-18. Shepperson uses the term Ethiopianism to refer specifically to secessions from mainstream nonconformist churches in Africa and not as a synonym for African nationalist liberation struggles.

6. Marcus Garvey, *Philosophy and Opinions of Marcus Garvey*, ed. Amy Jacques Garvey (London: Frank Cass and Co., Ltd., 1967). p. 39.

7. Ibid., p. 4.

8. The Ethiopian Empire scheme of sea captain Harry Dean, early in this century, does not seem to have been directed to the country of Ethiopia. Dean who claimed descent from Paul Cuffe, one of the first back-to-Africanists, once asserted: "I am an African and proud of it. There is not a drop of white blood in my veins." See Captain Harry Dean, *The Pedro Gorino* (Boston and New York: Houghton Mifflin Co., 1929).

9. J. Fred Rippey, "A Negro Colonization Project in Mexico 1895." *Journal of Negro History*, 6, 1 (January 1921): 66-73. In 1893 at a national convention of Afro-Americans summoned by Bishop Henry M. Turner, Ellis argued for

settlement in Mexico rather than Africa. The former had the advantages of greater proximity and greater civilization. See Edwin S. Redkey, *Black Exodus: Black Nationalist and Back-to-Africa Movements, 1890-1910* (New Haven and London: Yale University Press, 1969), p. 188.

10. See the editorial in the *African Methodist Episcopal Church Review*, January 1904. In 1903 Ellis delivered a letter from Menelik to Andrew Carnegie thanking the Scottish-born philanthropist for his "nobleness and generousness" and specifically for his gift to "African Americans of the United States assisting and aiding them to gain a higher sphere of civilization, knowledge, virtue and morality and educating them. . . . " The original letter is in The Carnegie Dumferline Trust in Scotland.

11. *Chicago Defender*, December 14, 1935.

12. Chicago Commission on Race Relations, eds., *The Negro in Chicago: A Study of Race Relations and a Race Riot* (Chicago: The University of Chicago Press, 1922), pp. 59-60.

13. Arna Bontemps and Jack Conroy, *Anyplace but Here* (New York: Hill and Wang, 1966), pp. 204-205.

14. *The Negro in Chicago*, p. 62. Also see E. U. Essien-Udom, *Black Nationalism—A Search for an Identity in America* (New York: Dell Publishing Co., 1964), p. 59. It is difficult to ascertain if the American-Ethiopian treaty in question is the commercial agreement negotiated in 1903. For additional information about the treaty, particularly W. H. Ellis' role in the American contacts with Menelik, see *The New York Times*, June 25, 1904, and July 17, 1904.

15. Roi Ottley, *New World A-Coming: Inside Black America* (Boston: Houghton Mifflin Co., 1943), pp. 106-107.

16. Ibid., p. 107.

17. See "Ethiopia '33" in *Crisis*, November 1933, p. 262.

18. William R. Scott, "Going to the Promised Land: Afro-American Immigrants in Ethiopia 1930-1935" (Paper delivered at the 14th annual meeting of the African Studies Association, Denver, Colorado, November 1971).

19. "Ethiopia '33," pp. 250-251.

20. Scott, "Going to the Promised Land," pp. 10-11.

21. Public Record Office, Foreign Office 371/19176: Secret Dispatch from S. Barton (British Legation in Addis Ababa) to Sir Samuel Hoare, November 21, 1935.

22. Ibid.

23. Ibid. The suggestion made by one historian that Rabbi Ford and W. D. Fard, founder of the Black Muslim sect, were one and the same has no basis in fact. It is predicated on the demonstrably false notion that Ford never went to Ethiopia, but went to Detroit instead. See Howard Brotz, *The Black Jews of Harlem: Negro Nationalism and The Dilemmas of Negro Leadership* (New York: Schocken, 1970), pp. 11-12.

24. Ottley, *New World A-Coming*, p. 107. For a readable account of Colonel

Julian's "madcap odyssey" through life, see John Peer Nugent, *The Black Eagle* (New York: Stein and Day, 1971).

25. Colonel Hubert Julian (as told to John Bulloch), *Black Eagle* (London: The Adventurers Club, 1965), p. 82.

26. Ibid., p. 84. Inexplicably, Julian notes that in May 1930 he sailed from Marseilles to Djibouti which he erroneously says was in French West Africa (p. 83).

27. *Daily Telegraph,* August 15, 1930.

28. *Daily Gleaner,* November 8, 1935.

29. Julian, *Black Eagle,* p. 112.

30. Ibid., pp. 114-118. Today Colonel Julian is board chairman of Black Eagle International Associates, international arms and ammunition dealers. The one-time opponent of Italian colonialism in Africa, almost three decades later during the Congo crisis, became a staunch supporter of Moise Tshombe, regarded by many as a tool of the imperialists. Indeed at the time of Tshombe's death, Julian was trying to ransom his Congolese friend from his Algerian captors. In addition, Julian who was formerly an aide to Garvey, today speaks contemptuously of the Black Power movement which was inspired by Garvey and which reveres the Jamaican. Colonel Julian, Personal interview, January 3, 1970.

31. Ottley, *New World A-Coming,* p. 111.

32. *Chicago Defender,* June 29, 1935. A week before the match, it was reported that Carnera had prophesied he would defeat Louis because the Detroit pugilist would be afraid to knock down a white man.

33. Ottley, *New World A-Coming,* p. 109.

34. *Afro-American,* September 28, 1935.

35. John Hope Franklin, *From Slavery To Freedom: A History of Negro Americans* (New York: Vintage Books, 1969), p. 574.

36. *Afro-American,* October 12, 1935.

37. *Amsterdam News,* October 12, 1935.

38. *Pittsburgh Courier,* October 12, 1935, and November 2, 1935.

39. Ibid., November 9, 1935.

40. Roi Ottley, *The Lonely Warrior: The Life and Times of Robert S. Abbott* (Chicago: Henry Regnery Co., 1955), p. 348; *Chicago Defender,* July 13, 1935.

41. J.A. Rogers, *The Real Facts About Ethiopia* (New York: J.A. Rogers Publications, n.d.), p. 44.

42. "The Smell of Mussolini," *Black Man,* July-August 1936.

43. *Black Man,* Late October 1935 and July-August 1936.

44. *Amsterdam News,* October 5, 1935.

45. *Afro-American,* September 21, 1935.

46. *Amsterdam News,* October 5, 1935.

47. *Afro-American,* October 5, 1935.

48. Ibid., October 12, 1935

49. Claude McKay, *Harlem: Negro Metropolis* (New York: E. P. Dutton and Company, Inc., 1940), pp. 166-167.

50. Ottley, *New World A-Coming,* p. 111. Dr. Bayen, who was the emperor's nephew, founded the Ethiopian World Federation Council in 1937. Its objectives included the preservation of Ethiopia's sovereignty and integrity and the dissemination of the ancient Ethiopian culture. Its motto was "Ethiopia Yesterday, To-day and Tomorrow." See Essien-Udom, *Black Nationalism,* pp. 60-61, 388-389.

51. Ottley, *New World A-Coming,* p. 112. Josephine Baker, the American Negro entertainer based in Paris, pledged her support to Italy. Among her reasons for favoring the Italians was that Haile Selassie kept his people in bondage and was not himself a Negro by blood. See *Chicago Defender,* October 5, 1935.

52. Quoted in McKay, *Harlem: Negro Metropolis,* p. 176.

53. *Black Man,* July-August 1936.

54. Ibid.

55. Harold Preece, "War and the Negro," *Crisis,* November 1935, p. 329.

56. *Afro-American,* October 19, 1935.

57. Ibid., September 28, 1935.

58. For the purposes of this discussion Guyana, formerly British Guiana, will be considered as part of the British West Indies.

59. *Barbados Advocate,* October 22, 1935.

60. *Daily Gleaner,* October 7, 1935.

61. Ibid., October 14, 1935.

62. Ibid., October 23, 1935.

63. The Rastafaris are discussed in chapter 4.

64. *Daily Gleaner,* October 15, 1935.

65. Public Record Office, Foreign Office 371/20154: UNIA petition enclosed in Edward Denham, Governor of Jamaica, to Colonial Secretary, November 13, 1935.

66. Ibid., Minute (author unknown), January 7, 1936.

67. *Daily Gleaner,* October 15, 1935.

68. *Barbados Advocate,* October 12, 1935.

69. Ibid., December 7, 1935.

70. P.R.O., F.O. 371/20154, A. C. Hollis to J. H. Thomas, January 6, 1936.

71. Ibid.

72. Ibid., Enclosed in S.M. Grier to Malcolm MacDonald, Colonel Secretary, October 28, 1935.

73. Ibid., John H. Pilgrim, Friends of Ethiopia Committee, to Edward Baynes, Administrator of St. Lucia, April 16, 1936.

74. Ibid., F.O. 371/20155, A.E. James, Secretary of the Friends of Ethiopia Committee, to A. Wallace Seymour, Acting Governor of Trinidad, May 9, 1936.

75. Ibid., F.O. 371/19175, D.R. Stewart, Acting Governor of St. Kitts, to the Colonial Secretary, November 12, 1935.

76. Ibid., F.O. 371/20154, Colonial Secretary to the Governors of His Majesty's Dependencies in East and West Africa, November 19, 1935.

77. *Barbados Advocate,* November 12, 1935. Many Africans were incensed

by the latest crime of the colonialists. While in London en route to the U.S. Kwame Nkrumah heard of Mussolini invading Ethiopia. "At that moment it was almost as if the whole of London had suddenly declared war on me personally. For the next few minutes I could do nothing but glare at each impassive face wondering if those people could possibly realize the wickedness of colonialism, and praying that the day might come when I could play a part in bringing about the downfall of such a system. My nationalism surged to the fore; I was ready and willing to go through hell itself, if need be, in order to achieve my object." Kwame Nkrumah, *Ghana: The Autobiography of Kwame Nkrumah,* (New York: Thomas Nelson and Sons, 1957), p. 29.

78. P.R.O., F.O. 371/20154, United Aid for Ethiopia to Gerald Campbell, May 27, 1936.

79. Ibid., Gerald Campbell to Ronald Lindsay, British Embassy in Washington D.C., June 1, 1936.

80. Ibid., United Aid for Ethiopia to Anthony Eden, June 5, 1936.

81. George Padmore, *Pan-Africanism or Communism: The Coming Struggle for Africa* (London: Dennis Dobson, 1956), p. 146.

82. George Padmore, "Ethiopia and World Politics," *Crisis* 42, 5 (May, 1935): 157.

83. C. L. R. James (J. R. Johnson), *Why Negroes Should Oppose the War* (New York Pioneer Publishers,?), p. 8.

84. James R. Hooker, *Black Revolutionary: George Padmore's Path from Communism to Pan-Africanism* (New York: Frederick A. Praeger, 1967), p. 42.

85. Padmore, *Pan-Africanism or Communism,* pp. 145-146.

4

BACK-TO-AFRICANISM SINCE GARVEY

Less than two years after Marcus Garvey's involuntary departure from American shores, the Great Crash occurred. President Herbert Hoover's optimistic assurances notwithstanding, the economic bubble burst and with it the hopes, dreams, and cherished myths of millions. America would never be the same. The nation began a seemingly irreversible descent to the depths of depression, the most calamitous in its history. Not until the United States went to war against the Axis powers was there any real recovery.

Corrosive in its effects on American society as a whole, the depression had an especially devastating impact on the black population. Their position in the economy had been marginal at best. Events in the 1930s were to bear out the truth of the old saying that blacks were the last to be hired and also the first to be fired. Disproportionately represented in the ranks of domestics, they soon discovered that the depression had made them expendable. Many blacks working in the agricultural sector of the economy had already undergone bad times in the 1920s. Already beset by financial hardships, they and their urban brethren were to be ravaged still further after 1929. As the New Deal began, in excess of two million Afro-Americans were on relief and black joblessness was two times the national average.[1]

Institutional racism added to the misery of blacks. Unions which had long been guilty of discriminatory and/or exclusionary practices were not about to mend their ways when jobs were so difficult to come by even for whites. Bigotry was also rampant in the implementation of President Franklin D. Roosevelt's relief and recovery programs which were usually controlled on the local level. When indigent blacks were shortchanged by the Federal Employment Relief Administration, there was little they could do about it. The National Recovery Administration (NRA), the Tennessee Valley Authority (TVA), and the Agricultural Adjustment Administration (AAA) were all accused of not treating blacks equitably but the complaints were to no avail. Discrimination in recruitment by the Civilian Conservation Corps was by no means uncommon and that agency was notably reluctant to put blacks in positions of authority. This deplorable situation prevailed despite the fact that the federal statute creating the CCC mandated equal employment opportunities. Afro-Americans even lost out when the long overdue Social Security Act was finally instituted in 1935: persons engaged in farm work and household labor were not covered by its provisions. This meant that millions of blacks did not qualify for coverage.[2]

Blacks had to devise ways and means of keeping body and soul together. The problem was sheer survival and it consumed their meager resources, their time, their attention, their physical and psychic energy. Little remained for fanciful schemes of resettlement in a faraway land which they had never seen and about which they knew next to nothing. What they knew or thought they knew about Africa rendered it unappealing.

During the lean years of the depression only a few new groups were formed to promote and implement a black exodus and their growth was negligible. Leadership was conspicuously absent. There was only one Marcus Garvey and he was in exile. In 1929 a dispute erupted between Garvey then based in Jamaica and many of his erstwhile devotees. At issue was the location of the UNIA headquarters. The dispute caused a rupture which never

was healed. Dr. Lionel A. Francis, a West Indian physician, became head of the UNIA branch in New York City. He had been practicing medicine in London when he "got hit by the Garvey bug." In 1920 he had joined Garvey in the United States. When the schism occurred, Bishop McGuire, Henrietta V. Davis, and other prominent former aides to Garvey supported the New York branch. For a time after the split, Dr. Francis continued to use the facilities of Liberty Hall.

He fought a long and bitter court battle with his ex-mentor over a $300,000 bequest made to the UNIA years before by Isaiah Morter, a prosperous black man who had died in British Honduras. Which branch of the UNIA was legally entitled to Morter's estate—that in New York or the Garvey-led organization? In 1939 Dr. Francis emerged victorious with the Morter legacy as his prize.

Although in calling an international convention of the UNIA in 1932, Dr. Francis had listed colonization and development opportunities in Africa as matters requiring immediate attention, by 1940 he was de-emphasizing the contribution Africa could make to the black American's salvation. "We don't advocate going back to Africa," he told an interviewer in that year. "We plan to solve the Negro problem in this country not by going to Africa. You couldn't even get in Africa if you went over there."[3] Instead the black nationalist physician put forward a ten-point plan aimed at making the black man self-sufficient in the United States. He planned on a membership of one million, but in 1940 he conceded that his organization had only seven hundred members.[4]

With the commanding figure of Garvey no longer on the American scene, fragmentation plagued the black-nationalist and back-to-Africa movement. A number of former disciples attempted to assume the Jamaican's mantle. One such was Arden A. Bryan who with Charles B. Cumberbatch in August or September 1932 formed the Nationalist-Negro Movement and African Colonization Association. Its motto was "For God, For Africa and For Humanity." The organization's center of

operations was in New York City, but in October 1933 it claimed to have an affiliate in Savannah, Georgia, and a prospective affiliate in Panama City. Total membership was put at five hundred. Many were West Indians. Only Cumberbatch had ever been to West Africa where he had visited Liberia and Nigeria at the time of World War I.[5]

Unemployment among the blacks was causing acute suffering. Hopes and aspirations were redirected to Africa, at least for a few. Because Liberia was encumbered with debt it was not regarded by the Nationalist-Negro Movement (NNM) as a suitable area for their activities. Instead they set their sights on the Cameroons and petitioned the League of Nations for land there.[6] From 1884 to 1916 Cameroon had been a German protectorate. Germany forfeited her African colonies after her defeat in World War I and Cameroon was divided into two League of Nations mandates, one under French administration, the other under British jurisdiction. Exactly which territory the NNM had in mind for colonization by blacks from the Americas is not clear.

When they were informed by the League that a request such as theirs could only be made by a member state, Messrs. Bryan and Cumberbatch turned to Great Britain to sponsor their cause before the League. They also hoped that Britain would finance their experiment in the Cameroons. If they were successful, they believed, racial tensions aggravated by economic distress in the United States, the West Indies, South and Central America would be relieved. British officials in New York with whom members of the NNM conferred were unimpressed. One official could not see why "these people want to mess up the Cameroons as their confreres have played havoc with Liberia."[7] A spokesman for the British consul-general had pointed out to the Negro Nationalist Movement visitors that until their membership was "infinitely more considerable" and more representative there would be no justification for sponsoring their cause at Geneva. Furthermore, even if their petition for the Cameroons were granted, it was extremely unlikely that any nation would be willing to fund such a project especially in troubled times. The atten-

tion of the NNM visitors was also drawn to the "fact" that if somehow it were possible for the group to realize its dreams, American and West Indian blacks long absent from the African continent would not prove to be immune to the diseases of the West African coast. They would suffer in their new homes as had the first settlers dispatched to Liberia by the American Colonization Society a century before. The visiting blacks left the meeting apparently unconvinced.[8]

Such overtures to the British by the NNM were fruitless. Nothing came of the petition to the League. British diplomats believed the organization to be a relic of Garveyism and of no importance whatsoever.[9] Indeed the NNM slipped into obscurity, sharing the unhappy fate of so many back-to-Africa groups.

At approximately the same time the NNM was in touch with British authorities in New York, members of the Pacific Movement of Chicago wrote directly to His Majesty, King George V, about the terrible living conditions of blacks in America. Whereas Bryan, Cumberbatch, and their followers had sought British support because large numbers of Africans and people of African descent lived under the Union Jack, the Chicago group felt that England had a particular responsibility because "when the first slaves were brought from Africa America belonged to England" and "it was through England that they were brought here."[10]

It was alleged that the forebears of most of the adherents of the Pacific Movement had come originally from various regions of Nigeria. Some it was acknowledged had come from other parts of West Africa. Although their letter mentioned that members had large families—seven or eight children—there was no indication of the size or strength of the organization. Given the numerous misspellings in the letter, it may be surmised that the authors were persons with little formal education.

The letter detailed the suffering of Afro-Americans. Lynchings in the South were given emphasis. Black patience was at an end. The writers stated that they no longer wished to remain in America where they were treated so cruelly: "This is not our country." They wanted to go to their native land, "back home"

to Africa where they would be treated as free people, not "slaves," as human beings, not "dogs." It was their belief that when blacks were removed from Africa there was an understanding that after a length of time (unspecified) they would be returned to their motherland. (This appears to be a variation on the providential thesis previously discussed.)

The letter also noted that the "Prince of Nigeria" had been a recent guest at the World's Fair and had supposedly been so struck by the mistreatment of Afro-Americans that he wanted to take their case to the League of Nations. The writers of the letter explicitly solicited British assistance in repatriating members of the Pacific Movement. Their luck was no better than that of the NNM. The letter was not even deemed worthy of acknowledgment.

One other outgrowth of Garveyism in the depression was the so-called Peace Movement of Ethiopia founded in Chicago late in 1932. It was to enjoy greater longevity, if not greater success, than competitive groups of the same ilk. "Ethiopia" as used in the name of the organization denoted not the kingdom ruled by Haile Selassie; rather it referred to the whole African continent. Actually the sole territorial target of its repatriation efforts was Liberia.

The Peace Movement expended much energy on its petition addressed to President Franklin D. Roosevelt urging that relief moneys earmarked for blacks be used to subsidize settlement in that West African country. Concentrating its efforts in Illinois and Indiana, within eight months the Movement was able to obtain four hundred thousand names on the petition—or so it claimed.[11] In the petition, members of the Movement described themselves as "simple minded, sincere, lowly, law-abiding workers who have maintained traditions of simple honesty, industry and frugality as much from choice as from necessity." They asked only for an opportunity in their "ancestral Africa" where they would "carve a frugal but decent livelihood out of the virgin soil and favorable climate of Liberia."[12]

Temporarily thwarted when the White House rejected its pro-

posal as impractical, the Peace Movement turned to the state of Virginia for assistance. And in 1936 the General Assembly of Virginia asked the United States Congress to aid in the colonization of people of African descent who elected to go to Liberia or somewhere else in Africa.[13]

There were those on Capitol Hill who looked with favor on schemes of this type to cut the racial Gordian knot, for example, Senator Theodore G. Bilbo of Mississippi. American politics have long been a spawning ground for racist demagogues. As such, Bilbo had few if any equals in the 1930s and 1940s. A fanatically intransigent champion of segregation, he contended that if the black race were to enjoy social equality, the "culture of the white race" would be destroyed. His fear of "mongrelization" was almost pathological.[14] Consistent with his belief in keeping the races apart, in April 1939 Bilbo introduced his "Greater Liberia" bill before the United States Senate. The bill provided for the voluntary resettlement of American blacks in West Africa. There was nothing novel in the measure. Bilbo was walking in the footsteps of Senators Butler and Morgan.

Support for Bilbo, the Negro-baiter, came in the pages of Garvey's *Black Man,* published in London. Garvey was impressed by Bilbo's "ability and his sincerity" and called the Mississippian "the real exponent of the suppressed Negro."[15] In America the black man's future was dark and dismal. What he needed was an opportunity to build his own civilization. Consequently American branches of the UNIA were entreated to continue their fight on behalf of the bill. Garvey thanked Senator Bilbo and Major Ernest Sevier Cox whom one historian has described as "perhaps the most important race theorist residing in the South in the period between World Wars I and II."[16] Cox was the man Garvey believed to be the prime mover of the colonization bill.

Enthusiastic backing for the bill came from the Peace Movement of Ethiopia working in concert with other black nationalists in Chicago. Three hundred fired-up back-to-Africanists set off for the nation's capital in broken-down vehicles, a number

of which were unable to transport their exhilarated passengers beyond the boundaries of Chicago.[17]

Bilbo was almost certainly guilty of hyperbole when he boasted that more than two million Afro-Americans had signed petitions endorsing his scheme. "The Man," as the redoubtable senator was called, was not cowed by Congressional failure to enact his bill. He told Gunnar Myrdal, Swedish author of the monumental work, *An American Dilemma,* that he would await more propitious circumstances and still greater black support for his plan.[18]

Little more was heard about the Peace Movement of Ethiopia. It did not pass out of existence but as so many organizations with small, dedicated memberships it lingered on. In February 1960 the *New Crusader,* the "Militant Voice of the Negro People," a weekly published in Chicago, carried an article by A. B. Baker. The piece announced that the Peace Movement of Ethiopia met every Sunday at noon on State Street.[19] Indeed, in 1968, Baker, "a skilled worker in the employ of the City of Chicago" and a James Hemphill were reported to be in Connecticut trying to drum up support for the Peace Movement. Speaking as a representative of two and a half million Afro-Americans, a self-appointed representative one suspects, Baker argued that repatriation would enable the black man to gain self-respect and would relieve the tensions which had led to riots "because the blacks could very easily have everything in Africa" that they were fighting for in the United States.[20] On their tour Baker and Hemphill were armed with literature stating that land in Liberia had been offered to black Americans.

Splinter groups such as the Peace Movement of Ethiopia have frequently given birth to other equally ineffectual splinter groups whose goals are not noticeably different from those of the parent organizations. This fissionlike process probably results in the main from personal feuds and petty rivalries which are exacerbated by the inability to make progress or to win new adherents.

The Ethiopian-Pacific Movement was the brainchild of Mrs. Mittie M. L. Gordon who had been one of the founders of the Peace Movement of Ethiopia. In 1941 Mrs. Gordon clashed with the federal government over her opposition to the Selective Service System. She categorically rejected the charge that she was discouraging males from performing their military service and claimed that her paramount concern was transporting Afro-Americans to Liberia. "Whites should remain whites and blacks should remain blacks. Africa is our country and that's where we want to go—to the soil of Liberia," she told federal authorities. A recipient of public assistance herself, Mrs. Gordon wanted welfare funds to be allocated to "transport all self-respecting blacks to Liberia."[21] Along with countless frustrated blacks, shadowy figures determined to abandon America for the land of their fathers, Mrs. Gordon faded into oblivion. Needless to say, her project made no headway at all.

It has already been shown that the 1930s were an economically troubled era for Caribbean blacks as well as for blacks in the United States. But, with the exception of the UNIA and one other movement in Jamaica, that of the Rastafarians, West Indian disgruntlement was not translated into back-to-Africanism. Jamaica, a Spanish possession prior to 1655 when it passed into British hands, has in the nineteenth and twentieth centuries produced its share of messianic and chiliastic cults.[22] Exotic religious cults are often much more than they appear to be. In Jamaica they have traditionally been reactions to a society which failed to meet the material and spiritual needs of many of its citizens.

To understand the origins of Rastafarianism one must recall that it was to Jamaica that Garvey had gone after his deportation from the United States in December 1927. He remained there until 1935 and it was during that period that Rastafarianism was born. The actual connection between Garvey and the Rastas is nebulous. According to legend Garvey di-

rected his followers to look to Africa where a black king would
be crowned. This would be their day of deliverance. The prophecy may be apocryphal but today it is widely credited by the
Rasta brethren who view Garvey as a "major prophet."[23] They
have appropriated the UNIA official song, "The Universal Ethiopian Anthem."[24] They have borrowed his motto, "One God,
One Aim, One Destiny"[25] and have incorporated the concept of
a black deity emphasized by Garvey and Bishop McGuire into
their philosophy.

Although the Rastas are somewhat heterogeneous in ideology,
they share certain fundamental tenets. Predominant is that Emperor Haile Selassie of Ethiopia is the living god, the returned
messiah. Daily prayers of the Rastas contain the supplication:
"So we hail our God, Selassie I, Eternal God, Rastafari: hear
us and help us and cause thy face to shine upon us thy
children."[26] "The Lion of Judah Shall Break Every Chain" is
the title of a Rasta song.[27]

Before his coronation in 1930, the emperor was known as Ras
Tafari. It was that coronation which was widely construed by
the brethren as fulfillment of the Garvey prophecy. To this day,
Coronation Day, the anniversary of the epochal event, is observed with much reverence.[28] Much publicity was given to the
event by the *Daily Gleaner,* the island's major newspaper. And
at the end of 1933, a Mr. Leonard Howell, one of the authors
of the theory of imperial divinity, sold approximately five thousand photographs of the emperor for a shilling each. He did the
proverbial land-office business. Their popularity was due to the
fact that buyers believed that the pictures could be utilized as
passports to Ethiopia.[29]

Haile Selassie, who claims lineal descent from Solomon and
Sheba, has never professed to be the god his Rastafari
worshipers fervently believe him to be. The emperor paid his
first and only visit to Jamaica in April 1966 and received a
tumultuous welcome.[30] Rastafarians were overcome with joy.
They were frenetic. His Majesty was moved to tears by his
reception. During his four-day stay he personally received many

of the brethren. Medals bearing the emperor's likeness were distributed. The visit was nothing less than a milestone for the Rastas who gained prestige as a consequence.

A second basic belief of the movement is that black men are destined to return to their African homeland. "Repatriation An Unfinished Business" is the name given to one of their poems. Emigration to almost any region of Africa would satisfy some, but for most, the Kingdom of Ethiopia is *sui generis* among African lands. Rastas are drawn from the lowest stratum of society, essentially the same stratum which has supplied manpower for back-to-Africanism in the United States. Many are unemployed or underemployed. Their economic prospects are poor. It is no surprise that they see Jamaica as hell and Ethiopia as heaven. Wishfully, they view their return as just a matter of time.

In September 1955 their hopes of repatriation were buoyed by a letter from the Ethiopian World Federation. The federation had originally been set up in 1937 by Dr. Malaku Bayen with headquarters in New York City "to secure justice and maintain the integrity of Ethiopia." Eighteen years later on a trial-basis five hundred acres of the emperor's personal property, "very fertile and rich land," was being donated to the "Black People of the West" who had assisted Ethiopia in her hour of peril. The land was in Arussi province around Shashamane. Mass migration was not encouraged by the government of Ethiopia. Skilled workers and persons knowledgeable about farming and imbued with the pioneer spirit were considered to be especially desirable immigrants. However, funds to facilitate settlement would have to be raised in Jamaica.

One disastrous attempt to effect repatriation occurred in 1959. It was reminiscent of the Howell fiasco more than twenty years earlier. The central figure was Reverend Claudius Henry, a Jamaican who had resided in the United States for a considerable period of time. Back in Jamaica he founded the African Reform Church and distributed thousands of certificates on which was printed a statement that began with the words: "Pioneering Israel's scattered children of African origin back home

to Africa." Fifteen hundred certificates were sold at a shilling each. For holders of these certificates no passport would be required to return to Africa.[31]

In October 1959 throngs of certificate purchasers who had disposed of their homes, their land, and other meager worldly possessions arrived in Kingston eager to depart for Africa. But the new messiah, Reverend Henry, had made no arrangements for transportation and literally hundreds, including women and children, were stranded in the capital, victims of their own gullibility and the chicanery of Reverend Henry who was subsequently imprisoned. So compelling is the Rastafarians' urge to repatriate that periodically they descend on the Kingston airport fully prepared to return to Mother Africa. These efforts amount to little more than futile, although desperately sincere, gestures.

By 1960 due in part to the Claudius Henry escapade, popular and governmental concern was rapidly growing. In July some prominent Rastafari brethren requested the University of the West Indies to study and report on the movement, its origins, and its aims. The request was speedily complied with. A team of investigators was assembled and in short order a report was published.[32] Among the investigating team's principal recommendations was that the Jamaican government should dispatch a mission to Africa to make arrangements for the immigration of Jamaicans. Preparations for the mission were to be made after immediate consultation with Rastafarians.

On April 4, 1961, the delegation consisting not only of Rastafarians but of various black nationalists set off on a two-month journey. Their itinerary included Ethiopia, naturally, Liberia, Nigeria, Ghana, and Sierra Leone.[33] According to the majority report filed by the non-Rastafarian members of the expedition, Ethiopia was very receptive to the idea of immigration from Jamaica by certain types of people. Encouragement for the objectives of the mission was also found in the quoted remarks of Dr. Azikiwe, then governor general of a relatively tranquil Nigeria, and Osagyefo Kwame Nkrumah, then prime minister of Ghana and one of Africa's most prestigious statesmen. President William V. S. Tubman of Liberia was also reportedly en-

thusiastic about receiving repatriated blacks. Indeed at that juncture he did not restrict his hospitality to skilled immigrants as did other African leaders.[34] Sierra Leonian officials were noncommittal at best about black immigration.

The Rasta minority report did not differ significantly in most respects. It was somewhat more passionate in tone and more spiritual in nature and it focused primarily on Ethiopia where the members of the commission had been given national robes. Despite the financial and moral support which the mission received from the Jamaican government, despite two subsequent missions to Africa in 1962 and 1964, despite the availability of the 1955 imperial land grant to the "Black People of the West" and the purported zeal of His Majesty, the emperor, for Ethiopia-bound emigration schemes, few Jamaican blacks, Rastafaris or others, have resettled there. In the last fifteen years perhaps eight black American families have gone over to try their luck but most found the going too rough and returned to the United States. It should be mentioned that a recently published piece claimed that the prolonged stalemate over the Ethiopian World Federation land cession had been ended. After repeated appeals to the imperial government, it was decreed that the coterie of Rasta settlers living on the land, a dozen souls in all supposedly, would be given twenty-five acres each. The major obstacle to resolving the resettlement problem in Ethiopia had been foreign pressures which, it was explained, had now eased.[35]

Over the past three or four decades there has been only a trickle of West Indian resettlement elsewhere in Africa,[36] although England since the end of World War II has witnessed a dramatic influx of "dark strangers" from the Caribbean. Literally thousands of West Indians served in the armed forces in Britain during the war. Countless others worked in war-related industries when labor was in short supply.[37] Some never returned to their sun-drenched home islands. Later they were joined by a steady stream of their countrymen seeking better jobs and also by Pakistanis, Indians, and other "coloureds." By the late 1950s the stream had become a flood, an unwelcome one to many Britons living in a highly homogenized nation and traditionally sus-

picious of outsiders.[38] A full-blown race problem was spawned, nurtured by racist myths and old wives' tales all too familiar to those cognizant of America's seamy record of race relations. The magnitude of the British problem necessitated the passage of civil rights legislation first in 1965. It also led to restrictive immigration laws which, in effect, redirected emigration-minded West Indians to the United States.

Immigrants from more than a dozen West Indian islands had previously flocked to the United States in the 1920s. At that time their status as British subjects permitted them to enter the country with comparative ease under the new quota system. Their energy and self-confidence had quickly enabled them to establish themselves in business and in professions out of all proportion to their numbers in the black community. Alterations in the American immigration laws in 1965 once again gave a strong fillip to West Indian migration. Reliable figures do not exist but there may be as many as two hundred and fifty thousand Jamaicans and thirty-two thousand Barbadians in New York City alone.[39] Canada has also served as a mecca of sorts to discontented and restless West Indians. A good percentage of those who have migrated to North America from the islands have been persons with college degrees, specialized skills, and technical training. Others, of course, have been individuals short on education and marketable skills. Significantly, for both groups their discontent and restlessness have not pointed emigrants toward the continent of their forebearers. Orde Coombs who was born on St. Vincent and now lives in New York where he works as an editor and a writer has offered a succinct explanation for this phenomenon: "The West Indian does not think of Africa because he is not concerned with nation-building. He is on this earth to reaffirm the validity of middle-class values, and America represents the triumph of the middle class."[40] But Coombs probably is not considering the lower strata of Caribbean societies. Given a choice of new homes, they might opt for Africa.

Malak, the hapless hero of Trinidadian playwright Derek Walcott's *The Dream On Monkey Mountain,* pursues in an African land of which he is the king the intangible goals of freedom and identity which have always eluded him. This theme may be escapist fantasy rather than one reflecting and revitalizing an African heritage. Rural folk in the Caribbean whose cultural baggage contains a miscellany of Africanisms are, in fact, not acutely conscious of happenings in Africa. Africa evokes for the preponderance of islanders images of slavery, savagery, and blackness.[41] Why then would they seek to emigrate there? Is it not more likely that the rural and urban poor using the middle class as their model might prefer the more tangible rewards of economic success—rewards more likely to be had in London, Toronto, or New York than in Africa. It is the considered opinion of at least one scholar, Roy S. Bryce-Laporte, that in the future it is by no means inconceivable that both the poor and the bourgeoisie of Jamaica including the Rastafaris may "shift their emphasis from the outside world to their homeland."[42] Perhaps the rising tide of black power which has already touched the shores of sundry Caribbean isles suggests that the phenomenon will not be exclusively a Jamaican one.

As far as the United States is concerned, back-to-Africanism is still alive, but only barely so. There are some organizational vestiges of Garvey's UNIA for whom repatriation remains the cardinal objective, for example, the African Nationalist Pioneer Movement (ANPM). Repatriation is the very heart of black nationalism as they interpret it. The ANPM with headquarters in New York was led by Carlos A. Cooks until his death in May 1966. Cooks, a native of the Dominican Republic, had previously been active in the UNIA.

According to the ANPM's current "administrator," Charles "Nwokeoji" Peaker, who describes himself as a "Man of Africa," his organization has no designs on or in America.[43] In 1961 the ANPM branded integration of the races a "sociological farce whose cheering section consists of myopic misfits, chronic

race panderers and professional Uncle Toms of the Tschombe [*sic*] school."[44] To the tiny membership of the ANPM, repatriation to the African homeland is the only permanent solution to the problems of the black masses in North, Central, and South America and in the Caribbean. With remarkable consistency, but with little actual success, the ANPM has devoted its energies to promoting "an orderly, peaceful exodus of *African people* out of America and *into Africa.*"[45]

In 1964 the ANPM wrote to the White House calling for the creation of an African Resettlement Bureau which would oversee a voluntary resettlement program. All necessary food, clothing, tools, and medical aid would be furnished by the bureau. Each adult applicant for resettlement would receive $1,000. Perhaps mindful of the Black Star Line, the ANPM also asked that the United States provide seaworthy ships with "ethnologically compatible" crews to transport the repatriates to their new homes.[46] These efforts were to no avail.

The ANPM has not put all its eggs in one programmatic basket. It is a leading sponsor of the Garvey Day celebrations held annually on August 17, the birthday of the man honored. A flyer announcing the celebration one year described Garvey as the "father of African Nationalism, Leader, Patriot, Organizer, Prolific Writer and Soldier Statesman." As part of the yearly observance there are eulogistic meetings. There are parades in which the uniformed African Legionnaires of the ANPM march. And there is a Miss Natural Standard of Beauty Contest which consciously rewards possession of those African physical features historically defined as unattractive by Caucasian societies.

ANPM manifestoes admonish residents of Harlem to "Buy Black," i.e., patronize black-owned business enterprises. Economic control of black communities by Afro-Americans is deemed imperative. Extremely race-conscious, the ANPM also derogates miscegenation which it calls "race suicide."[47]

Another back-to-Africa group is the African-American Repatriation Association (AARA). Philadelphia is the hub of their

activities. In March 1969, at their request, Congressman Robert N. C. Nix, Democrat from Pennsylvania, introduced a bill (H.R. 8965) in the House of Representatives. Congressman Nix is the oldest member of the black congressional delegation in Washington, D.C. His measure which was referred to the Committee on Foreign Affairs authorized voluntary repatriation of Americans of African descent and the funding of development aid to Africa. More specifically, the bill declared it to be the policy of the Congress to cooperate with independent African countries individually and collectively in furthering the "interests and welfare of large numbers of persons of African descent in the United States" who desire to settle permanently in independent African nations. The President was directed to negotiate for and purchase landsites on which the repatriates could live.[48]

In June 1969 the African-American Repatriation Association sent a petition to President Nixon in support of H. R. 8965.[49] Describing themselves as descendants of those Africans who had been kidnapped from Africa, who were brought to the New World in chains, and who were compelled to live and work without payment for three hundred and fifty years under conditions of cruelty, privation, and degradation, the petitioners asked for reparations to finance voluntary emigrationism and to aid African states. Also called for was the establishment by executive order of a Bureau of Repatriation to enable Congress to calculate the number of people desirous of going back home and the cost of resettling them.

The AARA whose president is Mustafa Hashim has argued that passage of the Nix bill would solve America's race problem once and for all by providing transportation, sustenance, economic opportunity, and homes in Africa for those blacks who want to leave and help in building the motherland. So long as Afro-Americans are denied the option of repatriation at government expense, self-determination does not exist. Integration, assimilation, separatism (in the United States) are all unacceptable: "the masses of the people want to repatriate."[50]

In a call for favorable congressional action on H.R. 8965 an

AARA flyer explained that the bill would help "Black people who are forced to stay in America by poverty, Black people who have been denied opportunity by discrimination, Black convicts who are forced to return to the same ghettos that produced them. . . . " By helping these people and others to return home the civil war facing America could be averted.

Mimeographed literature of the AARA presenting the case for repatriation evidences a familiarity with the back-to-Africa tradition. Paul Cuffe (spelled Kofi), Martin R. Delany, Henry Highland Garnet, Bishop Turner, and, of course, Marcus Garvey are cited and their programs explained. The venerable Garvey is given special attention. As a gesture of esteem for him the AARA has designated its meeting place the Marcus Garvey Center. In the June 1969 memorial to the chief executive, it was contended that the United States government had prevented Garvey from returning "our people to Africa *at their own expense* after having purchased ships, entered into communication with the Republic of Liberia and acquired land for settlement." Elsewhere it is stated unequivocally that Garvey in his battle to restore Africa to her rightful place of greatness and glory had the support of the masses of Afro-Americans. "They had no hesitation or second thoughts about undertaking this task."[51] No proof of any kind was given for this last assertion about pro-repatriation sentiment among black Americans.

The AARA's insistence that "our brothers in Africa are requesting, demanding, almost pleading for us to come home" should also be taken lightly. To prove that Afro-Americans are wanted and needed in Africa, statements of these African leaders past and present are quoted: Kwame Nkrumah, Sekou Touré, Joseph Mobutu, Leopold Senghor, Tom Mboya, William V. S. Tubman.[52] To the martyred Congolese premier, Patrice Lumumba, is attributed a remark with obvious emotional appeal to the downtrodden and forlorn: "There are legends among the tribes that our brothers and sisters were taken across the wide sea, and that one day they would return and when they return they would be supermen."

As of this writing Congress has not made it possible for Afro-Americans to become "supermen" in the land of their forefathers. It has not seen fit to appropriate money to facilitate their return "home" and is not likely to do so in the foreseeable future.[53]

The pull of Africa has been so strong for some Afro-Americans that they have not awaited governmental succor. They have reached out on their own. In December 1967 the New York *Amsterdam News* reported that 134 Afro-Americans had taken up residence in Liberia; by the very end of the year the total was put at 173. They described themselves as Black Hebrews or Hebrew Israelites,[54] members of the Abeta Israel Hebrew Center on Chicago's South Side. Most of the emigrants were young, in their twenties and thirties, but the contingent included one eighty-two-year-old woman. Some had Hebraized their names. According to a spokesman for the group it was their intention to surrender their United States citizenship, "if you can call it that—they really don't have a citizenship to give up."[55] Bitterness over racial oppression in America was apparent in the statement of one of their leaders: "We'd rather live in the jungles of Africa than in a house in Cicero [Illinois]."[56] Yet one reporter who visited the Israelites in Liberia said their motivation was "more religious than racial." They saw their emigration as fulfillment of divine prophecy.[57]

A small number of these pioneers returned to the United States within a few months. A few remained in Monrovia. The majority established themselves on a three-hundred-acre site near Gbatala in a snake-infested region, more than eighty miles from the capital. Bush was cleared, wells dug, and dwellings constructed in short order. Work was begun on a house of worship for the migrants. Most tilled the soil though they were generally lacking in agricultural experience. To raise money the expatriate group resorted to sundry enterprises such as operating a snack bar in Monrovia where the menu included "soul chicken" and an ice cream dish imaginatively advertised as "soul on ice."[58] The real attitude of the Liberian government toward the black

Jews has been shrouded in mystery. Whereas the *Amsterdam News* stated that it had been informed by the government of President William V. S. Tubman that immigrants were still welcome,[59] *The New York Times* wrote that unidentified Liberian officials were fearful that these blacks "could be the vanguard of large migrations from the United States that would upset the political balance here."[60] Life was difficult in the wilderness camp but a report published in November 1968 indicated that the doughty band was content in Liberia. About the same time they vowed to an *Ebony* correspondent, "We are here to stay."[61] A year later James A. A. Pierre, Liberian attorney general, expressed displeasure with the immigrants. He faulted them for not assimilating into Liberian society and said the group evidently had no "intention of working or becoming useful in the country."[62] A deportation order for seventy-five of the black Israelites was then issued, but subsequently rescinded.[63]

Nevertheless, approximately two years after they fled the United States seeking freedom in Africa, a second exodus was undertaken by about seventy of these black Jews. For them "permanent" residence in Liberia turned out to be rather temporary settlement. Indeed Mr. Ben-Ami, formerly Ben Carter, a spiritual leader of the sect, commented that their stay in West Africa was originally intended to prepare them for their return to Israel.[64] They advised Israeli authorities that they were bona fide Jews[65] and consequently were entitled to Israeli citizenship under the Law of the Return.[66]

Individual black expatriates may be found in many regions of the world. They have forsaken America for a host of reasons almost all tied to the race issue in one way or another. Some have chosen Africa to start new lives for themselves. Doyen of expatriates in Ghana is Robert E. Lee who went to West Africa in 1955 with his wife. Both are dental surgeons. Dr. Lee who has become a Ghanaian citizen and has learned the local languages believes that in Ghana "a black child grows up in an environment that is not set up to make him hate himself."[67] And Gloria Lindsey who has lived and taught in East Africa has ob-

served: "Being black in a black society changes the image you have of yourself."[68] Bill Sutherland, another black emigré who worked for the Ghanaian minister of finance and subsequently went to Tanzania, has been quoted as follows: "I feel that here in Africa there are opportunities for new experimentation, new values, a society which more represents what I am seeking than the society I lived in in the United States."[69] Clifford and Laverna Sharp left well-paying jobs as a skilled auto repairman and an experienced teacher to settle in French-speaking Guinea, once the provenance of New World slaves and now "the blackest country there is." They wanted to see and experience "this source of all blackness." The Sharps told a *New York Times* correspondent, "We all feel a need to soar in spirit" and that was not possible in America where blacks are a minority.[70] Many expatriates do not enjoy the same standard of living which they had attained in the United States. Nevertheless, the consensus of opinion seems to be that life in Africa is not a sacrifice, but what the Sharps called "an adventure in freedom."

To be sure, not all Afro-American travelers to Africa expect to sink roots there. Some go for short visits as did Richard Wright, the brilliant black novelist who, prior to his sojourn in the early 1950s, had not felt anything African about himself. He had no compelling urge to go to Africa. Yet, speaking to Ghanaians, he described himself as "one of the lost sons of Africa who has come back to look upon the land of his forefathers."[71]

Unquestionably, Africa has had a magnetic pull for some. The attraction of free Africa for the semi-free Afro-American has been clarified by John Oliver Killens, a Georgia-born black author who had no intention of permanently relocating. He has written of his journey:

Everywhere I went people called me brother . . . "Welcome American brother." It was a good feeling for me to be in Africa. To walk in a land for the first time in your entire life knowing within yourself that your color would not be held against you. No black man ever knows this in America.[72]

Even before the "winds of change" began to blow through Africa and long before "black power" became a familiar slogan of militancy, Paul Robeson commented:

> I think a good deal in terms of the power of black people in the world. . . . That's why Africa means so much to me. As an American Negro, I'm as proud of Africa as one of those West Coast Chinese is proud of China. Now that doesn't mean that I'm going back to Africa, but spiritually I've been a part of Africa for a long time.
>
> Yes, this black power moves me. Look at Jamaica. In a few years the white minority will be there on the sufferance of black men. If they're nice, decent fellows they can stay.
>
> Yes, I look at Senator Eastland [Mississippi] and say, "so you think you are powerful here? If only I could get you across the border."
>
> Although I may stay here the rest of my life, spiritually I'll always be a part of that world where black men can say to these crackers, "Get the hell out of here by morning."
>
> If I could get a passport, I'd just like to go to Ghana or Jamaica just to sit there for a few days and observe this black power.[73]

Robeson, as Essien-Udom has suggested, is exemplifying the need of the powerless for connection to a center of power.[74]

James Farmer, former national director of CORE, has characterized his first arrival in Africa as "perhaps a kind of religious experience—for I felt irrationally like falling on my knees to kiss the earth."[75] Farmer explained his intensely emotional reaction to setting foot on African soil in terms of the black American's "terrible search for identity." Only in this light can we comprehend why prior to his departure from the United States one Afro-American had given Farmer a bottle to fill with Nile River water and why another had pressed a wood box into his hands and asked him to fill it with earth from "Mother Africa."

It is by no means uncommon for black Americans to discover in Africa just how American they are in a cultural sense. Priscilla Stevens Kruize who lives in Ghana has observed that she had nothing in common with many Ghanaians, ". . . like being able to crack a joke and have someone really understand it."[76] Some like Mrs. Kruize learn that they do not fit in African

society. They may miss friends and family or it may be creature comforts, entertainment, favorite sports teams, or foods. In Mrs. Kruize's case, and this is surely not unique, what she missed was really more a matter of *black* American culture, soul food in particular.

Stan Whitehurst is a black American who spent two years in Togo as a Peace Corps volunteer. He worked on rural community development there. When he was assigned to West Africa, Whitehurst did not have the feeling that he was going home. He had no reason to think that his ancestors had been Togolese. Although many others thought that as a person of African ancestry he would have a keener understanding of the Togolese and their culture, Whitehurst concluded that he did not. He discerned in games, in foods, even in the carriage and gestures of people clues to surviving Africanisms in black America, but otherwise Togo was a completely foreign country and Whitehurst suffered a sort of culture shock.[77]

Generalizing about the responses of black Americans to Africa is perilous. Blacks who go to Africa have differing needs and desires. They possess different temperaments and widely divergent attitudes toward Africa. Moreover Africa is a variegated continent. Franco-phone countries do not offer the same experience as Anglo-phone nations. Living in radical Guinea or Ghana under Nkrumah was not the same as living in Liberia. And rural and urban settings may be worlds apart.

There are black Americans who cannot be too "choosy" about the nation to which they journey. Calvin C. Cobb, a black attorney and civil rights activist, was convicted of stealing in 1966 and received a suspended sentence. While on probation Cobb fled to East Africa with his family and persuaded the Tanzanian authorities that the United States sought his return for political and racial reasons. Tanzania's Vice President Rashidi Kawawa rejected America's request for extradition and Mr. Cobb announced that he would apply for Tanzanian citizenship.[78]

Another black fugitive who found asylum in Tanzania was

Robert F. Williams. All told, Williams who fled the United States after being charged with kidnapping in North Carolina in 1961, spent eight years in exile traveling to and living in Cuba, the People's Republic of China, and North Vietnam, as well as Africa.[79]

Discussing decisions by isolated individual blacks to emigrate to Africa is not the same as discussing back-to-Africanism as an organized movement. Used in the latter sense, back-to-Africanism as a way out of America's racial quandary has clearly ebbed in the 1960s and 1970s. Accurate estimates of the number of potential black Zionists in the United States today are extremely difficult to make. Floyd B. McKissick, former national director of CORE, has contended that although the movement receives little publicity, the Garveyites (presumably meaning believers in repatriation) are as numerous as the integrationists.[80] While not a back-to-Africanist himself, McKissick sees nothing wrong with the idea of returning to Africa "if one desires to go."[81] He points out quite correctly that many of the black people who do subscribe to this philosophy do not have the fare to get to Africa, lack the funds to purchase land or a home on arrival, and do not possess the requisite skills for living a productive life there. McKissick argues further that from the viewpoint of the independent nations of Africa, "it is desirable that many Afro-Americans return to their homeland." Consequently, in his *Black Manifesto* he has called for the Congress of the United States to enact legislation to finance technical training for American blacks to meet the technical needs of these developing nations.[82] To date, Congress has shown no disposition to heed his call.

For black nationalist Dan Watts, publisher of the monthly periodical, the *Liberator,* what he refers to as the "Noah's Ark" remedy is a fantasy. "We must discard the romantic notion of 'Back-to-Africa.' Returning to Africa is an individual solution not one for 22,000,000 people who have given their sweat and blood to the building of this country."[83] Watts is unable to calculate the strength of repatriationism but he does feel that many

Afro-Americans hold on to it as a necessary psychological prop. From time to time the middle-class Negro press publishes letters to the editor urging emigration. Typical was the letter which appeared in *Ebony* written by an Illinois black. He invoked Garvey's cherished name and claimed that "the only way we are going to get our freedom, justice and equality is to flee this country."[84]

But correspondence to white and black newspapers and magazines more than occasionally advances a diametrically opposed point of view. For example, in 1968 a black woman living in Long Island City asserted in a letter, "I am not moving to a black state in the South nor back to Africa. I will stay right here—in my country getting some of my share of the pie and helping others, white and black, to get theirs." This letter appeared in *The New York Times*.[85] Back-to-Africanists are not likely to write to the editor of that newspaper.

Precisely how many Afro-Americans would echo the views of the Long Island City black is not known. The letter to *Ebony* reflects utter despair over ever achieving first-class citizenship and full humanity here. The other indicates a dogged determination not to knuckle under to bigotry and a great reluctance to abandon the nation which blacks helped to build.

What is plain to students of black affairs is that in recent times those black spokesmen whose statements have been most quoted (and sometimes misquoted) by the fourth estate do not favor back-to-Africanism. Indeed, it is deemed so insignificant that they rarely discuss it. Manifestly, repatriationism has not been the policy of Roy Wilkins, A. Philip Randolph, or Bayard Rustin. It was not the program of Whitney Young or Martin Luther King. The Reverend Ralph David Abernathy, Dr. King's successor as president of the Southern Christian Leadership Conference, has no plans to go back to Africa until the English go back to England, the Italians to Italy, the Irish to Ireland, until America is given back to the Indians. Abernathy has expressed his love for Africa as his ancestral home but he isn't "going to run away from problems and move there." Rather

he intends to remain in the United States and "desegregate everything in it and fight for everything that the blood and sweat of black people have earned."[86]

Needless to say, the foregoing persons have been associated with the civil rights movement, the principal goal of which has been full equality and integration in the United States. None of these spokesmen could by any stretch of the imagination be categorized as separatists or black nationalists. Where do the best-known exponents of those philosophies stand on the question of repatriation? For the most part even they have not unequivocally advocated the African solution.

Pronouncements of the late Malcolm X on this subject are instructive. Actually, over the years repatriation had not been emphasized by Black Muslim leaders, including Malcolm. But in June 1963 at the invitation of Adam Clayton Powell, Malcolm sermonized on "The Black Revolution" to the mammoth congregation of Powell's Abyssinian Baptist Church. Speaking with typical reverence for the man who had redeemed him from a life of depravity and converted him to Islam, Malcolm informed his Christian audience that

> The Honorable Elijah Muhammed says that this problem can be solved and solved forever just by sending our people back to our own homeland or back to our own people, but that this government should provide the transportation plus everything else we need to get started again in our own country. This government should give us everything we need in the form of machinery, material, and finance—enough to last for twenty to twenty-five years until we can become an independent people and an independent nation in our own land.[87]

If Americans were fearful about repatriating blacks, territory in the "Western hemisphere" should be granted to enable the races to live apart.

On March 12, 1964, less than two weeks after he announced that he had left the Nation of Islam, Malcolm held a press conference at a New York hotel to explain his position and his plans. For one thing his religion was still Islam—for another, he still felt that his mentor and erstwhile leader, Elijah Muhammed, had the best long-term solution to the black man's

dilemma: "complete separation with our people going back home, to our African homeland." But in the meantime, mundane needs, such as food, clothing, shelter, jobs, and education, had to be met for twenty-two million Afro-Americans.[88] Addressing himself to the same topic on July 5, 1964, less than four months later, Malcolm saw a black exodus as extremely remote. He was speaking at a rally of his newly formed Organization of Afro-American Unity. During the discussion period Malcolm was asked why he had downgraded repatriation at a previous rally. Malcolm responded by saying that he wanted to go back to Africa, but his short-range program necessitated remaining in America. Restoring cultural and spiritual bonds between black people in the United States and blacks in Africa deserved top priority. A physical return to Africa, he had concluded after talking to African leaders, was premature. Afro-Americans would find themselves welcome in Africa, but that was not the point. From the pan-African perspective, black Americans could be most effective in the United States. Moreover, there were real impediments to a return home, notably the fact that blacks were not blackminded enough to want to go back. Even some black nationalists, Malcolm asserted, were not ready to go back.[89]

H. Rap Brown, for a time chairman of the Student Non-Violent Co-ordinating Committee (SNCC),[90] is one who has seen the United States as the black citizen's rightful place. It is here that the struggle for freedom must be waged. He minced no words and insisted, "For Black people it is not a question of leaving or separating—given our historical experiences, we know better than anyone that the animal that is america [*sic*] must be destroyed."[91]

In the past four or five years Eldridge Cleaver, the Black Panther party minister of information, has attracted a following of young, angry blacks. Like Malcolm whom he reveres, Eldridge is a "graduate" of America's penal system. In his best seller, *Soul On Ice,* he wrote that the "question of the Negro's place in America which for a long time could actually be kicked around as a serious question, has been decisively resolved: he

is here to stay."[92] In his *Post-Prison Writing and Speeches* he is more ambiguous. He draws a parallel between the contemporary situation of Afro-Americans and the circumstances in which European Jewry found itself in the 1890s when Theodor Herzl founded the modern political Zionist movement. Black Americans must do what the Jews did—build an organization, form a government, and later procure a land on which the government and people would be planted. Nowhere does he say where the land should be.[93] Cleaver seems to be arguing against the perpetuation of a colonial status hamstringing black Americans and arguing for black self-determination in this country. His numerous pronouncements on the race question, both written and verbal, all imply a resolution, perhaps a cataclysmic one, in "Babylon [The United States]." Faced with re-incarceration on a charge of assault with intent to murder, Cleaver himself sought sanctuary in Africa. He has been living in Algeria since 1968. Noteworthy also is the fact that all ten points in the 1966 Black Panther party platform and program demand drastic changes in the conditions under which blacks live in American society. Africa is not mentioned at all.

Another black militant who has taken up residence on the African continent is Stokely Carmichael. He lives in Guinea with his wife, the talented South African singer, Miriam Makeba. The Trinidadian-born black power activist was once chairman of SNCC. For a brief while he was honorary prime minister of the Black Panther party, but since 1969 he has been estranged from the Panthers. Carmichael has written that blacks need a land base and the best and fastest place to acquire one would be in Africa, specifically in Ghana.[94]

In 1970 Stokely rejected the notion that all blacks should go back to Africa at that point in time. However, "we all have to go back there sooner or later. If this white boy keeps on going the way he's going, a whole lot of people will be running as fast as they can to get there."[95] Interviewed in Conakry at the beginning of 1971 by a British journalist, Stokely explained that the long-term goal "is to create a milieu of thinking in Africa

that will allow the black person living in America to realize his place is in Africa. Similarly we must create a milieu of thinking in Africa so that the African would want to have his brother in America return to Mother Africa."[96] The foregoing pro-emigration statements are as unequivocal as any coming from a black who now enjoys a national reputation. But, it must be remembered, Stokely heads no organization which could possibly give substance to his proposals.

Separatism is by no means unpopular in the 1970s, but increasingly, it takes forms other than that of repatriation. Separatist-minded groups such as the Nation of Islam have been remarkably successful in forging their own economic institutions independent of the white man's. And in March 1971 the black nationalist Republic of New Africa declared the territorial independence of a twenty-acre area near Jackson, Mississippi. This was to be its capital called El Malik after the name Malcolm X took following his pilgrimage to Mecca. It was to be the nucleus of a much greater nation. Eventually the group hopes to control five southern states—Mississippi, Louisiana, Alabama, Georgia and South Carolina—one-tenth of the United States for the black tenth of the general population.[97] At present this goal seems impossible of attainment.

Separatism also manifests itself in crusades for community control. Blacks are more and more vocal in their demands that institutions of the inner city—the schools, the hospitals, the fire and police departments—be removed from white control. What Mayor Gibson and LeRoi Jones are attempting to do in Newark may well provide a model for the other black communities. As whites flee the manifold problems of our decaying urban areas for the suburbs, black majorities will emerge in a host of cities in the next few decades.[98]

Black nationalist developments in the foreseeable future are more likely to follow these lines than the path of emigrationism. The latter will almost certainly not die, but instead will feebly linger on, searching for but probably never finding a "black Zionist" of the stature of Bishop Turner or Garvey. And this

situation is unlikely to change except in the event of a race war which would transform into reality black nationalist fears of genocide. Such a holocaust, not as impossible as well-meaning whites believe, could be a powerful catalyst to the back-to-Africa movement, just as Hitler's persecution of European Jewry revitalized and crowned with success political Zionism.

Listening to Afro-Americans debate the merits of back-to-Africanism in the 1970s can truly be called a *déja vu* phenomenon. Arguments for and against emigration have scarcely changed since the antebellum period. Today's integrationists and the stay-at-homes of the last century sound remarkably alike. They should. They are ideological as well as racial brothers. The same, of course, may be said for those who advocate a return "home."

Historically, the so-called Negro establishment has opposed every back-to-Africa program. It has denounced the Pied Pipers of emigrationism, regarding them as misguided and unrealistic men at best and. charlatans at worst. But it is not really this denunciation that has kept Negroes in the United States. Why then, one may justifiably ask, has back-to-Africanism failed? Why, in sharp contrast, have Jews been able to create a national homeland in Israel and to achieve the ingathering of the exiles?[99] When Theodor Herzl convoked the First World Zionist Congress in 1897[100] he was as much a Don Quixote in the eyes of fellow Jews and Gentiles alike as was his contemporary Bishop Turner. Initially, political Zionism was no less chimerical than back-to-Africanism and it was rejected by Jewish elites—both secular and religious. Yet in little more than fifty years Israel was born. How was this possible?

Zionists had certain distinct advantages back-to-Africanists were lacking. In Eastern Europe at least, Jews were able to maintain their own cultural identity. They spoke a language (Yiddish) distinct from that of their Christian neighbors. Jews had a religious tradition which for centuries kept alive the hope for national redemption. Restoration of the "Chosen People" to the coveted land of their ancestors, which, it is claimed, God promised to them in his covenant with Abraham, was expressed

in countless poems, prayers, and sayings. "Next year in Jerusalem" was a traditional phrase uttered at the conclusion of the annual Passover *Seder.* Thus religious Zionism continuously rekindled the Zionist idea down through the ages.[101] In addition to Messianism and Herzl's political Zionism there was secular cultural Zionism in the nineteenth century. The revival of the Hebrew tongue as a modern vernacular was one of its cardinal accomplishments. Today Hebrew is the national language of Israel. Spoken by Oriental as well as European Jews, it is a strong unifying factor in that Middle Eastern state.

Pioneer Zionists were able to gain a foothold in Palestine at just about the same time Bishop Turner was promoting repatriation. Though there were reverses in their initial efforts to create viable colonies and Jewish settlers often returned to their dispersion, the Zionists surmounted the formidable obstacles confronting them including debilitating, sometimes deadly, diseases and starvation. Their triumph cannot be attributed merely to grit, heroism, and the willingness to make great sacrifices, virtues which it must be acknowledged the *Chalutzim* (pioneers) possessed in abundance. Bishop Turner had concentrated his talents on motivating Afro-Americans to relocate in Africa. No provisions were made for their survival once they got there. Essentially they were left to their own devices. During the seasoning process, the period spent acclimating themselves to new surroundings, a strange diet, and diseases to which they were as vulnerable as any Europeans, they had to fend for themselves.

Rank-and-file Zionists were poor but their settlements were taken under the protective wing of Baron Edmond de Rothschild whose largesse helped meet the basic needs of Jewish colonists. Schools, synagogues, livestock, tools, and, later, technical training were all provided as part of the baron's plan. Rothschild was not alone. Financial instruments such as the Jewish Colonial Trust and its subsidiary, the Anglo-Palestine Company, plus a Palestine land purchasing agency, the Jewish National Fund, all aided in the building of a secure foundation for the future Jewish state. All efforts were coordinated by the World Zionist

Organization. These various agencies had no counterparts in the back-to-Africa movement. Moreover, unlike the individualistic black Americans dispatched to West Africa by Turner and the handful who went there under other black auspices in the late nineteenth and twentieth centuries, the early Zionists pooled their resources in *kibbutzim* (collectives) and *moshavim* (cooperatives).

Other differences between black emigrationism and Zionism should be underscored. With the backing of men of extraordinary wealth and prestige and with the support of many Jewish intellectuals and persons of influence, the Zionist movement gained access to some of the most powerful governments in the world. Withal, only in the wake of the Nazi holocaust which pricked the conscience of the Western world did the United Nations sanction the flowering of Jewish national regeneration through the establishment of Israel.

Compare this, if you will, with the fortunes of back-to-Africanism. With relatively few exceptions it was scorned by the black press and by black intellectuals. Furthermore it lacked international diplomatic leverage. It had no influence with the British, the French, or the American government or any other government of major world powers. As a consequence by turns it has been ignored by the League of Nations[102] and the United Nations.

Back-to-Africanists could not call upon black millionaires for assistance. Money to finance transportation to Africa and to enable black emigrants to establish themselves there has always been in short supply. Naturally, blacks who have earned reasonably good incomes have also been the most reluctant to relinquish the bird in the American hand for the two in the African bush.

Black despair in some of America's darkest moments led to African fever, but in other critical periods, despair produced apathy and resignation. Compounding the dilemma was the knowledge that Africa was not the heaven that Bishop Turner, Chief Sam, and their fellows said it was, a knowledge confirmed by returning emigrants.

During certain periods in American history, e.g., Reconstruction (1865-1877) and the civil rights era of the 1950s and 1960s, black hopes were buoyed by legal advances. There was progress albeit of an incremental nature. Still it was sufficient to generate optimism about the future of black people in the United States. Beyond that, for many blacks there has been an emotional, indeed a patriotic, attachment to the only country they have known. There is much in the general American culture that is familiar and therefore dear. When absent, it is sorely missed by blacks. Attachment to the subculture of the ghetto may be even stronger. With its soul food, its argot, and its biting yet comforting humor, its sights and sounds, it cannot be replicated, not even in Africa. Some would say especially not in Africa.

In restrospect, back-to-Africanism may properly be adjudged a failure, but its longevity and the fervor with which it has been espoused by its proponents must not be underestimated. Writing of the response of the black masses to Garveyism, Gunnar Myrdal, in his classic survey of the *American Dilemma,* observed: "It tells of a dissatisfaction so deep that it amounts to hopelessness of ever gaining a full life in America."[103] Myrdal's observation is applicable to the entire back-to-Africa movement. Thus, its failure notwithstanding, the movement should be a constant reminder of America's promise to her black citizens, a promise still unfulfilled.

NOTES

1. John A. Salmond, "The Civilian Conservation Corps and The Negro," ed. Bernard Sternsher, *The Negro In Depression And War—Prelude To Revolution* (Chicago: Quadrangle Books, 1969), pp. 78-90.
2. Ibid. Also see Leslie H. Fishel, Jr., "The Negro in The New Deal Era" in Sternsher, ed., *The Negro in Depression and War,* pp. 10-12.
3. Ralph Bunche, The Programs, Ideologies, Tactics and Achievements of Negro Betterment and Interracial Organizations—A Research Memorandum. Unpublished Study Conducted for the Carnegie-Myrdal Project. Vol. 2, p. 419.
4. Ibid., p. 423.
5. Public Record Office, Foreign Office 371/16618: Memo in Campbell to Wiggin, October 31, 1933.
6. Ibid. Arden Bryan and Charles Cumberbatch to Sir Ronald Lindsay, Brit-

ish Ambassador to the U.S., September 18, 1933.

7. Ibid. Gerald Campbell of British Consulate General to A. F. H. Wiggin of British Embassy, Washington, D. C., October 2, 1933.

8. Ibid.

9. Ibid.; British Embassy, Washington, D. C., to the American Department, Foreign Office, October 4, 1933. Bryan was an old Garveyite. In a letter dated January 4, 1921, Garvey acknowledged Bryan's efforts and thanked him for his good work.

10. Ibid., F.O. 371/17585: Pacific Movement of Chicago to His Majesty, King George V, December 14, 1933.

11. A second petition to the White House allegedly carried almost two million names.

12. Bunche, 3, 427.

13. Ibid., 428.

14. For a full exposition of his racial philosophy see Theodore G. Bilbo, *Take Your Choice: Separatism or Mongrelization* (Poplarville, Mississippi: Orleans House Publishing Co., 1947).

15. Apparently the feeling was mutual. In his book Bilbo referred to Garvey as a noted and world-renowned leader. He also applauded Bishop Turner. Bilbo, *Separatism or Mongrelization,* pp. 254, 268.

16. I. A. Newby, *Jim Crow's Defense: Anti-Negro Thought In America, 1900-1930* (Baton Rouge: Louisiana State University Press, 1965), p. 61.

17. Arna Bontemps and Jack Conroy, *Anyplace but Here* (New York: Hill and Wang, 1966), p. 209.

18. Gunnar Myrdal, *An American Dilemma* (New York: McGraw-Hill Book Company, 1964), II, p. 806.

19. *New Crusader,* February 27, 1960.

20. *African Opinion,* August-September 1968, p. 2.

21. Bontemps and Conroy, *Anyplace but Here* p. 209. Mrs. Gordon had been president of the Chicago division of UNIA for some years. See Theodore G. Vincent, *Black Power and the Garvey Movement* (Berkeley: Ramparts Press, 1971), p. 130.

22. The leader of one in the 1920s was a prophet named Bedward who claimed to be a black reincarnation of Christ. He eventually died in an asylum for the deranged. Leonard E. Barrett, *The Rastafarians—A Study in Messianic Cultism in Jamaica* (Rio Piedras: Institute of Caribbean Studies, 1968).

23. M. G. Smith, Roy Augier, Rex Nettleford, *Ras Tafari Movement in Kingston, Jamaica* (Kingston: Institute of Social and Economic Research—University College of the West Indies, 1960), p. 8.

24. The words were written by Rabbi Ford and a collaborator.

25. Barrett, p. 63.

26. Ibid., p. 131.

27. George Eaton Simpson, *Religious Cults of the Caribbean: Trinidad, Jamaica and Haiti* (Rio Piedras: Institute of Caribbean Studies, 1970), p. 212.

28. Ibid., p. 217.

29. Smith, Augier, and Nettleford, *Ras Tafari Movement*, p. 10.

30. Barrett, *The Rastafarians*, pp. 122-123.

31. Ibid., pp. 84-85, and Kingsley Martin, "The Jamaican Volcano," *New Statesman*, March 17, 1961.

32. This was the Smith, Augier, Nettleford publication.

33. This information is drawn from Barrett, *The Rastafarians*, pp. 90-94.

34. However, according the minority report, he did not cotton to Rastafari beliefs.

35. *African Opinion*, January-February 1971.

36. By the 1950s the Gold Coast, soon to become Ghana, had a West Indian population that may have reached 200. Quite a few were from Trinidad. A handful were actually in West Africa before the beginning of this century. After the fall of Nkrumah some of Ghana's West Indians moved to Tanzania.

37. See Sheila Patterson, *Dark Strangers—A Study of West Indians in London* (London: Penguin, 1965), pp. 44-45. For an interesting study of Caribbean emigration to various regions see Graham Norton, "The West Indies As Centres For Migration — Black British Adventurers," *The Round Table*, No. 242 (April 1971); 273-281.

38. Perhaps the majority of Jamaicans and Barbadians migrated to England when those islands underwent tremendous economic growth. Many of the migrants were skilled.

39. *The New York Times*, October 28, 1970. In 1965 under the old national origins quota system 2,100 Jamaicans immigrated to the United States. In 1970 under the liberalized immigration act the number of Jamaican immigrants was 15,309.

40. Orde Coombs, "On Being West Indian in New York," ed. Floyd B. Barbour, *The Black Seventies* (Boston: Porter Sargent Publisher, 1970), p. 184.

41. David Lowenthal, "Race and Color in the West Indies," *Daedelus*, 96, no. 2 (Spring 1967): 602-603. In Trinidad despite the Nigerian "Shango" faith practiced in the countryside, Africa was not consciously a part of the cultural or social life of the island. Eric Williams, the prime minister, has attempted to generate popular interest in Africa. Shortly after Trinidad became independent, the entire cabinet paid state visits to several African countries.

42. "The Rastas," *Caribbean Review* (Summer 1970), pp. 3-4.

43. Charles Peaker, *Black Nationalism* (New York: African-American Publications, 1967), p. 86. There have been and still are countless splinter groups advocating back-to-Africanism in one form or another. The following were just a few active in the 1960s. The Universal African Nationalist Movement, centered in Harlem, was led by Louisiana-born Benjamin Gibbons who since 1949 has campaigned for the voluntary repatriation bill introduced by Senator William Langer of North Dakota. The United African Nationalist Movement headed by Georgia-born James Lawson met weekly in its headquarters in Harlem's Hotel Theresa. The movement's motto has been "Africa for the Africans—Those at Home and Those Abroad." Lawson has tried to promote economic self-determination in black communities and has maintained liaison

with African delegations to the United Nations. Lawson also attended the 1958 All-African Peoples Conference in Ghana. *African News and Views,* published in New York, frequently editorialized in support of back-to-Africanism. In May 1962, for example, it said that peoples of African descent in the United States should go home to Africa at least financially and mentally, and physically if possible.

44. *African Opinion,* June-July 1961, p. 12.

45. Peaker, *Black Nationalism,* p. 86.

46. Ibid., p. 64.

47. John H. Bracey, Jr., August Meier, and Elliott Rudwick, eds., *Black Nationalism in America* (Indianapolis and New York: Bobbs-Merrill Co., Inc., 1970), p. 487.

48. H. R. 8965. The five black Congressmen who commented publicly on the bill were decidedly cool to it. Outspoken Shirley Chisholm of New York said, "Win or lose we are part of this country." Even the sponsor, Congressman Nix, did not really favor the bill. He acted on behalf of constituents.

49. Reprinted in *African News and Views,* July 1, 1969.

50. *The Case For Repatriation* (Philadelphia: African-American Repatriation Association, n.d.), p. 7.

51. Ibid., p. 4.

52. At least a few of these seem to limit their invitations to skilled American blacks, those least likely to be members of AARA.

53. On March 1, 1971, Mr. Nix introduced H.R. 5250 in the House of Representatives. Essentially the same as his earlier repatriation measure, it was duly referred to the Committee on Foreign Affairs which took no action on H.R. 8965. Bills calling for repatriation and reparations have also been introduced into Congress on behalf of the "Self-determination Committee" in California and other back-to-Africa groups.

54. *The New York Times,* September 20, 1967.

55. Ibid.

56. Ibid., January 18, 1968.

57. Era Bell Thompson, "Are Black Americans Welcome in Africa," *Ebony,* January 1969, pp. 44-46.

58. *The New York Times,* November 6, 1968.

59. *New York Amsterdam News,* December 23, 1967.

60. *The New York Times,* January 18, 1968.

61. Thompson, "Are Black Americans Welcome in Africa," p. 46.

62. *The New York Times,* November 12, 1969. Quoted from *The Liberian Star,* November 4, 1969. Difficulties also developed over the question of citizenship.

63. An article published in New York in a black nationalist periodical was critical of the action of the Liberian government. External pressures were suspected. See *African Opinion,* March-April 1970.

64. *Jerusalem Post,* February 10, 1971.

65. *The New York Times,* November 23, 1969.

66. Their Judaism, the black explained, was four hundred years old. However, their religious origins have still not been clarified by the Ministry of Religious Affairs. Therefore the rabbinate has not officially recognized them as Jews and their legal status in Israel is uncertain. They were settled in Dimona in the Negev desert. Because of the confusion over their status they did not qualify for immigrants' housing. According to a piece in the *Jerusalem Post* in February 1971 their accommodations were inadequate, but in general they were faring quite well. Textile mills provided employment. Their children attended local schools and they appeared to be accepted by their Israeli neighbors. Yet in August 1971 Mr. Ben-Ami held a news conference at which he complained about jobs, housing, and "Jim Crow policies similar to what we left behind." The early contingents were followed by a number of other black Israelites who came directly from the United States. The later arrivals have been at a disadvantage in competing for work, for homes, and for educational benefits because they were accorded only tourist status. Moreover as the Dimona black community grew, friction with the townspeople developed and the Israeli authorities became uneasy about a continuation of the black influx. In October 1971 over twenty black Israelites were deported immediately upon arrival in Israel allegedly because they were destitute and would become public charges. They had come directly from the United States. Their deportation left approximately two hundred black Israelites in Israel. See the *Jerusalem Post,* February 10, 1971; *The New York Times,* August 31, 1971 and October 8, 1971; *Providence Evening Bulletin,* October 7, 1971.

67. Ernest Dunbar, *The Black Expatriates—A Study of American Negroes in Exile* (New York: E. P. Dutton and Co., Inc., 1968), p. 78.

68. Ibid., p. 33.

69. Ibid., p. 103.

70. *The New York Times,* December 8, 1968.

71. Richard Wright, *Black Power—A Record of Reactions in a Land of Pathos* (New York: Harper and Brothers, 1954), pp. 4, 77.

72. John Oliver Killens, *Black Man's Burden* (New York: Pocket Books, 1969), p. 157.

73. Carl T. Rowan, "Has Paul Robeson Betrayed the Negro?" *Ebony* (October 1957).

74. E. U. Essien-Udom, *Black Nationalism—A Search for an Identity in America* (New York: Dell Publishing Co., 1965), p. 69.

75. James Farmer, "An American Negro Leader's View of African Unity," *African Forum,* 1, no. 1 (Summer 1965): 69-70. In 1961 when Jesse Owens, black hero of the 1936 Olympic Games, visited the Ivory Coast he thanked God for allowing him to be "on the soil of my ancestors." Curiously, Owens, a long-time FBI man, has been the object of much black nationalist scorn in recent years. According to Julius Lester, Fannie Lou Hamer wept when she was in Africa, "because she knew she had relatives there and she would never be able to know them. Her past would always be partially closed."

76. Dunbar, *The Black Expatriates,* p. 64.

77. Stan Whitehurst, personal interview, December 16, 1970.

78. *New York Amsterdam News*, December 23, 1967.

79. *The New York Times*, August 23, 1969 and September 9, 1969. While he was living abroad Williams was named president of the Republic of New Africa. He has since left that separatist group.

80. Floyd B. McKissick, *A Black Manifesto* (New York: National Congress of Racial Equality, 1967), p. 5. Harold Cruse doubts the sincerity of those who profess to want to return to Africa "because if they did they would have already left and would not be on the urban scene lulling other disgruntled and unhappy Blacks to sleep with dreams and romances about 'Our Homeland.' " Sincere emigrationists, he believes, "would be engaged in the politics of organizing Black 'pioneer' groups to return to Africa with 'dual citizenship' status comparable to the status of Israeli Jews. They would be trying to make 'Back to Africa' a political issue." See Harold Cruse, "Black and White: Outlines of the Next Stage," *Black World*. May, 1971, p. 38.

81. McKissick, *A Black Manifesto*, p. 8.

82. Ibid.

83. *Liberator*, October 1965, p. 3. A contributor to the *Liberator* who intends "to go home one day" is John Soares. Soares does not foresee a mass exodus but he writes, " . . .if we are going to wear Dashikis, speak Swahili and take African names in our rejection of things Western, why don't we go all the way? We certainly can be truer Africans there than here." *Liberator*, September 1968.

84. *Ebony*, December 1966. See *Ebony*, August 1969, for a letter in support of H. R. 8965, a bill that "will be the end of begging for a crust from the loaf of white bread."

85. *The New York Times*, March 11, 1968.

86. *Ebony*, June 1970.

87. Benjamin Goodman, ed., *The End of White World Supremacy—Four Speeches by Malcolm X* (New York: Merlin House, Inc., 1971), p. 74. Malcolm thought that Black Muslims made the best returnees: ". . . when we go back among Africans, our feelings are the same as the Africans; our objectives are the same as the Africans," (p. 77) Also see Essien-Udom, *Black Nationalism: A Search for an Identity in America* (New York: Dell Publication Co., 1964), p. 207.

88. George Breitman, ed., *Malcolm X Speaks—Selected Speeches and Statements* (New York: Grove Press, Inc., 1966), p. 20.

89. George Breitman, ed., *By Any Means Necessary—Speeches, Interviews and a Letter by Malcolm X* (New York: Pathfinder Press Inc., 1970), pp. 104-105.

90. SNCC changed its name to the "Student National Coordinating Committee" in July 1969.

91. H. Rap Brown, *Die Nigger Die* (New York: Dial Press, Inc., 1969) p. 135.

92. Eldridge Cleaver, *Soul On Ice* (New York: A Delta Book, 1968), p. 114.

93. Eldridge Cleaver, *Post-Prison Writings and Speeches,* ed. Robert Scheer (New York: Random House, Vintage Books 1969), pp. 67-69.

94. Stokely Carmichael, "Pan-Africanism—Land and Power," Reprinted from the *Black Scholar* (November 1969), p. 7.

95. Stokely Carmichael, *Stokely Speaks—Black Power Back to Pan-Africanism* (New York: Random House, Vintage Books, 1971), p. 206.

96. For the immediate future he proposed self-determination in predominantly black communities. *The New York Times,* February 6, 1971.

97. See Brother Imari Abubakari Obadele I, "The Republic of New Africa—An Independent Black Nation," *Black World,* May 1971, pp. 81-89.

98. According to the Census Bureau, blacks now constitute a majority in six cities including Newark. Eight additional cities have a population that is forty percent black. Fifty percent of America's blacks are to be found in fifty cities. One-third of the total black population is concentrated in just fifteen cities. *The New York Times,* May 19, 1971.

99. Black emigrationism to non-African destinations has been paralleled by "territorialism" in Zionist history. Territiorialists favored colonization but were not Palestinocentric. In other words they sought to separate the national resolution of the Jewish problem from the age-old longing for Palestine. Jewish colonies in Chaldea, El 'Arish (Egypt), Cyprus, Mozambique, the Congo, and Kenya were all considered as havens for persecuted European Jews at a time when Palestine was unavailable.

100. For a comparison of Herzl and Garvey see Arnold Rose, *The Negro's Morale: Group Identification and Protest* (Minneapolis: University of Minnesota Press, 1949), p. 43.

101. Although religious faith had sustained the Zionist idea many extremely devout Jews opposed Herzl and political Zionism steadfastly maintaining that restoration of the Jews to the "promised land" could only be accomplished by divine intervention on their behalf. Any human effort would be tantamount to blasphemy, a terrestrial flouting of God's will.

102. The League of Nations mandate for Palestine which began in 1923 recognized the fundamental principle of the 1917 Balfour Declaration and provided for the "establishment in Palestine of a National Home for the Jewish people."

103. Gunnar Myrdal, *An American Dilemma* (New York: McGraw-Hill Book Company, 1964), II, 749.

5

THE VIEW FROM AFRICA

Up to now emigrationism, essentially a New World Negro phenomenon, has been discussed without reference to the attitudes
of Africans. Where do they stand on the question of back-to-
Africanism? If Afro-Americans were to emigrate in droves to
the mother continent, just how welcome would they be in African countries? It is natural, if not necessarily justifiable, to assume that the doors to black New World immigrants would be
open much wider in the post-independence era than they were
in the colonial era. Before the "winds of change" began to blow
through Africa, white imperial powers were suspicious and probably rightly so of subversive Afro-American influences. Black
American visitors and expatriates, often of the black nationalist
stripe, were viewed as a potential fifth column.

Now that most of Africa is free of European shackles, politically if not economically, it is rather difficult to ascertain just
how eager black African politicians are to have black immigrants from the western hemisphere. Not only does there appear
to be a diversity of expressed opinion on this matter among African leaders but, in at least one case, there is a discrepancy between word and deed. Generally speaking, sporadic, small-scale
immigration is differentiated from wholesale immigration. A
distinction is also made between skilled and educated immi-

grants and those who might conceivably become public charges in countries which are grappling with the ever rising demand by their own nationals for jobs, schooling, and housing. Ebenezer M. Debrah, the current Ghanaian ambassador to the United States, who has evinced great interest in the black American community, has bluntly told black audiences that "if a group of 500 American blacks suddenly came to Ghana, we couldn't absorb them."[1]

A survey of African opinion on the question of back-to-Africanism was published by *Ebony* magazine in January 1968.[2] *Ebony* had sent a reporter to interview a variety of African leaders. President Joseph Mobutu of Zaire, formerly the Congo (Kinshasa), was one interviewee who would permit, even encourage a flood of Negro immigrants from the United States. He asserted that the Congo, one of Africa's largest countries in area, could accommodate as many as a hundred million persons.[3] As long as the immigrants were hard-working and were not coming to "make politics," it was not necessary that they possess job skills. It should be added hastily that prior to, during, and subsequent to Belgian rule, an infinitesimal number of black emigrants actually made the Congo their destination.

President Tubman of Liberia, an Americo-Liberian himself, used less astronomical figures than his Congolese counterpart, but was no less enthusiastic about an influx of black Americans. "You Negroes belong here," he stated. "You had no business being there to begin with." Space for half a million blacks could be found in Liberia and no insurmountable problems would be created. New arrivals would not be concentrated in one place. They would be dispersed throughout the country. Notice of their coming should be given the government which was prepared to care for the newcomers for three months, to make it possible for them to become citizens and to make twenty-five acre land grants to them.[4] President Tubman's terms seem most generous. But it may be surmised that the Hebrew Israelites who gave up Liberia for Israel would not be very sanguine about the future for black Americans in Liberia.

President Hastings Kamuzu Banda of Malawi who has lately been under fire from fellow Africans and from many blacks in the United States for his rapprochement with the Republic of South Africa, has said that eight million Afro-Americans could be accommodated in his central African land. But the Scottish-trained physician turned politician noted sarcastically, "I don't think they would fit in. We haven't got a cinema you know."[5]

Emile Zinsou, who in June 1968 had become president of the former French West African colony of Dahomey, also put out the welcome mat to those willing to labor for African development. But he was troubled by what he characterized as the black American's complete loyalty to the United States, a characterization that myriad black nationalists would surely call ill-informed and probably insulting. In any event Zinsou managed to hold power for only seventeen months.

Senegal's gifted poet-politician, Leopold Senghor, Ghana's General Joseph Ankrah, who succeeded Kwame Nkrumah, and Milton Obote, Uganda's head of state until he was toppled by a coup d'etat in January 1971, all agreed that the Afro-American's battle for justice and equality had to be fought in the United States and could not be won by emigration.[6] Without doubting the sincerity of those other African leaders who cordially and blithely invited mass black American immigration, it may be hypothesized that were the question to become a real instead of an academic one, the invitations might well be qualified. They might even be withdrawn.

The most volatile African comment on the desirability of back-to-Africanism was made by the late Tom Mboya. Mboya, born into the Luo tribe, was an influential member of the Kikuyu-dominated Kenya African National Union, Kenya's major political party. He was generally considered pro-Western in outlook. When he made his controversial comment, Mboya was a young, dapper, and extremely articulate minister for economic planning and development of Kenya. The time was March 1969, the place the Countee Cullen branch of the New York Public Library in Harlem. Mboya, who was shortly to fall victim to

an assassin's bullet in Nairobi on July 5, 1969, had delivered
a one-hour address on the formidable economic and social problems that beset Africa in the post-independence era. Those remarks caused no difficulty. The audience seemed receptive to
Mboya. But when he briefly gave his views on the movement
of Afro-Americans to Africa, he stirred up a hornet's nest.
Mboya said that he did not believe in such a movement because
"we should not run away from the struggle."[7] The Kenyan
added: "I also believe that the cosmopolitan atmosphere which
has been established in Africa and elsewhere must be established
all over. Africa has shown the white nations that there is no
place for racialism. We are, I think, we can pride ourselves with
a Government. . . . " At that juncture he was abruptly cut off
by the audience which was crowded with members of the African
Nationalist Pioneer Movement and other black nationalists. One
irate woman repeatedly cried out, "You're not the same Mboya
we fought for—we fought for Kenya." Another voice demanded
the guest speaker be ejected from the room. In vain Mboya
pleaded for order from the podium. Pandemonium reigned.
There were boos and other expressions of displeasure. Eggs were
hurled at Mboya by one uninhibited critic. "His aim was as bad
as his manners," the planning minister was subsequently to
write.[8] Order was not fully restored until the police arrived. Later the director of information for the ANPM, Cecil Elomba
Brath, who had been in the audience sharply disagreed with the
speaker regarding emigrationism: "Black people should go and
help build Africa so that all black people can have a homeland."
He explained further that many in the audience "knew that
Marcus Garvey had lectured Jomo Kenyatta in London and had
taught Nkrumah."[9] Mr. Brath himself is a cultural nationalist
who has actively promoted African clothing and hair styles. He
is also director of the African Jazz Art Society and Studios.[10]

As might be expected, reactions to the incident and to the
Kenyan's opinions varied greatly. Mr. Odeyo Ayaga, head of
the East African Student Union in the Americas, accused
Mboya of being a spokesman for the forces of conservatism in

African political life. Mboya's position was designed to avoid
the humiliation that a mass departure of American blacks would
cause the United States. On the other hand, Mr. Ayaga, a student at the Fletcher School of Law and Diplomacy, stated: "If
we are to be self-sufficient, we must rely on black scientific
brains and must create an atmosphere in Africa to welcome
blacks from America. They did not choose to be where they are
and have every right to return to Africa."[11]

During the following weeks there were other adverse responses
to the speech. James Leopold, a contributor to *African Opinion,*
a bimonthly which serves as a clearinghouse for widely scattered
back-to-Africa groups, noted sardonically that presumably the
Kenyan was "dragged into the African Community of Harlem,
New York City, to announce the scheme that his abductors were
unable to put over themselves." But, Leopold went on to say,
Mboya was rudely brought to his senses. The "former promising
brother" was taught a lesson it was hoped he would never forget.
Leopold also quoted a statement attributed to Mboya when he
came to the United States a decade earlier. Then, he purportedly
informed Afro-Americans: "You may come home whenever you
like; Africa is your heritage. You are wanted and needed."[12]

The episode was the subject of no fewer than three articles
in the black nationalist monthly, the *Liberator.* In the May 1969
issue, Selwyn R. Cudjoe endorsed Mboya's thesis "that our
battle is here where our forefathers gave their very lives as a
sacrifice to American capitalism."[13] The following month
Michael Knashie Searles seemed to concede that an influx of
black Americans into Africa would not strengthen the liberation
movements there. However, because the black man's struggle is
global in scope, "the idea that if Africans living in America
migrate to Africa it would mean 'running away from the struggle' is preposterous."[14] Although Sangha Wanyandey Songha,
a Kenyan student who had been living in Harlem for three years,
was appalled by the rudeness shown Mboya, he emphatically
disagreed with his countryman. He categorically declared that
Africa could "accommodate all her sons now scattered around

the globe." It was suggested that discussions about African integration of black Americans be undertaken under the aegis of the Organization of African Unity. A black return appeared much easier to Songha in 1969 than in Garvey's time, but one impediment was that Afro-Americans seemed to love America more than their ancestral land.[15]

Mboya's speech drew accolades from Bayard Rustin, the longtime civil rights advocate who coordinated the 1963 mammoth march on Washington. He is currently executive director of the A. Philip Randolph Institute. Rustin wrote to *The New York Times* that Mboya should be congratulated for destroying the African illusion harbored by some blacks, blacks whose native land is the United States and whose social problems will have to be solved in this country.[16]

Evidently stung by the March 1969 affair, Mboya soon elucidated his views. A scant four months had elapsed when *The New York Times Magazine* section carried an article of his. The piece was later reprinted in a collection of his speeches and writings published posthumously.[17] Mboya also wrote an essay clarifying his position for black readers. It was published in *Ebony.*[18] Mboya's clarifying articles underscored the universality of the black man's struggle of which the liberation of African lands and the civil rights movement were integral and interrelated parts: "black people cannot be fully free if there remains any part of the globe where a black man is denied his rights."[19] Within the borders of the United States the objective of the struggle ought to be equality of opportunity and equal treatment. Mboya noted that he had not found a "single African who believes in a black demand for a separate state or for equality through isolation."[20] As for Africa, Mboya wrote that Afro-Americans should look there "for guidance—and for a chance to give guidance—but not for escape." Individual blacks who wanted to live in Africa should not be rejected. Opportunities for *trained* Afro-Americans were plentiful in African nations and such persons were particularly welcome. A mass movement he thought impractical. He neither feared nor anticipated an exodus

of blacks from the United States to Africa,[21] and he opposed a proposal to bestow automatic Kenyan citizenship upon black Americans.

The latter proposal was incorporated in a motion introduced in October 1968 in the National Assembly of Kenya by the Honorable Mark Mwithaga, the member for Nakuru. In view of the fact that Afro-Americans and blacks of the Caribbean are the indigenous people of Africa "who did not leave the continent of their own accord, but as slaves," the government was called upon by Mwithaga to

A) treat them as the dispossessed sons and daughters of Africa

B) introduce a bill for amendment to the Constitution to grant them absolute and automatic citizenship in Kenya and

C) ask the Organization of African Unity countries to do likewise.[22]

The concept embodied in the motion is comparable to that underlying the Law of the Return enacted in 1950 by the state of Israel which entitles virtually every Jew in the Diaspora to an entry visa and Israeli citizenship. Debate on Mwithaga's motion took place on October 4, 1968, and reveals a great deal about conflicting African views on the relationship between Afro-Americans and their African cousins. Mwithaga led the fight for his own motion on the floor of the Assembly. He could not comprehend why Kenya offered citizenship to Asians and European settlers, but did not encourage Afro-American immigration. Kenya would benefit from the "black potentiality there in manpower, scientists, research experts and so on." Moreover, a sense of racial affinity coupled with humanitarianism moved him to try to help American blacks. Mwithaga lashed out at certain unnamed persons who propagandized that Africans were indifferent to the plight of American Negroes. He invoked the name of Marcus Garvey and said that the Jamaican had been

proved right by history. Many Afro-Americans had always desired to return to their motherland but "the way has not been paved, the way has not been found, and the receiving centers have not been found." If Kenya were to accept New World blacks, he predicted, "they would organize ways of coming out here, especially those who find that America is not their home."[23]

Another M.P., Mr. Mbogoh, supported the motion, going even further than Mwithaga. He thought it desirable that the Asian population which dominates the commerce of Kenya and the Caucasian population should organize respectively "Go Back to India" and "Go Back to Europe" movements.[24]

Particularly vociferous in his opposition to the motion was the minister for information and broadcasting, Mr. Osogo. Apart from the Sahara desert, he could see no African land that could adequately accommodate twenty million people. The population of Kenya, in excess of ten million souls, was already short of land. He was unwilling to add to the rolls of the landless and the unemployed, the more so in light of the fact that the forebears of Afro-Americans were not East Africans. Perhaps somewhat inconsistent with his concern over a flood of twenty million blacks from America was Mr. Osogo's contention that Afro-Americans were happy where they were. Many American Negroes dissociated themselves from Africans whom they condescendingly regarded as "very low people."[25] Another speaker, Mr. Kamau, also commented that "they [Afro-Americans] do not . . . even like to be called Africans and they would not like to come back to Africa."[26]

Many members observed during the course of the debate that Afro-Americans were not desirous of returning to Africa. Of course, this observation is accurate for the vast majority of blacks. Mr. Matano, the assistant minister, vice president's office and ministry of home affairs, explained to the National Assembly that American Negroes were "doing very well." Indeed, "I would not be surprised," he said, "if before long we see the President of the United States an Afro-American."[27] Even the

most polly-annish black American could only respond to such
an assertion with amused incredulity.

The consensus of opinion in the National Assembly seemed
to be that mass repatriation was a practical impossibility. Room
could not be found for two hundred thousand immigrants, stated
one speaker.[28] Another charged that Mr. Mwithaga would look
askance at as few as a hundred newcomers who would take jobs
away from his constituents, the inhabitants of Nakuru.[29] Opinions voiced during the debate strongly endorsed the idea that
the United States and the islands of the Caribbean were the
rightful homes of New World blacks. They were entitled to first-
class citizenship there and there was general agreement that
Kenyans had a moral obligation to help them attain that citizenship.

According to Kenya's *Hansards,* Tom Mboya did not
participate in the October 1968 debate. However, his views were
articulated in January 1969 when he said he opposed granting
automatic citizenship on the basis of race. Under the constitution, whites and blacks could qualify for Kenyan citizenship
as individuals. Black American visitors were welcome, but mass
migration would not be encouraged.[30]

Mwithaga's motion was rejected. Although he promised to
continue to press his ideas because of the racial situation in the
United States, passage in the near future is unlikely. That the
motion was introduced is significant nonetheless because it
reveals what might be considered a pan-Negro outlook on the
part of some Africans.

It must be understood that positions taken by legislators, in
Africa as elsewhere, may differ from those of persons who are not
elected officials. In 1953 the black journalist, Era Bell Thompson,
went on a trip to Africa. She was asked by one African, "Why
does not our brother come to teach us the things they have learned
in America, how to operate our business or to farm our land?"[31]
In 1962 the distinguished black American scholar, J. Saunders
Redding, went on a lecture tour of African universities. Upon
his return to the United States he discussed his impressions of

Africa and its people. The question put to him most often by African university students was: "Why don't more American Negroes come out to Africa?" They were especially keen about attracting Afro-American faculty, physicians, and technicians and were quite knowledgeable about those Afro-Americans who had previously gone to Africa, e.g., the man who founded the first school for deaf-mutes in Ghana.[32]

University-trained young Africans are probably the most pan-African-minded. In 1970 when the Pan-African Students Organization and the Students Organization for Black Unity convened at Howard University, a resolution was adopted which called *inter alia* for a treaty to be signed between African governments and the United States government to guarantee all human rights to Africans born in this country, i.e., to Afro-Americans. Even if the United States were unwilling to sign such a treaty, African governments were to grant automatic citizenship to all diaspora Africans. No person of African descent desirous of "Coming Back Home" should be denied citizenship. Travel documents and transportation were to be provided by the Organization of African Unity.[33]

Attitudes towards automatic African citizenship for New World blacks and African sentiments about the desirability and feasibility of back-to-Africanism may not faithfully reflect the full range of African feeling about bonds with blacks in the diaspora. Extensive field work conducted in Dahomey and elsewhere in West Africa forty years ago by Melville Herskovits revealed to that eminent anthropologist Africa's vivid memories of the Atlantic slave trade. Oral tradition perpetuated such memories which were an integral part of the ancestor worship prevalent in West Africa. Dahomeans had specific designations for the various lands to which their manacled forefathers had been carried in one of history's largest and certainly one of its cruelest population movements. Reverence for enslaved ancestors was evident in this Dahomean prayer.

Oh, ancestors, do all in your power that princes and nobles who today rule never be sent away from here as slaves to Ame'ica, to Togbome, to Gbulu,

to Kankanu, to Gbuluvia, to Rarira. We pray you to do all in your power to punish the people who bought our kinsmen whom we shall never see again. Send their vessels to Whidah harbor. When they come, drown their crews, and make all the wealth of their ships come back to Dahomey.[34]

In response to this prayer chanted to the accompaniment of blood being poured over altars to the dead, a chorus elaborated on the extent to which the European malefactors must make restitution.

The English must bring guns. The Portuguese must bring powder. The Spaniards must bring the small stones which give fire to our firesticks. The Americans must bring the cloths and the rum made by our kinsmen who are there, for these will permit us to smell their presence. Long live Dahomey.[35]

When food was given to the spirits of the dead, those who had passed on in distant countries, those whose names had been forgotten, and those whose names were not even known were all included.

Herskovits discussed totemic groupings with Dahomean elders and discovered further African consciousness of the slavery days of yesteryear and of its pitiful victims. At one point an old man exclaimed, "You have nearly all of the people of this family in your country. They knew too much magic. We sold them because they made too much trouble."[36]

African conceptions and not infrequently misconceptions of Afro-America were fostered by black American missionaries and also by Africans who had gone to the United States to study at Negro colleges and universities. The American experience of the second group often helped to nurture ideas and plans for African liberation. John Chilembwe, Kwame Nkrumah, and Nnamdi Azikiwe are just a few cases in point. The role that black Americans would play in the African freedom movement was occasionally fantastically overblown. George Shepperson has written of the highly romanticized picture of black Americans as liberators of colonial Africa which emerged in the post-World War I period.[37] This occurred after James E. K. Aggrey (1875-1927), a pioneer educator from the Gold Coast

who had spent several years in the United States both as student and teacher, visited Africa for the Phelps-Stokes foundation in 1921. In the Union of South Africa and in Nyasaland, Africans thought that Aggrey was the harbinger of an Afro-American invasion which would emancipate the blacks. Whites would then get their "comeuppance" for the wrongs they had perpetrated. They would be quickly expelled. Another rumor that was circulated in Nyasaland prophesied that the black American saviors would arrive in aircraft. When they dropped their bombs, miraculously only Europeans would be killed. In the 1920s it was commonly believed by the natives in southern and central Africa that all or almost all Americans were black.[38] During the course of the hysteria caused by the Kimbangu "religious" upheaval in the Congo, preachers were reported to have foretold that colored Americans would come to deliver their Congolese brothers from European bondage.[39] Of course this was the epoch of Garvey who, it was believed, was partially responsible for the ferment among the Congolese natives in the decade after World War I. Black American missionaries had allegedly disseminated subversive publications, some religious in nature, along with the *Negro World* in Kinshasa and Stanley Pool.[40] Years later during the 1947 rebellion in Madagascar, a bloody uprising which passed almost completely unnoticed in this country, there was talk among the Malagasy that black American soldiers had landed with weapons for the use of the rebels.

The preceding can be very misleading. Africans sailing across the Atlantic to study, work, and travel harbored widely divergent notions and expectations about Americans of African extraction. Stereotypes ran the whole gamut from glamorous saviors to childish buffoons and would depend on a wide variety of factors. These would include previous educational experience, political sophistication, religious affiliation, exposure to American films and newspapers, acquaintance with Africans who had already been to the United States, even a chance meeting with a black American in Africa.

Starting in 1935 Kwame Nkrumah spent ten years in the

United States studying, teaching, preaching, and working at odd jobs such as peddling fish on street corners. When he initially laid eyes on Harlem he felt at home immediately and "found it difficult to believe that this was not Accra." From his autobiography one gets the clear impression that the young Nkrumah's relationships with Afro-Americans were warm and friendly. He liked them and the feeling was reciprocated. At Lincoln University, a predominantly Negro college in Pennsylvania, classmates voted him the most interesting student in 1939, the year in which he received his undergraduate degree. In 1945 the year in which he left the United States, Nkrumah, who had been teaching at his alma mater, was voted "the most outstanding professor of the year."[41] This is a far cry from Harold R. Isaacs' unqualified statement that Africans who came to schools in America were "looked upon as barbarians or ex-barbarians who had become snobbish Europeans. At Negro schools, they were made to feel this prejudice most explicitly and painfully; they were isolated, made the butt of harsh jokes."[42]

Generalizing about what Africans coming to the United States anticipate and experience is an exercise fraught with danger. John Nagenda, an East African writer, came to America in the mid-1950s. His attitude towards Afro-Americans was "one largely of non-interest, tinged with a desire not to notice them overmuch."[43]

In sharp contrast was the case of R. Mugo Gatheru, a young Kikuyu, who had arrived here in 1950. In his poignant *Child of Two Worlds* he recalled a drive through Harlem and remembered being surprised at the number of black faces he saw. "I wanted to stop and go over to one of them and say: 'I am your brother.' I was naive. I felt I'd like to start telling them about their brothers in Kenya."[44]

At first Gatheru believed that his adjustment would be easier if he selected for friends more black Americans than white Americans. He soon discovered otherwise. "They all behaved alike. I had then to start approaching all of them on the basis of human beings, white and black, and not on the basis of race. In other words, the very fact that the American Negroes looked

like my tribesmen did not imply that I could understand them automatically."[45]

Black Americans too have learned that a common pigmentation and a shared history of oppression by whites does not ensure mutual understanding. Reports of friction between black Americans and African students in the United States are nothing new. A study of African students conducted in 1960 led to these conclusions. One out of five African students even in predominantly Negro colleges in the South reported that they had no black American friends. Thirty-one percent of the African sample thought they were receiving worse treatment than American Negroes. The proportion was smaller in the North—18 percent. Almost two out of three claimed "that American Negroes and Africans had difficulty in getting along."[46]

A recent attitudinal survey carried out at two large universities—one predominantly black, the other predominantly white—also turned up evidence of serious disharmony between the two kindred black groups. The survey was undertaken by Joseph Neale, a dean in the International Student Office of American University.[47] His conclusions were based on interviews with students and faculty and on a questionnaire distributed to a hundred Afro-American students and an equal number of African students at each institution. Neale found that black foreign students were often loath to associate themselves with black American militancy particularly if that required a commitment to violence. Others claimed that they had tried to involve themselves but had been rebuffed as "outsiders."

For their part American blacks were resentful of what they perceived and construed as feelings of superiority by Africans. Lack of concern about the plight of American Negroes was cited as another source of tension. Almost two-thirds of the Afro-Americans in the sample interviewed believed that the black students from overseas did not want to meet them and did not understand their problems. Hostility was also generated by the alleged eagerness of the African to differentiate himself from his

black American cousin. As a foreign black he knew he would be given preferential treatment by white Americans. Before dashikis and bubas became the vogue among younger blacks, African garb conferred a special status on a black who would *ipso facto* enjoy privileges and immunities denied Americans of African extraction. With reference to this situation, simultaneously ludicrous and irritating, Malcolm X once admonished a black audience to recognize that they were nothing but Africans living in America.

In fact, you'd get farther calling yourself African instead of Negro. Africans don't catch hell. You're the only one catching hell. They don't have to pass civil rights bills for Africans. An African can go anywhere he wants right now. All you've got to do is tie your head up. That's right, go anywhere you want. Just stop being a Negro. Change your name to Hoogagafooba.[48]

Whites have been accused of deliberately discouraging positive relations between the two black groups. David Mpongo, a graduate student at Lincoln University from Zimbabwe (Rhodesia), has claimed that when he first came to the United States in 1966 he "was given a white host family by the director of my program. . . . He told me that the Negroes don't like you. But I went out on my own and found a Negro family that accepted me."[49]

It is possible that the Neale study overstates the problems Africans and Afro-Americans experience in interacting with one another. Whatever degree of mutual suspicion and antagonism does exist can be attributed in large measure to the indoctrination to which each has been subjected. White America has exercised cultural hegemony to the fullest extent, and thus created the Afro-American's stereotyped imagery of Africa and Africans. Africans have been all too cognizant of the patronizing reaction they have received from some Afro-Americans. Back in 1951 a Nigerian student at Morehouse College, Akinsola Akiwowo, poetically voiced his concern in the pages of the quarterly *Phylon:*

Shall I sing your song, Africa
In this strange land of hate and love?
Shall I sing to those whose forebears
Were torn away from you long ago?
For they know you not, but believe
All the strange and gory stories
They oft have read and seen in films:
Apes, thick jungles, and men with spears,
And nude women with pancake lips.
They have not seen how, what, you are;
That long estrangement shuts their eyes...
Some say you are a thing of shame![50]

If Africans have an image problem in the United States then
it cannot be denied that the black American has had an image
problem in Africa. As a schoolboy in his native Uganda, John
Nagenda remembers that one called somebody a "Nigger or
even Negro" only at his peril for "it was an unfriendly act to
point out your racial relationship to American Negroes."[51] All
too often the Negro has been seen through the distorted lens
of motion pictures produced for white America. What John
Nagenda recalls is "some flashing-teethed, eye-rolling, broken
shouldered, perpetually perplexed nigger [who] brought drinks
to Clark Gable."[52] Hollywood's habitual portrayal of American
blacks solely as bellboys, janitors, stable boys, clowns, indolent
and carefree children aroused the ire of the Legislative Council
in Ibadan, Nigeria, back in March 1949. Epithets such as
"Nigger," "Sambo," "Jig," "Coon," and "Snowball," not un-
commonly used to identify blacks on screen, were also objec-
tionable. Nnamdi Azikiwe at the time advocated censorship of
those films which characterized persons of African descent "in a
derogatory and humiliating manner, because they tend to create a
spirit of resentment and bitterness on the part of Africans, thus
embarrassing race relations in this part of the world."[53]

Of late a *somewhat* more realistic portrayal of Negroes in the
cinema and contact between waves of young Africans traveling
to America for an education and black Americans appear to

have provided a much needed corrective. Negroes who have made their way "back home" as Peace Corps volunteers, AID personnel, tourists, or "permanent" exiles have also played a vital part in changing the "Stepin Fetchit" buffoon stereotype.

Half a century ago James Weldon Johnson, writing in the *New York Age,* speculated wishfully, "It may be that the day is not far off when the new Negroes of Africa will be demanding that their blood brothers in the United States be treated with absolute fairness and justice."[54] That day has arrived. It may have arrived as early as June 1960 when the Third Annual Conference of the American Society of African Culture met in Philadelphia. Participating as speakers and commentators were more than a score of Afro-Americans, West Indians, and Africans. In his closing address Jaja Wachuku, at the time Speaker of the Nigerian House of Assembly and subsequently minister of foreign affairs and commonwealth relations, pledged never to turn his back on "blood of my blood and flesh of my flesh." He was talking about black Americans. "The interests of twenty million American Negroes are entwined with those of two hundred million kith and kin in Africa." An African was an African regardless of where he was in the world. Defining some of the benefits of pan-Africanism, Wachuku urged American Negroes to "appreciate that as long as our continent exists and thrives, as long as there are African states respected in the world community of nations, they themselves will have a full growth—which is what they require. Their full contribution will be appreciated, their role of human beings will be greater. That's all we want."[55]

The day James Weldon Johnson had prophesied had certainly arrived by 1963 when Birmingham, Alabama, exploded. Birmingham was a city so pathologically consumed with Jim Crowism that a few years earlier a book about white rabbits and black rabbits had been banned. In April 1963 leaders of that industrial city's black community of one hundred fifty thousand (two-fifths of the population) launched an intensive desegregation campaign. There were sit-ins and protest marches

which culminated in mass arrests by the outraged authorities. The use of police dogs and high pressured fire hoses early in May heightened emotions and on May 12 two bombings in the black section touched off rioting.

May 1963 was also the month when a summit conference of independent African states was held in Addis Ababa. African unity was the subject of paramount interest but the black demonstrations in Birmingham, the police brutality, and the jailings were widely discussed both on and off the conference floor. Nigeria's foreign minister was not alone in coupling South Africa and the United States as nations which practiced the odious policy of apartheid. Simultaneous with the conference, Amharic newspapers and the *Ethiopian Herald,* an English-language newspaper which is an official publication of the Ethiopian government, charged that in the United States "to be black is still a crime." America's version of "civilized apartheid" had to be fought, said the *Herald.*[56]

The inhuman treatment of black Americans in Birmingham provoked Milton Obote of Uganda to write a letter of protest to President John F. Kennedy in which he said that the eyes of the world were focused on Alabama. Obote stated that it was particularly incumbent upon countries that projected themselves as leaders of the free world to guarantee freedom to all of their citizens, regardless of color. Those Afro-Americans who had been the targets of water hoses in Birmingham, Obote called "our kith and kin."[57]

At the May 1963 Addis Ababa conference a resolution was adopted which expressed "the deep concern aroused in all African peoples and governments by the measures of racial discrimination taken against communities of African origin living outside the continent and particularly in the United States of America."[58] When the Organization of African Unity met in Cairo in July 1964, the assembled heads of state and government recorded their disturbance over "continuing manifestations of racial bigotry and racial oppression against Negro citizens of the United States."[59]

When the duly elected Julian Bond was prevented from taking his seat in the state legislature of Georgia because of his vocal opposition to American policy in Vietnam, the chief United Nations delegates of fifteen African countries, in effect, took up the cudgels on his behalf. A luncheon was given at the UN in Bond's honor and the African representatives were joined by Dr. Martin Luther King as well as the entertainer, Harry Belafonte. Achmar Marof of Guinea objected to the idea that the Africans' action constituted interference in a purely domestic American matter. Because Africans believe race friction on their continent poses one of the greatest dangers to stability, Marof explained, they didn't want to miss a chance to improve race relations in the United States. Chief S. O. Adebo, Nigeria's permanent representative to the UN, described his attendance at the luncheon as "a gesture of support for equal rights."[60]

For all intents and purposes the presence of Tanzanian and Zambian delegates at the 1967 CORE convention was similarly motivated. African students as well as officials of African nations represented at the United Nations have also attended Black Muslim functions.

Chief Adebo once offered an African view of the black revolution in an article published by the New York chapter of CORE. He accentuated the need for cooperation between the African and the Afro-Americans. An essential prerequisite for this cooperation would be the removal of misunderstanding between the two peoples on the grass-roots level, a misunderstanding fostered "by centuries of lack of intelligent communication." Chief Adebo also wrote that the "African must recognize the American Negro as his brother, and American Negroes must acknowledge Africa as their ancestral home and Africans as their kith and kin." The Nigerian assured his readers that the unfortunate happenings in the South "have been a matter of as much concern to African leadership in Africa as they have been to the American Negro directly affected here."[61]

A few years later at the congress of African peoples convened in Atlanta, a Guinean representative, El Hajj Abdoulaye Toure,

speaking in French, told his predominantly black American audience, ". . . that Mother Africa thinks of her sons and daughters in America and she is with you in your struggle."[62] Malcolm X once pointedly asked the parliament of Ghana, "How can you condemn Portugal and South Africa while our black people in America are being bitten by dogs and beaten with clubs." After his speech he claimed to have heard "Yes! We support the Afro-Americans. . . morally, physically, materially if necessary!"

Malcolm X returned from his journey to West Africa convinced, once and for all, that the "black Africans look upon America's twenty-two million blacks as long-lost brothers! They love us! They study our struggle for freedom!"[63] Clearly, a reservoir of sympathy and concern for the tribulations of Afro-Americans exists in Africa. Of that there is little doubt. But how can African governments assist in the black "revolutions" in the United States? Diplomatic pressure offers one possibility.

In 1964 Malcolm had attended an OAU conference as an observer. In that capacity he submitted a memo requesting that the predicament of twenty-two million American blacks be brought to the attention of the United Nations by the Africans, "their elder brothers." Malcolm stated:

If the United States Supreme Court Justice, Arthur Goldberg, a few weeks ago, could find legal grounds to threaten to bring Russia before the United Nations and charge her with violating the human rights of less than three million Russian Jews, what makes our African brothers hesitate to bring the United States government before the United Nations and charge her with violating the human rights of twenty-two million African Americans?[64]

During the summer of 1967 representatives of SNCC were able to participate in a conference on racism, colonialism, and apartheid sponsored by the United Nations in Kitwe, Zambia. SNCC's role had been made possible by the efforts of the delegations of Tanzania and Guinea. James Forman, then international affairs director of SNCC, considered SNCC's participation in the Kitwe meeting as a "milestone in the liber-

ation of Black people in the United States" because "it represented the first time in the history of the United Nations that people of African descent now living in the United States had the opportunity to raise questions and discuss within a forum of the United Nations some aspects of our general condition in the United States."[65]

Racial oppression in the United States can undoubtedly be spotlighted by Africans in that world body. The government of the United States can be embarrassed, but diplomatic pressure by the international community may be futile. It has had little effect on racial practices in the Republic of South Africa. Moreover, in that unhappy land it is *de jure* segregation that has inflamed world opinion whereas in the United States legal equality is not the fundamental issue. That already obtains in theory if not in practice. In any event, enforcement of constitutional guarantees of equality and of civil rights legislation is only part of the solution. At this juncture in our nation's history only the massive expenditure of funds to close the gap between white America's standard of living and that of black America can resolve the racial crisis. What is required is a national dedication which cannot be fostered, much less coerced, by black African countries. African spokesmen will surely continue to prod the United States to expedite solutions to the racial dilemma. Some will periodically issue statements affirming their racial bonds with black Americans and recognizing racism as their common enemy. A few more "militant" than the rest may emulate Julius Nyerere's Tanzania which permitted SNCC to post a representative to Dar es Salaam, or Algeria which has allowed Eldridge Cleaver and the Black Panthers to open an Afro-American Information Center in downtown Algiers. Still other states will have to be content with safer, less dramatic actions which convey their good intentions.

In 1971 Houphouet Boigny's Ivory Coast named a street in its capital, Abidjan, for Jesse Owens, the hero of the 1936 Olympics held in Berlin.[66] The honor was bestowed on Owens because his track and field victories were an eloquent rejoinder

to Hitler's malodorous theories of white supremacy. Such gestures of pan-Negroism, particularly on the part of a relatively
moderate African state, are praiseworthy. They also serve to
remind us of the fact that even interested nations are limited
in the assistance they can give to American blacks. Stark political and economic realities are the limiting factors.

Actually, Afro-Americans, their colonial relationship to white
America notwithstanding, may be in a position to do more for
independent black Africa than vice versa. Back in 1960 Jaja
Wachuku asked a black American assemblage why the "ten
American Negro millionaires" of whom he had heard did not
contribute to the development of Africa.[67] Nine years later, after
most of Africa had severed the bonds of colonialism, Dr. Zinsou
commented to an *Ebony* reporter, "Compared to Africans you
are privileged. The problems of Dahomey are many. We need
trained people, money. You are much richer than little Israel
or Formosa who are sending people to help us. Help in any form
will be welcome."[68]

When he was in Central Africa several years ago, Clarence
Jones, now publisher of the *Amsterdam News,* the largest black
weekly in the United States, was told by Zambian officials that
they wanted Afro-Americans to act as a lobby for African
causes.[69] Because Zambia lacked skilled manpower in all fields,
President Kenneth Kaunda in 1970 personally invited black
Americans to work in his developing country. Lesotho's chief
representative at the United Nations has publicly stated that he
would like to replace the more than one hundred British expatriate civil servants with Afro-American technicians. The latter he
thought would be less condescending and more involved. "I'm
sure that a black person shares many of the things we suffer
and he will feel for us and then he will apply himself even better." With their scanty resources, liberation movements are in
dire need of black American succor. In October 1971 officials
of the South West Africa Peoples Organization (SWAPO)
besought the *Amsterdam News* to publicize Namibia's need for
assistance.[70] Afro-Americans could help by protesting to the

United States government about continued South African administration of the one-time German colony in defiance of a World Court verdict. Publicity could be given to the Namibian cause by the formation of "Friends of Namibia" committees, the SWAPO spokesmen suggested.

Recently, David Thebehali, a young college-educated Bantu who is a member of the advisory council of Soweto, the huge black ghetto astride white Johannesburg, advised black South Africans to relocate in and develop the Bantu or rural tribal homelands.[71] If help were needed, Afro-American doctors, dentists, economic experts, etc., should be called upon. Black Americans may not be keen about contributing to the policy of separate development particularly if they understand that the tribal homelands envisioned for the black South Africa majority constitute only 13 percent of the nation's land. But it is undeniably true that Afro-Americans possess many of the skills if not the capital needed to develop the considerable economic potential of some black African countries. Will they choose to utilize their skills for Africa's benefit? Conceptions and misconceptions about the land of their forefathers will certainly help to determine the extent of Afro-America's role in African development.

NOTES

1. "The Irrepressible Envoy from Ghana," *Ebony*, November 1970, p. 74.

2. Era Bell Thompson, "Are Black Americans Welcome in Africa?" *Ebony*, January 1969.

3. Ibid. According to the census bureau there are now twenty-two million black Americans who constitute 11 percent of the population of the United States. There has long been suspicion in many black circles that the black American community has been undernumerated.

4. Ibid. Tubman's own mother, Elizabeth Rebecca Barines Tubman, emigrated to Liberia from Atlanta with her parents, ex-slaves, during the Reconstruction era.

5. Ibid. As a young man Banda studied at a black high school in Ohio, at Indiana University, at the University of Chicago, and at Meharry, a black medical college in Tennessee. He completed his medical studies in Edinburgh.

6. Ibid., Senghor also commented, "Naturally Negroes are welcome in Senegal," but he did not expatiate.

7. Accounts of the incident may be found in the *Amsterdam News*, March 29, 1969 and *The New York Times*, March 23, 1969.

8. Tom Mboya, "The American Negro Cannot Look to Africa for an Escape," *The New York Times Magazine*, July 13, 1969, p. 30.

9. *Amsterdam News*, March 29, 1969.

10. *The New York Times*, March 25, 1969.

11. Ibid.

12. James Leopold, "Mboya Shown 'Like It is,'"*African Opinion*, May-June 1969, p. 5.

13. *Liberator*, May 1969, pp. 10-11.

14. Ibid., June 1969, p. 6.

15. Ibid.

16. *The New York Times*, April 12, 1969.

17. Mboya, "The American Negro Cannot Look to Africa for an Escape"; Mboya, *The Challenge of Nationhood* (New York and Washington: Praeger Publishers, 1970), pp. 221-232.

18. Mboya, "Mboya's Rebuttal," *Ebony*, August 1969, pp. 90-91, 94.

19. Mboya, "The American Negro Cannot Look to Africa for an 'Escape," p. 44.

20. Ibid., p. 34.

21. Ibid., pp. 43-44, and Mboya, "Mboya's Rebuttal," p. 91. Because Zambia lacked "skilled manpower in all fields," President Kenneth Kaunda in 1970 invited black Americans to work in his developing country. *The New York Times*, August 2, 1970.

22. Kenya National Assembly, Senate. *Official Report*, Vol. 16, 1968, p. 1650.

23. Ibid., pp. 1655-1656.

24. Ibid., pp. 1658-1659.

25. Ibid., pp. 1661-1662.

26. Ibid., pp. 1663-1664.

27. Ibid., pp. 1674-1675.

28. Ibid., p. 1674. Kenya which had an estimated population of 11,250,000 by mid-year 1970 is one of the few African nations where there is a rapidly growing realization of the need to increase birth control so as to improve living standards.

29. Ibid., pp. 1666-1667.

30. Quoted in Thompson, "Are Black Americans Welcome in Africa," p. 50.

31. Era Bell Thompson, *Africa, Land of My Fathers* (Garden City, New York: Doubleday and Company, Inc., 1954), p. 114.

32. *AMSAC* [American Society of African Culture] *Newsletter*, September 1962, p. 5.

33. Maina Kinyatti, "African Students Take Charge," *African Opinion*, January-February 1971, pp. 2-3.

34. Melville J. Herskovits, *The New World Negro-Selected Papers in*

Afroamerican Studies, ed. Francis S. Herskovits (Minerva Press, 1969), p. 87.

35. Ibid.

36. Ibid.

37. George Shepperson, "Notes On Negro American Influences On The Emergence Of African Nationalism," ed. Okon Edet Uya, *Black Brotherhood— Afro-Americans and Africa* (Lexington, Massachusetts: D. C. Heath and Co., 1971), p. 226. This useful Shepperson article was originally published in the *Journal of African History,* 1, 2 (1960): 299-312.

38. George Shepperson, "Nyasaland and the Millenium." *Black Africa—Its Peoples and Their Cultures Today* (London: Macmillan & Co., 1970), ed. John Middleton, p. 235.

39. Raymond Leslie Buell, *The Native Problem in Africa* (Hamden; Connecticut: Archon Books, 1965) II, 603. The Buell book was originally published in 1928.

40. Jabez Ayodele Langley, "Garveyism and African Nationalism," *Race,* 11, 2 (1969): 169.

41. Kwame Nkrumah, *Ghana: The Autobiography of Kwame Nkrumah* (New York: Thomas Nelson and Sons, 1957), pp. 30-34, 42. On one occasion which Nkrumah described, he felt embarrassed by his identification with black Americans. Shortly after he came to America he attended a service at the Abyssinian Baptist Church in Harlem in the company of a white friend, a Dutchman. The service was noisy, emotional, and, Nkrumah thought, "undignified." "As we left the church I tried to apologize but he seemed surprised at this and said, with all sincerity, that it was the most beautiful thing he had seen so far in any church" (p.30).

42. Harold R. Isaacs, "A Reporter at Large—Back to Africa," *The New Yorker,* May 13, 1961, p. 135

43. John Nagenda, "Pride or Prejudice? Relationships Between Africans and American Negroes," *Race,* 9, 2 (1967): 162-163.

44. R. Mugo Gatheru, *Child of Two Worlds—A Kikuyu's Story* (Garden City: Anchor Books, 1965), p. 148.

45. Ibid., p. 151.

46. Robert D. Cohen, "African Students and the Negro American—Past Relationships and a Recent Program," *International Educational Cultural Exchange,* 5, no. 2 (Fall 1969): 77-78.

47. "Exchange of Persons," *Intercultural Education,* 1, no. 10 (November 1970): 17-18.

48. George Breitman, ed., *Malcom X Speaks—Selected Speeches and Statements* (New York: Grove Press, Inc., 1966), p. 36. This speech entitled "The Ballot or the Bullet" was delivered in Cleveland in April 1964.

49. *The New York Times,* April 12, 1971. It is noteworthy that in the 1960s an Afro-American and a Ghanaian formed the Association of African and Afro-

American students at Harvard and Radcliffe. A Nigerian student was its first president.

50. Akinsola Akiwowo, "Song in a Strange Land," *Phylon,* 12, no. 1 (First Quarter, 1951), pp. 36-37.

51. Nagenda, "Pride or Prejudice?" p. 159.

52. Ibid.

53. Nnamdi Azikiwe, *Zik-A Selection From the Speeches of Nnamdi Azikiwe* (Cambridge University Press, 1961), pp. 152-153.

54. *New York Age,* May 12, 1923.

55. Jaja A. Wachuku, "The Relation of AMSAC and the American Negro to Africa and Pan-Africanism" in *Pan-Africanism Reconsidered* (Berkeley and Los Angeles: University of California Press, 1962), pp. 361-376.

56. *The New York Times,* May 19, 1963.

57. Ibid., May 24, 1964.

58. Resolutions of the Summit Conference of Independent African States, May 1962. Quoted in Colin Legum, *Pan-Africanism—A Short Political Guide* (New York: Frederic A. Praeger, 1965), pp. 296-297.

59. Resolutions of the First Assembly of the Heads of State and Government of the Organization of African Unity, July 1965. Quoted in Legum, p. 305.

60. *The New York Times,* January 22, 1966.

61. Chief S. O. Adebo, "The Black Revolution: An African View," *Rights and Reviews,* Winter 1966/67, pp. 33-34.

62. Alex Poinsett, "It's Nation Time," *Ebony,* December 1970, p. 100. Africans are not at all reticent about expressing disapprobation of individual black Americans and their policies. For a speech he delivered in Tanzania Stokely Carmichael was severely criticized by South Africa's banned African National Congress (ANC). Stokely was condemned as a racist troublemaker and his speech was termed "Meaningless and arrogant demagoguery." Lee Richard Gibson, "South African Toms Denounce Stokely," *Liberator,* 7, no. 12 (December 1967): 10.

63. Malcolm X and Alex Haley, *The Autobiography of Malcolm X* (New York: Grove Press, 1966), pp 356, 361-362.

64. Breitman, ed., *Malcolm X Speaks,* p. 75.

65. "James Forman Of S.N.C.C. Addresses the United Nations," *Liberator,* 7, no. 12 (December 1967): 8.

66. *The New York Times,* May 4, 1971.

67. Wachuku, "The Relation of AMSAC and the American Negro to Africa and Pan-Africanism," p. 369.

68. Era Bell Thompson, "Africa's Problems—The Other Side Of the Story," *Ebony,* July 1969, p. 121.

69. *Amsterdam News,* October 16, 1971.

70. Ibid.

71. *The New York Times,* July 13, 1971. One South African writer has written about the degree to which his countrymen have been inspired by black American literary, musical, and athletic achievements. See Ezekiel Mphahlele, "The Blacks," *Africa Today,* 14, no. 4 (August 1967): 22-25.

6

AFRO-AMERICA'S AFRICAN RENAISSANCE

Throughout human history psychological scarring has been one of the most common sequelae of long-term persecution. Contrary to his own best interests and against his will and better judgment, the victim of prejudice and discrimination often internalizes the grossly perverted stereotype foisted upon him by the oppressor. This is not peculiar to blacks. Many Jews, even chauvinistic ones, feel complimented when told that they do not look Jewish. On some level they have accepted the grotesque hook-nosed image of Jews.

For a few centuries blacks have been indoctrinated with the psyche-searing canard that their African forebears, along with contemporary Africans, belong to a naked, spear-wielding savage race incapable of progressive development without the tutelage of whites. The melancholy truth is that historically large numbers of American blacks, almost certainly a majority, have subscribed consciously or subconsciously to this insidiously dangerous and fallacious idea.

A few short decades ago Paul Robeson met Afro-Americans who were convinced that the black man in Africa "communicated his thoughts solely by means of gestures, that, in fact, he was practically incapable of speech and merely used sign language."[1] In 1937 Carter G. Woodson, founder of the

Association for the Study of Negro Life and History, remarked that Negroes welcomed the theory of a complete cultural break with Africa "for above all things they do not care to be known as resembling in any way these 'terrible Africans.' " [2] James Egert Allen, a black historian, a teacher for many years, now retired and a long-time booster of Negro History Week, reminiscing about his initial failures in the 1920s and 1930s to promote the study of the black heritage, recalls that "black school teachers, for the most part, wanted nothing to do with Africa or the study of Africans." They insisted they were just citizens of the United States.[3] Why should the teachers have thought that their American citizenship which was second-class to begin with was incompatible with an acknowledgment of their African past? Considering the prevailing picture of Africa and Africans and the depiction of Garveyites as "monkey chasers," such an acknowledgment would understandably have produced great discomfort among the black bourgeoisie.

Whenever possible some black Americans have identified themselves with white people and with European civilization. Stokely Carmichael among others has chided his "brothers" for having gone to the cinema and identified with Tarzan against the "nigger," the "black savage."[4] Unwillingness by blacks to associate with Africa and Africans has been bound up with self-hate induced by the white man, Malcolm X once observed. Early in 1965 he commented, "we have been a people who hated our African characteristics. We hated our black heads, we hated the shape of our nose, we wanted one of those long dog-like noses. . . ; we hated the color of our skin, hated the blood of Africa that was in our veins."[5] On a previous occasion he had cited the pejorative image of Africa as one impediment to the success of a back-to-Africa plan. "How would you go about getting 22 million people to go to a place they think is a rotten, insect-infested jungle?" he asked rhetorically. "How would you go about getting them to go back when they cringe when you use the word African or Africa."[6] Avid black nationalists are not necessarily exceptions to Malcolm's caustic criticism.

Essien-Udom has perceptively written that Black Muslims have not greatly stressed Africa in their recruitment campaigns owing to the fact that many black Americans continue to conceive of sub-Saharan Africa as a "vast-jungle" and that conception, a gross misconception actually, generates feelings of mortification and degradation. Alternatively, Elijah Muhammad has fostered an inoffensive psychological association with Asia and the Middle East.[7]

One of the most eloquent synopses of popular Afro-American images of Africa and Afro-Americans was contained in Era Bell Thompson's thoughts on her 1953 visit to the "dark continent."

> Until a few months before, Africa had been the last place on earth I wanted to visit. Until a few years before, my knowledge of the continent, like that of most Americans, both black and white, was geared to concepts handed down by Livingstone and Stanley nearly a hundred years ago. . . . Had anyone called me an African I would have been indignant. Only race fanatics flaunted their jungle ancestry or formed back-to-Africa movements—and they were usually motivated more by a king complex than by any loyalty to black genes.
>
> When I saw bare-toed African students walking down Chicago boulevards in their flowing robes and colorful head cloths, I, too, shook my head and murmured, "My people!" If there was the skeleton of a chief in my family closet, he was Cherokee, not Kru; Black Foot, not Yoruba or Fulani. I was proud of my red and white blood, ashamed of the black, for I grew up believing that black was bad, that black was dirty and poor and wrong. Black was Africa. I did not want to be an African. . . . [8]

Miss Thompson traced the denial of her African ancestors and her detestation of her motherland back to her childhood years.

Why should black Americans have thought differently about Africa? They were educated in white-run school systems and exposed to racist histories of Africa, a continent allegedly without a past worth studying before the European providentially appeared on its shores. White cultural hegemony, encompassing not merely schools, but movies, newspapers, and books, created the "savage in the jungle" myth which led Afro-Americans in the main to find Africa and its people distinctly odious.

There were always plenty of exceptions, persons who nurtured

positive attitudes toward Africans, who shared a pride in their African past and demonstrated a concern for the continent's future. Many, but certainly not all, were Garveyites or votaries of Du Bois' Pan-African ideology. J.A. Rogers' numerous writings proclaimed the contributions to world civilization that had been made by Africans, continental and diaspora alike. Arthur Schomburg, a black bibliophile born in Puerto Rico, amassed an extraordinary collection of books by and about Africans and Afro-Americans. Africana was featured in a bookstore operated on Harlem's 135th Street early in this century by George Young, an ex-pullman porter. Works by and germane to blacks have been the specialty of Lewis Michaux, a black nationalist, in his bookstore on 125th Street for decades now. It was in the 1920s that a Mississippi black, William Leo Hansberry, was doing seminal work in the then academically unsanctioned field of African civilization. Although recognition of Hansberry's labors was very slow in coming, when a school of African Studies was established at a Nigerian university (Nsukka), it was named in his honor, thanks to one of his former students, Nnamdi Azikiwe. An African theme was also crucial to the Harlem Renaissance. These facts taken together with the shock and revulsion registered over the Italian incursion into Ethiopia suggest a great diversity of feeling for and about Africa. Even within individual blacks there were conflicting and contradictory emotions vying for supremacy. Ambivalence may have been the norm.

By and large, overt black American interest in Africa was very limited for a long time. As late as the mid-1950s when readers of *Ebony* were queried about the topics that they wished to read about, in a list of ten Africa occupied last place. Within an amazingly brief span of time a metamorphosis occurred. In 1956 Kwame Nkrumah paid a visit to the United States. Chicago's black belt and the Harlem community gave him an extremely enthusiastic welcome. Similarly, Sekou Touré of Guinea received a very warmhearted reception when he came to this country in 1959. In 1957, of course, Ghana was born, the first new independent nation in black Africa in the post-World War

II era. Other states followed at a rapid pace thought wholly unrealistic by the colonial powers just a few years earlier. It was the headlong rush toward freedom in Africa that radically altered the thinking of Afro-Americans regarding their black brothers. The smell of freedom was in the air. It wafted across the Atlantic following the route onc: involuntarily taken by African slaves.

No single postwar independence struggle in Africa caught the imagination of the American public to quite the same degree as Kenya's Mau Mau (1952-1960). British authorities euphemistically spoke of the period of the "Emergency." To white Americans who, on the whole, found it sanguinary and frightening, and to countless black Americans who found it awe-inspiring, it was always Mau Mau, an obscure name for a hotly debated phenomenon cloaked in mysterious secrecy. Considered a religious aberration by some, a peasant's revolt by others, it was, in the minds of its participants and supporters in Kenya and abroad, a justifiable anti-colonial nationalist movement spearheaded by the Kikuyu tribe. Its ultimate success in expediting decolonization added the word *Uhuru* (freedom) to the pan-African lexicon.

Although the number of Mau Mau-connected European fatalities has been grossly exaggerated by Western films, novels, and newspaper stories,[9] there is no gainsaying the fact that the Mau Mau uprising was ruthlessly violent. Both its nature and the fruits of Kenyan sovereignty which it yielded earned a special place for Mau Mau in the hearts of black Americans, particularly black nationalists. By comparison, legalistic and nonviolent direct action techniques such as sit-ins aimed at effecting integration in the United States looked weak, hesitant, timorous, ineffective, even shameful to some Afro-Americans.

Vicarious satisfaction could be drawn from the courageous exploits of the Mau Mau. Toward the end of 1956 the *Chicago Defender* published an editorial, "Victory for the Mau Mau," which left no doubt about where its sympathies lay. The whole rebellion was called daring and was chalked up to racial discrim-

ination compounded by economic wrong. Jomo Kenyatta was depicted as "the brilliant, fearless European-trained Mau Mau leader."[10] "We will not, and must not support the British overlords in Kenya," Paul Robeson said in 1953. The athlete-entertainer-political activist vowed, "We will fight to free Kenyatta."[11]

In their revolutionary rhetoric time and time again Afro-Americans have admiringly referred to Mau Mau, sometimes by design to instill fear in "Mr. Charlie." Stokely Carmichael once observed: "To most whites, black power seems to mean that the Mau Mau are coming to the suburbs at night. The Mau Mau are coming, and the whites must stop them."[12] In December 1964 speaking to a racially mixed audience in a Harlem church, Malcolm X hailed Jomo Kenyatta and Oginga Odinga, then his vice president. (The two men have since gone their separate ways.) Malcolm predicted that the judgment of historians would be that the Mau Mau were "the greatest African patriots and freedom fighters that the continent ever knew." There was a lesson for Afro-Americans to learn from their brothers in Kenya. Then Malcolm opined that Mau Mau was just what was needed in Alabama, in Georgia, indeed in New York City.[13]

The insurrection in Kenya stimulated the formation of a group called the Harlem Mau Mau. It has been led by Charles Kenyatta who was once a bodyguard for Malcolm X. Mr. Kenyatta, a bearded man partial to khaki military tunics cut a redoubtable figure, especially when backed by six or so youthful followers armed with machetes. Actually, as far as the police in Gotham were concerned, the membership of the Harlem Mau Mau was microscopic.[14]

Throughout the latter half of 1960 and the better part of the next year, Congo (Kinshasa), or the Belgian Congo as it was known in the colonial period, occupied center stage in the theater of world affairs. Afro-Americans fixed their gaze upon a distant black land as it underwent a bloody and excruciating ordeal. Out of the welter of tribal and neocolonial politics emerged

Patrice Lumumba who, by dint of his martyrdom, became one of the brightest stars in the constellation of black heroes. His murder caused shock waves across black America at the beginning of 1961. The previous year on a visit to the United States he had deeply impressed blacks at Howard University in Washington, D. C., and elsewhere. An unswerving foe of imperialism, he became well liked because of statements such as this: "Africans built America. They are the reason America has become a great world power. If Africans can achieve that in the new world, they can achieve it in their own continent."[15]

News of Lumumba's slaying led to a riot by black Americans in the visitors' gallery of the United Nations, the most serious disruption inside the headquarters of the world organization since its founding. In addition there were marches, demonstrations, and picketing, all to protest Lumumba's death which was seen as a lynching with global ramifications. James Baldwin considered the killing of the former Congolese premier as "surely among the most sinister of recent events."[16] He intended to go to the United Nations gallery but was unable to do so. Superficial commentators attributed the disturbances to communist influence. But James Reston in a column aptly titled "Copper Sun, Scarlet Sea, What Is Africa to Me?" recognized the pan-African implications of the protests. Afro-Americans were chafing at the glaring inconsistencies between the American government's pontifications to the world about democratic ideals and the day to day mistreatment of blacks at home in the United States. Blacks were beginning to feel that they were involved in a broader battle. The partial liberation of Africa had augmented the black American's frustration and caused him to fuse his own struggle to that taking place in Africa. Hence, Reston concluded that there was no longer a need to pose Countee Cullen's question about the meaning of Africa to Afro-Americans.[17]

Prodded and emotionally buttressed by political ferment in Africa, black Americans initiated and quickly escalated the process of redefining themselves within the American context and of reassessing their relationships to Africa and its inhab-

itants. One result was what may properly be termed an African
cultural renaissance. Its manifestations were diverse. Black
Americans, not all nationalists by any stretch of the imagination, eschewed the use of the word "Negro," as it applied to
them. It was a "slave name" foisted on the black man by his
oppressor, a name which by implication denied the Afro-
Americans a homeland across the Atlantic and a heritage. "Negro" was employed as a term of opprobrium interchangeable
with "Uncle Tom." Invidious semantic distinctions were made
between "Negroes" unable or unwilling to divest themselves of
the old slave mentality and "blacks" or Afro-Americans proud
of their African past and of being black. The latter insisted on
being called black (even when their skin color was truly brown
or tan) or Afro-American or African-American. A few wanted
to be referred to as simply Africans.[18]

On university campuses black culture associations and Afro
clubs proliferated. Some of these adopted African names. They
lobbied, occasionally with force, for the addition of African-re-
lated courses to the school curricula. These curricula reforms
were seen as an antidote to the "intellectual imperialism" of
Europeans. Black survival was anchored to consciousness of
Africa and its culture. Essentially, then, the purpose of black
campus organizations has been to emphasize blackness and race
pride. As a member of the Afro-American Students Union at
the University of California (Berkeley) put it:

We decided to remember our African heroes, our American heroes and our culture. We decided to stop hating ourselves, trying to look like you, bleaching
our hair, straightening our hair. In high school, I used to hold my big lip in.[19]

This anti-assimilational pattern of thought percolated down to
black high school students, even junior high school students.
And it was verbalized. A case in point is the Swahili squabble.

Kiswahili or Swahili as it is popularly known is a lingua
franca spoken widely in East Africa from Kenya down to
Mozambique. Its grammar is Bantu. A sizable percentage of its
vocabulary is Arabic, not surprising in view of the historical role

played by Arabs in the area especially in towns dotted along the Indian Ocean. In fact the name of the hybrid language is derived from the Arabic word for "coast." Originating on the East African littoral the language spread to the interior. Words of Portuguese, German, East Indian, and English origin found in Swahili are a reminder of the parts played by these peoples in East African history. Not only is Swahili a living language, the official one in Tanzania, but it can boast an impressive literature including prose and poetry. Almost forty years ago Paul Robeson, who achieved remarkable proficiency in African tongues, wrote, "It is astonishing and, to me, fascinating to find a flexibility and subtlety in a language like Swahili sufficient to convey the teachings of Confucius."[20]

In the 1960s with the upsurge of interest in and identification with black Africa by black Americans the use of Swahili became *de rigeur*. Swahili words and phrases began to appear in magazine advertisements particularly those for cosmetics purveyed in the black community. Advertisements for Afro Sheen, a hair product, featured catch phrases such as *wantu wazuri*, translated as "beautiful people" and *Upendo ni pamoja* which was rendered as "Love is together." Accompanying the Swahili copy were photographs of groups of black men and women with Afro hairdos. *Harambee*, a Swahili word that is a favorite slogan of Jomo Kenyatta's and is Kenya's national motto, is usually translated as "let us all pull together." It has also been widely used by black Americans. The African-American Teachers Association in New York City incorporated the term in its organizational emblem. In 1968 *Harambee* was adopted as its name by a black development group in the Detroit area. A nonprofit toy manufacturing division of Operation Bootstrap in Watts was given the Swahili name *Shindana* (to compete or contend). Among its products are black dolls with Negroid features draped in African garments. Swahili names have been bestowed upon a few of the dolls: *Malaika* (angel) and *Tamu* (sweet).[21] Renaming has not been confined to the inanimate in black America. One black actress assumed the name Tatanisha.

Tatanisha in Swahili means "to perplex."

Among black students the Swahili movement blossomed quickly. A few years ago the controversial dormitory at Antioch College's Afro-American Studies Institute was dubbed Nyumba Umoja (Unity House). The center for blacks at the University of Pennsylvania was designated the Nyumba ya Ujamma (House of the Family). At the Bronx Community College the black student organization was called *Simba* (lion or warrior).

Demands that Swahili be taught at secondary schools and universities were heard with increasing insistence and stridency. Such a demand caused what one writer described as a "veritable, linguistic war" in Washington, D.C. In November 1967 William Howard Taft, a secondary school in the Bronx, announced its intention to add Swahili to its curriculum. With jubilation and considerable exaggeration, the Negro student who had initially suggested to the school principal that the course be offered characterized the announcement as "the most revolutionary accomplishment in the history of New York State." The youth's hyperbole is significant in itself. It reveals the concern among blacks, especially the more militant, with the cultural heritage of black people which, they charge, has been "distorted, minimized and in some cases outrightly suppressed."[22] Further evidence of this concern was provided by Floyd B. McKissick, then national director of the Congress of Racial Equality (CORE), when he returned from a two-week trip to sub-Saharan Africa during the summer of 1967. At a press conference, McKissick explained why his organization would foster the study of Swahili in public schools. "We have Spanish, French and German in our schools, white languages. We want Swahili, a black language."[23]

Critics of Swahili point out that for its vocabulary the language is deeply indebted to Arabic, the tongue of the people who for centuries operated the iniquitous East African slave trade.[24] There are those who argue that Swahili is a poor linguistic choice for Afro-Americans because it is an East African tongue and the provenance of black slaves in the United States

was, with very few exceptions, West Africa. Dr. Lorenzo Turner, an Africanist of note and a recognized black authority on linguistics, has reservations about the selection of Swahili which he imputes to ignorance of the fact that bondsmen in the New World originated in Yoruba- and Hausa-speaking regions in West Africa.[25] The rejoinder offered by a black free-lance writer is that "West Africans are not separate from East Africans in either color, culture or linguistics."[26] Interestingly Ron Karenga, the California-based cultural nationalist, is alleged to have chosen Swahili for his Us group because it is not peculiar to any single tribe and thus facilitates Afro-American identification with the whole of Africa.[27]

The practical value of Swahili has been questioned by many in both black and white communities who feel that underprivileged black children should first learn to read, write, and speak English properly. As long as blacks remain in the United States, "American English" is a more functional medium of communication than Swahili, an Afro-American wrote to *The New York Times.*[28] A letter to the Negro press asked that it be remembered that the textbook on "How to make an Atom Bomb" was not written in Swahili.[29] Proponents of the East African language are, of course, not chiefly interested in its usefulness. For them it is rather a matter of "self identity" and of "improving the badly eroded self image of black people."[30] Beverly Coleman writing in *Black World* explained that she had long been uncomfortable because "Afro-Americans are, perhaps, the only ethnic group which does not have a linguistic vehicle with which to perpetuate our heritage; that, until recently, most of us didn't even know we had a heritage (other than slavery) to perpetuate."[31]

For many Black Panthers who are Marxist-oriented and indifferent to and often hostile to cultural nationalism the discovery of a black heritage is of little importance. Ray "Masai" Hewitt, minister of education, Black Panther party, addressing himself to the educational needs of black people, commented in an inter-

view "We don't mean to get hung up studying Swahili for the next 16 semesters while we are being oppressed, suffer unemployment, low paying jobs, high taxes, high cost of living, war after war and police brutality." At the time of Hewitt's interview with *The Black Panther* in 1969, he had just returned from a trip to Africa. In the course of his travels he had met Africans engaged in revolutionary struggles. Whenever "we told them that there were brothers here studying Swahili for the revolution they burst out laughing," "Masai" said, "To them it was the funniest thing they ever heard."[32] Eldridge Cleaver has also been quoted to the effect that it is far more important for a black man to read Marx than to learn Swahili. Cleaver, though he describes himself as an Afro-American, "I'm Afro and I'm also American," has taken middle-class cultural nationalists to task for turning black pride into a kind of fetish. Black awareness was a good and necessary development but it was a transitional phase and not an end in and of itself. Cleaver has faulted the cultural nationalists for "thinking that once you learn how to speak Swahili or wear African clothes or let your hair grow long and grow out a natural or an 'Afro,' that you're free." Ron Karenga was scored for teaching that without doing these things, without acquiring a speaking knowledge of Swahili, black people could not be free. To Eldridge's mind that line of thought was naive and pointed up the basic difference between cultural nationalism and revolutionary black nationalism.[33] Linda Harrison, a Panther in the East Oakland, California, office, has also sneered at the people who think that a common tongue, Swahili, could make all blacks brothers. Cultural nationalists, she wrote in *The Black Panther,* "want a culture rooted in African culture; a culture which ignores the colonization and brutalization that were part and parcel; for example, of the formation and emergence of the Swahili language." But the gravamen of the charge against the cultural nationalists was that their philosophy was fanciful and was oblivious of political realities. Wearing African clothing could not end exploitation or truly emancipate black Americans.[34]

Panther and other critics notwithstanding, in the 1960s African fashions became a fairly common sight at black gatherings. They were worn by both sexes. Although undiscriminating observers frequently labeled all African garments dashikis (or danshikis), a loose-fitting West African outfit popularized by Nigerian diplomats at the United Nations, there were bubas, djellabas, caftans, and agbadas. Geles, turbanlike head wraps, proved popular among black women.

Before his disappearance in April 1970, H. Rap Brown was often seen clad in African clothing. Stokely Carmichael commonly appeared in a flowing Nigerian agbada. Of course the African vogue was not limited to black nationalists. The year 1967 witnessed the opening of an apparel shop in Harlem devoted exclusively to African garb. In September 1968 Boston public schools were kept in turmoil for almost a week by black students demanding the right to wear African dress. It was a matter of black consciousness, of blacks proclaiming their Africanness and simultaneously repudiating white values. Not all Afro-Americans take African clothing styles seriously. Although he has expressed his approval of black Americans searching for cultural ties to Africa, Roy Wilkins has regarded "these Hollywood Africans with the dashikis" as frivolous.[35] Ironically then, both Black Panther spokesmen, so-called "revolutionaries," and the executive director of the "moderate," "bourgeois" NAACP were less than enthusiastic about some facets of the African renaissance in black America. Although they differed sharply about means and ends, both organizations felt that cultural nationalism would divert attention from the real problems facing black America. Despite much criticism, however, the African craze grew swiftly.

By the mid-1960s a stroll along Seventh Avenue in Harlem offered opportunities to purchase African shampoos, African candles, African beads, and African earrings. In 1970 *Essence,* a new magazine responding to the new fashion predilections of its readers, carried a piece on Masai jewelry.[36] Sculpture and other objets d'art from Africa decorated more and more black homes.

An ancient Egyptian symbol of life, the ankh, a cross with a loop at the top, was fashioned and proudly displayed by black youth. Africa Ltd., a crafts shop in New York City, sold musical instruments from Ethiopia and Nigeria, masks from the Ivory Coast, and a variety of African games, dolls, and carved wood chess sets. Prince Thomas, an African-American from Mississippi who ran the shop, once complained lightheartedly, "We can't keep these Benin bronzes in stock—they sell too quickly."[37] Africana had become something of a fad for whites. For blacks it was considerably more. It was a redefinition of blackness. Again black opposition to a preoccupation with Africana was expressed by Bishop Stephen G. Spottswood, chairman of the board of directors of the NAACP, who in his keynote address to that association's 1970 annual convention noted that a black architect had been working on a theory that Afro-Americans "should have distinctive type housing—one which adequately accommodates their tribal instincts inherited from our African past—reductio ad absurdum!"[38]

One of the most popular expressions of black pride has been the bouffant "African" hair style, called an Afro, a bush, or a natural. Young radical blacks, male and female, were the trend-setters but before too long "establishment"-oriented brothers followed suit. Even the barber at the highly respectable Harlem YMCA started advertising haircuts "African-style." It offered an alternative to the white coiffures which the nationalists held demeaning to black people and usually unsuitable for black hair. Initial unwillingness on the part of U.S. military authorities to allow young black recruits to wear their hair Afro style led to considerable racial friction. In 1969 the commandant of the Marine Corps retreated somewhat and sanctioned a modified version of the Afro cut. It failed to satisfy black Marines. Early in 1971 forty-nine military barbers and beauticians underwent a hairstyling course under the direction of a well-known black hair stylist.[39]

Civilian life offered additional options. Africanization of the hair was simplified by the marketing of Afro wigs. Obviously

not all blacks have hair that is amenable to the natural look. The Afro has not been universally acclaimed by any means. There has been disapproval and not just by American blacks. The government of Tanzania has actually banned Afros.[40] After some urbanized, educated African women began sporting naturals in East Africa, a writer for the *Tanzania Sunday News,* a newspaper owned by the government, denounced the trend, contending that the style was wholly foreign to the continent.[41] It was a kind of cultural neocolonialism, an unwelcome import from the "land of drug takers and draft dodgers" that would undermine the African personality. Black Americans in Tanzania were deeply disturbed by the journalistic attack. One who responded in a letter to the editor which he signed "Pan-Africanist" conceded that the natural was not typically African. But, he wrote, the style was a "direct manifestation of the African-American's effort to cast off imperialist oppression from his makeup, from his mind and from his body."[42]

Whether the Afro is authentic is really immaterial. As two black psychiatrists, William H. Grier and Price M. Cobb, have convincingly argued, it represents a repudiation of the painful, humiliating, and completely unnecessary hot-comb hair-straightening ordeal. It constitutes an unqualified rejection of the self-deprecating notion that straight hair is attractive and tightly-knit hair is ugly—a value spawned by white American society and largely internalized by black Americans. Such a rejection, as Grier and Cobb have pointed out, is "psychologically redemptive."[43] Finally it signalizes a determination to be accepted as they are and for what they are—blacks not dusky imitations of whites.

As has already been noted, black hair fashions have long been a controversial topic in certain quarters. Black nationalists of the Garvey stripe have continuously decried the "conking" or straightening practice. Carlos Cook of the African Nationalist Pioneer Movement is supposed to have taunted women passing his street-corner speaker's platform as follows: "Your hair has more intelligence than you." "In two weeks," he prophesied

"your hair is willing to go back to Africa and you'll still be jivin' on the corner," an allusion to the ephemeral quality of the hair-straightening process.[44] Cultural nationalist Cecil Elombe Brath has spoken with contempt of "Congo blondes" and "Zulu redheads."[45] In his autobiography, the late Malcolm X gave a lively description of the pain he endured to "conk" his hair using lye and other ingredients. Years later upon mature reflection he pronounced the habit "my first really big step toward self-degradation."[46]

The decade of the 1960s was a propitious period for the Afro to achieve popularity. It was a time in America when hirsuteness became a vehicle for making philosophical and political statements. Among blacks the drift away from hair straightening has lost little of its momentum with the onset of the 1970s. Indeed some other innovations have been introduced. Shaving the head and braiding or "corn-rowing" the hair, practices with African precedents, have been seen with increasing frequency. This is not to say that the overwhelming majority of blacks are content not having the "good" hair of whites. Middle-class Negro publications still carry advertisements for hair processing. In 1968 the proprietors of a black-owned beauty salon in downtown New York reported that 70 percent of their customers were black. Nine out of ten ignored the Afro look and had their hair straightened.[47] Not long before his tragic assassination, Martin Luther King commented adversely on this practice in Louisville, but when by the hundreds black women arrived at a fund-raising function with processed hair and blonde wigs, the reverend kept silent about the subject.[48]

Thus Africanness touched large sectors of the black American population, but it did not completely saturate the community. At the same time it is fair to describe the reversal of many black attitudes as sudden and dramatic. For example, in the 1960s certain Afro-Americans began to familiarize themselves with African music and a few actually learned to play indigenous African musical instruments. Some also learned to do African dances, dances which they had ignored for decades. Ismay Andrews was

one of the black artists who pioneered in the teaching of bona
fide African dances in the United States. Years ago when she
was giving dance lessons at the Abyssinian Baptist Church in
Harlem, Miss Andrews was reproached by the black parents
who asked "why I was teaching that African mess, that's what
they called it; *African Mess."* This kind of parochialism faded
markedly in the black revolution.

Among the most curious issues on the ballot in America's
1968 elections was a proposition to change the name of East
Palo Alto, California, to Nairobi, after the capital of Kenya,
located some ten thousand miles away. The community in question had a population which was approximately 70 percent black
at the time. Excluded for all practical purposes from white
neighborhoods, the large body of black migrants to the bay area
had been funneled into East Palo Alto. Backers of the measure,
including many teenagers, fervently believed that the name
change would increase the pride of American blacks in their African past. Donald Ried, the young Afro-American who initiated
the campaign to alter the community's name, argued that many
American communities were named after European cities: "The
lack of place names in America which are of African origin
tends to reinforce the general acceptance of the dangerous belief
that Americans—real Americans—are people of European descent and that people of African descent are not really
Americans at all."[49] The proposition, which received national attention, was defeated by a vote of 3,052 to 1,262.

Despite the defeat, sympathizers as far away as New York
addressed mail to Nairobi, California. Undaunted by their electoral setback the local Black Business Coalition pressed forward
with its pet project, the Nairobi Village Shopping Center which
was being built by the UMOJA Construction Company. Located in the commercial complex are the Nairobi Book Store
and the Nairobi House of Music.[50] In the educational sphere
there are Nairobi day schools and a Nairobi College.

Why do the blacks of East Palo Alto select Nairobi instead of
Lagos or Accra or some other major West African capital city

one may logically ask? The one-time railhead on the Uganda railway, Nairobi (the Masai word meaning "cold"), barely existed before the turn of this century. It was largely a creation of the British who controlled it politically while the East Indians dominated it commercially. The choice of Nairobi by the California blacks may signify just how deep an imprint the bitter struggle for independence in Kenya left on the black American consciousness.

Poignant gestures of pan-African loyalty are sporadically made by black individuals deeply disillusioned with the white world. Even in death they reach out for a black identity. Arch Foster was working in a community development program in North Carolina when at the age of thirty-eight he lost his life in a swimming mishap. Foster's oft-stated wish to be buried beyond the borders of the United States was carried out by his widow. It was decided to have an African-style funeral and to inter his remains in Guyana.[51] African dancing, African drumming, and African folklore were all part of the last rites. Prayers were offered in Yoruba and Swahili. Mrs. Foster, garbed in white and bearing the symbolic African calabash, led the cortege. Her husband's epitaph, soon to be inscribed on a stone marker, read, "We are an African People, Arch Foster."[52]

Ralph Featherstone, a SNCC activist, was killed in March 1970 by an explosion that demolished the automobile in which he was sitting. His funeral service also had an African motif. There were lively African chants and the deceased was dressed in African clothing as were a number of those who attended the ceremony. The body was to be cremated and the ashes sent to Africa.[53]

Marriage signalizes what is probably the major milestone in the individual's journey from womb to tomb. In virtually all human societies it is enveloped in ritual, linking the couple to a particular people and a particular tradition. When Stokely Carmichael, the Trinidadian-born black nationalist, took South African-born Miriam Makeba as his wife, a wedding reception was held in an appropriately pan-African milieu. The bride im-

plored her ancestors to bless the union while the groom's "personal pastor" directed his prayers to long-deceased bondsmen in America and to tribesmen in Africa. The couple were dressed in African raiment. Caribbean and African delicacies were served to the guests. Diplomats from a number of African countries attended the festive event which was held in the New York home of the ambassador from Tanzania. Achmar Marof, the Guinean envoy, saluted the union as "the beginning of stronger ties between black people on both sides of the Atlantic."[54]

Another manifestation of the Afro-American's wide-ranging quest for an identity has been the multiplication of Africa-oriented black nationalist splinter groups and cults. One example is the Yoruba Temple located in New York which practices an ancestor-worshipping West African voodoo religion.[55] Their Friday night religious rites conducted for the most part in fluent Yoruba include offerings to a myriad of deities. Replete with rhythmic, repetitive drumming and sometimes a sacrifice as well, the services are modeled on those historically held in West Africa. One can easily discern the pan-African element in the ritual. In the obeisance paid to noteworty African figures, continental and diasporan, past and contemporary, *Ojubas* (we bow down to you) are chanted to Nat Turner, Harriet Tubman, Jean Jacques Desallines, a hero of the Haitian independence struggle, Marcus Garvey, W.E.B. Du Bois, Patrice Lumumba, and Malcolm X.[56]

Spiritual leader of the Yorubas is Baba (priest) Ofuntola Oseijeman Adefunmi. In 1967 he claimed a following of one hundred and twenty. Originally a resident of Detroit, Baba, before converting to the Yoruba faith, was living in Greenwich Village. He was loath to identify with blacks. The catalyst that eventually led to his transformation into a thoroughgoing black nationalist was Ghana's acquisition of independence.[57] As Ogboni (keeper of ancestral customs) and as priest of the Yoruba Temple of New Oyo (the West African name with which he has rechristened Harlem),[58] Adefunmi has instructed his disciples to immerse themselves in African culture and to adopt

African instead of western life styles. He has called for the Africanization of "our names, our hats, our clothes, our churches, our religions, our schools, home, furnishings, businesses, holidays, games, arts, social functions, our manners and customs, etc., etc., etc."[59] Without Africanization black liberation could never be complete; emulating European mores is unnatural, asinine, and abasing. Many Yorubas have selected African names and wear African vestments. Yoruba wedding ceremonies in Chicago as well as New York have been patterned after centuries-old Nigerian nuptials.[60]

Adefunmi has involved himself and his organization in the always volatile New York City school system. He has loudly championed the inclusion of African history in the public school curricula: "Black children should be taught the histories of the glories of the African nations of Ashanti, Dahomey and Yoruba . . . just as all children are taught European history. We have black counterparts to Charlemagne and Queen Mary."[61] In May 1966 the Yorubas led a march through Harlem to protest the discharge of a black nationalist from his teaching post.

Members of the Yoruba Temple have been conspicuous at the annual commemorative services honoring Malcolm X. At a graveside program the year after the assassination, Adefunmi beseeched the spirit of Malcolm and other deceased blacks to aid the people of Harlem in solving their problems. [62] Wearing billowing robes and intoning Yoruba phrases, members of the Yoruba Temple were present in February 1967. On that occasion Adefunmi said that Malcolm was preeminent among American blacks because of his commitment to "complete freedom and self-determination."[63]

Quintessentially cultural nationalists, the Yoruba leadership is also political-minded. Adefunmi is a believer in Africanizing politics along with just about everything else. Therefore early in Yoruba Temple history, he brought into being the Alajo party. Its twin purposes were to train black leaders and to petition the United States government to indemnify black people. Almost

nothing has been heard of the party since its formation more than a decade ago.

In 1965 in the riot-torn Watts district of Los Angeles, a black nationalist organization with the unlikely name of "Us" was born. Ron Karenga, its founder, has a mandarin-type mustache and has his head shaved clean. He holds a master's degree in political science from UCLA. A student of African languages himself, the redoubtable Karenga has encouraged the study of Swahili among his followers and others in Watts. One of the principal objectives of Us is to enable black people to evolve their own customs, different from those of the dominating white man. To this end Karenga, who sports a buba, a short toga, has his supporters wear special clothing. For this reason, also, the members of Us practice a self-created African religion and adopt African names. Karenga's disciples also observe Negro holidays. One, Dhabihu, meaning "a sacrifice" in Swahili, commemorates the death of Malcolm X whom Karenga quotes frequently.[64] Karenga tells his enthusiastic, often youthful audiences that they are Afro-Americans and not Europeans. "Have you ever seen a Chinese named Jones or a Japanese named Whitfield?" he asks to the delight of his listeners.[65]

Karenga is given credit for inspiring a fellow cultural nationalist, writer LeRoi Jones, to create BCD (Black Community Development and Defense), a black cultural organization. The time was early 1968, the place Newark. BCD recognized "Africa as the Motherhood and its people as our people." Culture, in this case black culture, is seen as the force that motivates liberation and unity. At the Duka Kitabu ("bookstore" in Swahili) which BCD operates in East Orange, New Jersey, African statues and African attire are sold along with black literature. Most members of the organization are youthful. The males, called *Simbas,* are drilled in martial arts. Members don African habiliment, speak Swahili whenever possible, observe traditional African customs, and forsake their European names for Arabic and African ones.[66] Jones prefers to be addressed and referred to as Imamu Baraka.

Africa is at the core of the program which the playwright de-
vised for the African Free School, a federally supported educational experiment in Newark. Pictures of Julius Nyerere of
Tanzania and of Baraka himself and sketches of African villages
adorn classroom walls. Pupils are familiarized with African
geography and African history. Using fabric imported from the
mother continent, pupils learn to make African clothes. They
are taught how to string African bead necklaces. There is also
instruction in elementary Swahili. In the catechistic teaching
technique employed at the school, words such as *tafadhali*
(please) and *asante* (thank you) are often heard.[67]

Given the rapid growth of interest in African clothing, acces-
sories, hair styles, customs, religions, and languages, it is only
logical that more and more Afro-Americans yearn to see the
continent firsthand. Some are searching for their roots. Others
are merely curious. Seldom do they intend to stay in Africa.
Few actually do remain. Nevertheless the fact is that travel
agents reported a boom in overseas travel by black Americans
in the late 1960s. Despite airline fares which are often
prohibitive, the West Indies and Africa have been the destinations of an ever increasing number of Afro-American travelers.
One travel agency in Atlanta specializing in African tourism offers "Ebony Tours" open only to blacks. Treading the soil of
independent black states in the Caribbean and in the "mother
country" can be a psychologically rewarding experience. It has
been described as spiritually liberating and has been compared
with the exhilaration most American Jews feel when they first
set foot in the state of Israel. A visit to Gorée, the tiny island
across from Dakar, capital of Senegal, and similar points of departure to the New World for innumerable slaves centuries earlier, provides a more sobering experience.[68] According to a hotel
official in the Ivory Coast, the number of black Americans
vacationing in his nation has been steadily rising. Vacationers
in their twenties and thirties predominate. Usually they travel
in groups, one of which puzzled the Ivorians with the "Black
and Proud" motto on their shirts.[69]

Black American students have also been gravitating to Africa. Not infrequently they are sent under the auspices of a Negro college sometimes as part of a student exchange. For example, Fisk University in Nashville sent eleven students to the University of Abidjan in the fall of 1970. Private contributions made possible an earlier trip by twenty-five New York ghetto youths (seventeen to twenty-four years of age). One returning youngster felt that he had been duped prior to his journey by those who led him to believe that Africans would wear naturals and would all be clad in dashikis. Blackness, however, should still be emphasized, he felt, despite what had seemed to be a deception. Another member of the party came back much more of a pan-Africanist: "Now I see myself not only as a black American but as one of the millions of black people throughout the world."[70] Twenty girls from a black community in the Chicago area were sent on a "cultural safari" to Liberia in 1969. It proved enlightening and unforgettable. A sixteen-year-old was stunned by the irony of the fact that "we wear African clothes to look like them . . . they wear miniskirts to look like us."[71]

There is then a stream of black Americans to sub-Sahara Africa—tourists, students, Peace Corps volunteers, A.I.D. and other government personnel, and black entertainers. However, the percentage of Afro-Americans who wend their way back to Africa in one capacity or another is minute. Ted Joans, a poet and musician who now lives in Africa, has chided all of his black American brothers and sisters for not making a pilgrimage to Africa. He is particularly hard on "Afro-hip chicks and cats, who are not getting their funds together for the trip"; "lazy-Black-niggers," Joans has branded them. "I pour a big libation to the ancestors who will haunt them into coming to Africa for a trip." He suggests that they replace the lyric "I'm Black and I'm proud" with "I'm *back* and I'm proud!"[72]

Contemporaneous with the black American-African rapprochement of the 1960s was the emergence of a black power movement. Actually the one could hardly be isolated from the other. Black pride was a pivotal element in both. Anxious about

the political reverberations of black power, the white press has sometimes been rather callous, shortsighted, and unfair in judging the African cultural renaissance in this country. A minor incident is illustrative.

Harlem is unquestionably the heart of black America, and 125th Street and Seventh Avenue is indisputably the heart of Harlem. Cognizant of this fact, street-corner orators have historically established their pulpits at the crowded intersection. Rallies have customarily been held there. At a 1967 gathering commemorating the life and death of Marcus Garvey, a proclamation signed by the then borough president of Manhattan, Percy E. Sutton, was read redesignating the intersection "African Square" for the day. This seemingly inoffensive gesture incurred for the articulate Mr. Sutton the wrath of *The New York Times*. In a sharply critical editorial, "Black Power Square," the *Times* lashed out at Sutton (a black man himself but certainly no nationalist), accusing him of kowtowing to black nationalists and of trying to clamber aboard the black nationalist bandwagon. The editorial was wholly insensitive. Sutton was acknowledging Harlem's rediscovered pride in Africa. His action may have been politically expedient but in and of itself it was quite harmless. Streets, avenues, and squares in New York City have been temporarily renamed on countless occasions. The *Times* editorial noted that at the outdoor rally Charles Kenyatta had prophesied bloodshed that would make Detroit, where there had already been extensive ghetto violence, "look like a teapot."[73] This may have been the true source of the *Times'* anger and the real reason for the brickbat aimed at Sutton.

Politics and culture were deeply enmeshed at the Pan-African Cultural Festival held in Algiers in the summer of 1969. Black Americans were well represented there. The festival also drew delegates from well over a score of independent states. There were spokesmen for liberation movements too. Dressed in African attire, the Afro-Americans were not easily distinguished from continental Africans. Although there was nothing novel about blacks from the United States attending pan-African

conclaves abroad, the North African meeting was different in a sense. George Shepherd, an American scholar, has written that Algiers "may well signal a new phase in African-American relations." Generally speaking, participants from the United States were not the internationally known black intellectuals who had been conspicuous at previous festivals and conferences. Rather they were revolutionaries eager to use the 1969 festival for political purposes. For them the African art, dance, and theater were of secondary importance. Throughout the proceedings Eldridge Cleaver and the Black Panthers enjoyed the limelight and were, in effect, recognized as the principal representatives of Afro-America, according to George Shepherd. The Algerian government and, to some degree, the Organization of African Unity were "clearly establishing a direct political link between Africa and the American continent." For the Africans the festival was not simply a cultural fete as the secretary-general of the OAU indicated when he said of the meeting that it had "raised the curtain on the greatest event that Africans ever conceived, worked out and offered to the world in the framework of its revolutionary fight against foreign domination and its various effects."[74]

Unable to advance rapidly enough toward their goal of full equality in the United States, black nationalists have widened their angle of political vision to embrace the developing, non-white areas of the globe. Although blacks are a distinct minority here, "colored" peoples are a sizeable majority on the planet. By forging bonds with the Third World, with Africa in particular, Afro-Americans hope to acquire some political muscle on the international scene in order to ameliorate their domestic situation. Such hopes underlie the expansion of pan-Africanism in black America. This is evident in the speeches and writings of several black spokesmen.

Owing in large measure to firsthand experiences in Africa, Malcolm X evolved in his last years into an articulate exponent of pan-Africanism or "global black thinking," as he put it. Malcolm was convinced that black organizations and their leaders

had made their most grievous error in neglecting to "establish direct brotherhood lines of communication between the independent nations of Africa and the American black people."[75] While visiting West Africa he elaborated on this thesis in a talk at Ibadan University.

> I said that just as the American Jew is in political, economic, and cultural harmony with world Jewry, I was convinced that it was time for all Afro-Americans to join the world's Pan-Africanists. I said that physically we Afro-Americans might remain in America, fighting for our Constitutional rights, but that philosophically and culturally we Afro-Americans badly needed to "return" to Africa—and to develop a working unity in the framework of Pan-Africanism.[76]

He was all but canonized by African students. Nigerian Muslim students registered him in their society as an honorary member. When they also bestowed upon him the Yoruba name "Omowale," "the son who has come home," Malcolm was profoundly moved. "I had never received a more treasured honor," he wrote in his autobiography.[77] Malcolm was ecstatic after seeing Nigerians opening their own communications agencies. In Ghana the local press gave Malcolm red-carpet treatment. He was unexpectedly given the chance to address the parliament of Ghana. He also spoke at the University of Ghana, Legon, and at the Kwame Nkrumah Ideological Institute. Everywhere he attempted to give a truthful assessment of the plight of Afro-Americans. Colonialism, be it political, economic, cultural, or psychological, was his favorite whipping boy. Whether the colonial struggle was waged in Africa or America made no difference. This pan-African theme formed an integral part of his conversation with Osagyefo Kwame Nkrumah: "We discussed the unity of Africans and peoples of African descent. We agreed that Pan-Africanism was the key also to the problems of those of African heritage."[78]

In July of 1964 Malcolm attended the Organization of African Unity Conference held in Cairo. Describing the black people of the United States as "your long-lost brothers and sisters," he entreated the independent African states to assist him in bring-

ing the problem of the Afro-American before the United Nations. "Your problems will never be fully solved until and unless ours are solved. You will never be fully respected until and unless we are also respected . . . Our problem is your problem."[79]

For Stokely Carmichael pan-Africanism is the highest expression of black power which he defines as the organization of black people with liberation as their major objective. "Pan-Africanism," he wrote in his last book, "is grounded in the belief that all African people wherever we may be are one . . . ."[80] Blacks in the United States, he insists, are Africans, not Afro-Americans, not black Americans, not Americans at all. Pan-Africanism is global in scope, not tribalistic, not restricted geographically or linguistically. Stokely agreed with Kwame Nkrumah that there is a single African nation despite the wide dispersal of African peoples. Wherever they are in the world, blacks share a common oppressor. Wherever they reside, they are confronted by the same problems: racism, imperialism, and landlessness. In a message which Stokely sent from Guinea for delivery at Malcolm X University in October 1969, he asserted that blacks in the United States "will never be a strong, proud, free people unless we liberate Africa and take from America what America is trying to protect."[81] Blacks need a land base. Therefore priority should be given to the freeing of Africa, "the richest and most beautiful continent in the world," but a continent which is grievously suffering because of exploitation.[82] In sum, the central thesis of Stokely's ideology, an ideology deeply rooted in the teachings of Du Bois, Garvey, and Malcolm X, is that a common bond exists among Africans in the United States and between them and their brothers in the beloved motherland. Racism in the United States cannot be dealt with effectively until blacks here develop this sense of community.

LeRoi Jones has written in the same vein. Pan-Africanism does not mean repatriation to Africa—"black people, ca. 1970 ain't going anywhere." Africa is still very much in the picture but it is not to be the locus of a mass relocation. Instead Africa should become "a unified power base to demand respect for

black people the world over—this is Pan-Africanism, because wherever we are we have a commonalty based on our common struggle."[83]

On April 26, 1969, James Forman presented a black manifesto to the National Black Economic Conference in Detroit.[84] After declaring "We are an African people" living in the "most barbaric country in the world," Forman proceeded to offer his solutions to the economic dilemmas of black people. His program contained a strong dose of pan-Africanism. Among the projects Forman proposed was a United Black Appeal which would be charged with the responsibility of developing cooperative businesses in the United States and in "Africa, our Motherland." The United Black Appeal would be expected to create a Black Anti-Defamation League to guard the African image of blacks. It would also be incumbent upon the United Black Appeal to support liberation movements in Africa. Forman adumbrated the scope of the black American commitment as follows: "We are so proud of our African heritage and realize concretely that our struggle is not only to make revolution in the United States but to protect our brothers and sisters in Africa and to help them rid themselves of racism, capitalism, and imperialism by whatever means necessary, including armed struggle."[85] Funding for these and other undertakings[86] was to come from five hundred million dollars in reparations to be paid to black people in the United States by the white churches and synagogues. On May 4, 1969, carrying an African walking stick, Forman interrupted religious worship at the Riverside Church in New York City to dramatically publicize his call for reparations.

Pan-Africanist spirit pervaded the air at Howard University in May 1970 when approximately two thousand persons attended the second annual conference of the African Heritage Studies Association. Most were faculty and students from the United States and from Africa. The theme of the parley was "Africanism—Toward a New Definition"; the ambitious objective was the unity of black people.[87]

Atlanta was the site of the international Congress of African Peoples in September of 1970. It drew twenty-five hundred delegates. Perhaps 90 percent were American blacks. They reflected almost the whole political spectrum of black organizations but nationalists predominated. African students were present. So were five spokesmen for the Australian aborigines and a member of the parliament of Bermuda. Highly visible African clothing contributed to the pan-African tone of the meeting. Haywood Henry, a lecturer in black studies at M.I.T. and Harvard, who served as chairman, succinctly summed up the primary purpose of the Atlanta conference: "to unite black people, not only in America, but in Africa, and the Caribbean, in Australia, Mexico, South America and all over the planet earth." To this end, at a workshop on political liberation, LeRoi Jones, who played a central role in the proceedings, proposed the formation of a World African Party.[88] A year later at the Eastern Regional Conference of African Peoples which convened in Newark, a resolution was passed calling for the creation of such a party. Counted among the thousand delegates to this regional gathering were a member of the Tanzanian mission to the United Nations and a representative of Frelimo, the Mozambique liberation movement. Two of the resolutions adopted by the convention called respectively for the establishment of an "African skills bank" to assist independent African countries and the creation of a teacher training center to teach educators how to exemplify the "African personality."[89]

Throughout the ranks of the delegates there was considerable distress over an article which had been published by *The New York Times* on September 5. Easily inferable from the piece authored by William Borders, a correspondent for the *Times*, was the idea that Afro-American feelings of solidarity and kinship with Africans were not reciprocated, that the two black peoples were estranged. Haywood Henry rated the article "unbalanced and biased." From LeRoi Jones' point of view it was "white boy stupidity." The *Times* was contemptuously dismissed as a "racist tool of degradation" of all black people by the conference.

A public apology was demanded and black people were admonished to boycott the newspaper.[90]

At the end of 1970 Portugal's surprise attack on Guinea served to fan the flames of pan-Africanism. In December, the month following the abortive raid, the Federation of Nationalist Organizations was quickly given life. Members of this coalition were both African and Afro-American organizations and included: South-West Africa Peoples Organization, Mozambique Liberation Movement, Nigerian Students Union, Cecil Brath's African Jazz Art Society Studios, African-American Teachers Association, and other African-minded black activist groups.[91]

The 1967 program of CORE underscored its desire to cement ties with Africa. At its annual convention held in July 1967 in Oakland, California, CORE resolved to develop a program for "one-to-one contact between our black brothers at home and in the mother country."[92] They proposed to give the program a Swahili name, "Umojo Makono [sic]" which CORE has freely translated "Hands together in Brotherhood and Unity." Among the initial measures which were projected were a pen-friend plan and African history study groups. With the same end in mind, Floyd McKissick was exploring the feasibility of charter flights to Africa. "You have excursion fares to Europe but not to Africa. If that isn't racism!"[93]

In January 1969 Wilfred T. Ussery, a CORE official, announced that his organization was mapping a campaign to mobilize black American support for guerrilla movements in sub-Saharan Africa. Arrangements were being made for leaders of African revolutionary causes to visit black communities where they would personally appeal for financial aid, for medical supplies, for weapons, even for volunteers. Ussery called the Africa liberation movement, the "epitome of black power."[94]

During the 1960s CORE itself had become more closely identified with the black power philosophy in the United States. Finally in September 1970, Roy Innis, a Virgin Islander by birth, who had succeeded Floyd McKissick as national director, proclaimed officially that CORE was abandoning integration and

was instead espousing black separatism in its unswerving quest for racial equality.[95] Without self-determination, racial equality would be permanently elusive.

Accompanied by CORE aides, Innis undertook a month-long journey to sundry east and west African states during the summer of 1972. In Kenya they were the guests of President Kenyatta at a state reception. They in turn honored *Mzee* [96] by presenting him with a CORE lifetime membership plaque which bore these pan-Africanist words of tribute: "In recognition of your leadership in the nationalist struggle of African people in Africa and the Western Hemisphere."[97] A CORE chapter is to be formed in Kenya.

Fresh from his peregrinations, Innis said that blacks, though widely scattered, were a single family. Afro-Americans, being better off financially and more technologically advanced, had a responsibility to their family members who were in Africa. Innis pledged that CORE would soon set up a United African Appeal and he called upon blacks in the United States to invest in sub-Saharan Africa, to build commercial bridges to Africa, and to organize themselves so that they might effectively influence the government in Washington to look more favorably upon African countries. The CORE director also revived the concept of dual citizenship for American blacks.[98]

That angry black militants in the United States should identify with independent Africa is not surprising. As Dan Watts has correctly noted, "In the past . . . with a few exceptions, identification with Africa has been a substitute for identification with America."[99] Historically, when conditions for Negroes worsened, consciousness of Africa was heightened. Today what is noteworthy, if not completely surprising, is the solicitude about Africa expressed by Negroes fully committed to integration into the American social fabric.

This solicitude has been manifest in the American Negro Leadership Conference on Africa (ANLC). First organized in 1962, this body comprises virtually the entire range of black opinion in the United States from the Urban League to SNCC.

At its initial biennial meeting, the ANLC rejoiced over the success of the African peoples who had recently won their independence. More importantly, the conference addressed itself to the unfree regions of Africa and proclaimed that the American Negro community had a special responsibility to press the United States government to formulate a dynamic African policy. Calling for energetic action to assist Africans to win their freedom, the ANLC observed that the civil rights struggle at home could not be separated from the color problem abroad. Reaffirming its "ethnic bond with and historic concern for the peoples of Africa," the conference passed resolutions condemning apartheid, criticizing the South African position on South West Africa, supporting the African nationalists in Mozambique and Angola, opposing the continuation of the Central African Federation as it was then structured, and calling for the unification of the Congo including Katanga as an integral part. In addition, there was a resolution urging greater participation by American Negroes in American programs, both governmental and private, in Africa.[100]

Two years later at its second conference the organization passed another series of resolutions regarding the freedom struggle in southern Africa. The delegates also urged more direct involvement by American Negro universities in Africa. Specifically, the universities were asked to institute courses in African studies, especially in those languages which would facilitate communications with Africans. Exchange programs for the faculties of African universities and their American Negro counterparts were also recommended.[101]

A third conference held in January 1967 asked predominantly Negro universities and colleges to enroll more African students. At the same time it decided to provide African nations with a roster of colored Americans willing and able to contribute their skills to Africa.[102] To be sure, the ANLC has done more than pass resolutions. During 1967 its executive director, Theodore E. Brown, paid two visits to Africa, primarily to employ his good offices to end the civil war in Nigeria. Regrettably, his

efforts were to no avail and the internecine bloodletting continued unabated.

Following in the footsteps of its most illustrious founder, Dr. Du Bois, the NAACP has consistently refused to turn a blind eye to the racial injustices perpetrated against Africans. When the white settler regime in Rhodesia unilaterally declared independence of Britain in November 1965, the executive committee of the NAACP's board of directors adopted a resolution stating that the time was right for the United States to impose any sanctions except intervention by American troops. At the same time it was stated that there was precedent for assisting countries that did take military action against Salisbury. Furthermore the committee explicitly urged an embargo on all commerce with Ian Smith's rebel government.[103]

Tenacity on the part of the NAACP regarding the Rhodesian crisis *may* have paid a few small dividends in 1970. A telegram to Secretary of State William Rogers in March from John Morsell, the assistant executive director, remarked on the "all-too-visible" weaknesses of the Administration in regard to the rights of Negro Americans and asked the government to show good faith by ending its diplomatic support for Rhodesia, specifically by withdrawing its consulate from the Rhodesian capital. Four days later the United States government announced that the consulate in Salisbury would close shortly. Of course the exact role of the NAACP in bringing about this action is a purely conjectural matter.[104] Concern for Zimbabwe[105] by the leaders of the NAACP is not at all conjectural.

Quite logically, the largest and oldest civil rights organization has also taken a highly jaundiced view of South Africa's racial policies, intervening whenever possible on behalf of the nonwhite population. For example, it pleaded for the release from custody of Robert Sobukwe, head of the banned Pan-African Congress, who had been convicted of incitement and had been given a three-year sentence. Although Sobukwe had finished serving his prison term in 1963, he was detained indefinitely without charge or trial by the minister of justice under the General Law Amend-

ment Act passed the same year with Sobukwe in mind. At its 1971 convention the NAACP passed a resolution "vigorously" protesting the sugar quota allocated to South Africa. Under the Sugar Quota Act certain designated nations are apportioned shares of the American market to which they sell their sugar crops at prices significantly above world-market levels.

Dr. Martin Luther King conceived of the black American as a hybrid, the offspring of two cultures—Africa and the United States. An indefatigable worker for human rights, Dr. King was best known for his ceaseless efforts to win racial justice for blacks in the land of his and their birth. Nevertheless he understood that racism was not a phenomenon peculiar to this nation. In *Afrikanerdom* racism was endemic. Dr. King was not satisfied with upbraiding the white supremacist government in Pretoria. He scolded the United States and Great Britain, self-described western democracies, for pursuing economic policies beneficial to South Africa. He took Britain to task for its woefully inadequate response to the Rhodesian rebellion. Portugal was indicted by the reverend for fostering "slave labor" in Angola.[106]

As revealed in a little publicized interview with C. Z. Sulzberger of *The New York Times* back in December 1964, the president of the Southern Christian Leadership Conference (SCLC) commented in true pan-African fashion that "until African problems are solved, our problems will not be solved." In the past, the Nobel Prize winner explained, black Americans had not contributed sufficiently to African development. This was due to two factors: their shame about their African descent and the absorption of their energies by the struggle in the United States. Dr. King put forward concrete proposals to mobilize black support for Africa. He wanted black churches and other black community institutions to invest in Africa. He wanted blacks to press Washington to sponsor a "Marshall Plan for Africa," and he recommended that blacks make their skills available to Africa by joining the Peace Corps.[107]

Reverend Jesse Jackson, a disciple of Dr. King's who until

his resignation in December 1971 was director of Operation Breadbasket, the economic arm of SCLC, has also voiced pan-African sentiments. Jackson attended the 1970 Atlanta conference. Afterwards with characteristic bluntness he defined pan-Africanism as an "antidote to white genocide. An attempt to organize all of the people of Africa and of African descent to protect themselves against genocide."[108]

The desirability of Africans and Afro-Americans making common cause has also been starkly expressed by John Oliver Killens. He has observed that nonwhites throughout the world and blacks in the United States have shared a common experience of subjugation by whites. They have all been "niggerized." "And all of us are determined to 'deniggerize' the earth."[109] From all indications, the determination is not spurious. It is very real.

In this climate of black opinion, the White House's snub of President Kenneth Kaunda in the fall of 1970 understandably irritated many black Americans. The diplomatic blunder in question reminded them of the low priority that is given both Africa and Afro-America by *their* government. Mr. Kaunda was in the United States to speak to the General Assembly and reportedly was eager to confer with President Nixon. No mutually convenient appointment could be arranged. President Nixon was only able to see the Zambian at the hour when the latter was scheduled to address the United Nations. The American chief executive was then devoting much of his time to campaigning for Republican candidates in the upcoming elections. Black Americans were perturbed and insulted by what was indubitably an act of discourtesy to one of the African continent's most respected statesmen. They had good reason to feel upset. Is it conceivable that Mr. Nixon would have behaved with comparable tactlessness and insensitivity had the foreign dignitary been the chief of state or head of government of Israel, Ireland, or Italy, three nations with strong ethnic bonds to segments of the American populace? Quite possibly the White House failed to appreciate black America's expanding empathy for Africa—not

that the government has ever evinced a genuine desire to satisfy the legitimate needs and aspirations of African-derived Americans.

An ad hoc committee of Afro-Americans Concerned About U.S. Policy in Africa, with Dr. Elliott Skinner, former ambassador to Upper Volta serving as coordinator,[110] expressed its displeasure with America's shortsighted attitude toward Africa, an attitude symbolized by the Kaunda incident. The committee, consisting mostly of black scholars, did so in an open letter to the President of the United States.[111] Eight explicit requests were registered.

1) develop a meaningful aid policy for Africa.

2) accord due respect to all African officials visiting the United States.

3) disassociate the United States economically and politically from South Africa as long as that country pursues a policy of Apartheid—a policy which threatens both international peace and security and American domestic tranquility.

4) urge the United Kingdom not to resume arms sales to Africa, and not to compromise with the minority regime in Zimbabwe.

5) withdraw landing rights granted by the United States to South African Airways in violation of the United Nations General Assembly resolution.

6) discontinue military aid to Portugal under the Azores and NATO treaties and thereby make it impossible for her to wage repressive war against nationalist movements in Africa.

7) discourage the publically acknowledged American private investment in Portugal's slave empire.

8) honor your pledge in the "State of the World" message to help Africans (in this case Guinea) to help themselves when they are threatened by outside forces attempting to subvert their independent development.

This pan-African trend has continued apace. In February 1972 twenty-seven Afro-Americans, mostly scholars, many with long ties to Africa, met in Puerto Rico to explore ways and means by which they could influence American foreign policy to the advantage of black Africa. Delegates to the National Black Political Convention held in Gary, Indiana, the following month called for the United States to end its complicity with European repression in Africa.

Talk has been supplemented by direct action. In March 1972 Afro-American students placed five hundred black crosses in Harvard Yard to dramatize their opposition to Portuguese misrule in Angola, Mozambique, and Guinea-Bissau. The protesters alleged that Harvard University owned shares in the single largest American firm in Portuguese Africa, the Gulf Oil Company. When the United States lifted its ban on the importation of Rhodesian chrome in defiance of the United Nations embargo, hundreds of Afro-American students from Southern University, a black school in Baton Rouge, set up picket lines at a Louisiana port. Their laudable efforts to obstruct the unloading of shipments of Rhodesian chrome while ineffectual were evidence of burgeoning pan-Africanism.

Black elected officials have also refused to remain silent about United States-African relations. Congressman Charles C. Diggs of Michigan is just one member of the so-called congressional black caucus who has been vocal about his conviction that United States policy in Africa is sadly remiss. Diggs is chairman of the House Foreign Affairs Sub-committee on Africa. He has deplored the absence of executive direction and has lamented the less than encouraging record of Congress in coming to terms with our responsibilities to black Africans. He has talked of a "glaring racial credibility gap" in foreign policy where Africa is concerned. In a speech which he delivered in Chicago in June 1970,[112] Diggs faulted the government for its sympathetic policy towards the Republic of South Africa. *Inter alia* Diggs was upset by the sugar import quota worth $5 million annually in subsidies which has been granted to South Africa in the face of its

despicable racial discrimination. A second complaint of the Congressman's was directed at "the absence of black America from our foreign policy" involving Africa. Inasmuch as "black freedom is indivisible," Diggs called for Afro-Americans to join the battle for freedom in Africa's white redoubt. That battle, he said, was "an important part of the struggle for cultural, social and political liberation" in the United States. Victory here at home might only come when Afro-America had effectively aided and abetted African nationalist movements. Diggs specifically asked for medical and educational assistance for these movements. Pan-Africanism, the interlocking of African and black American aspirations, was evident not only in the ideas advanced by the Congressman but also by his choice of language. Talking about the need to improve U.S. foreign policy in Africa, he said: "we must help end landlordism in the international ghetto because ownership in the economies of the third world must revert to those societies."

When black members of the House of Representatives led by Congressman Diggs presented President Nixon with an enumeration of more than sixty recommendations germane to minority group problems, Africa was not forgotten.[113] Listed among the major ones was a recommendation that United States-South African relations be overhauled with a view to isolating the land of apartheid. Another asked that parity with other regions of the world be accorded Africa insofar as economic aid was concerned.[114]

On a subsequent junket to southern Africa, Diggs visited Bantu areas including Soweto where he was simultaneously serenaded and eulogized by hundreds of schoolchildren: "The black man who is lion hearted is here today. Perhaps he will help us with our difficulties." Touched by his greeting in Soweto, Diggs claimed that it "demonstrated the commonality of interests between us." In light of the "appalling amount of racial injustice" found in South Africa, Diggs was not content with denouncing the apartheid system. He conferred with officials of American corporations which operate in South Africa (Detroit-

based auto makers as it happened), hoping to mitigate the conditions of black workers. Diggs intends to continue his efforts in this direction.[115]

Corporate involvement in South Africa is a potent force militating against the adoption of a hard anti-apartheid line by this government. Investment in South Africa exceeds the combined American investment in the rest of the continent. More than 375 U.S. firms, including industrial giants, have an economic stake in South Africa.[116] This financial consideration plus the conception of South Africa as a bastion of anti-communism has more than neutralized the influence exerted by Afro-Americans rankled by the dehumanizing treatment meted out to the non-European population.[117] Relentless, carefully coordinated activities to change this deplorable status quo is imperative, but the task is herculean.

Black Americans, private individuals and public officials alike, who in manifold ways are lending a helping hand to Africa, are part of a time-honored tradition. Historically, ethnic, racial, and religious communities in the United States have lobbied on behalf of their kinsmen in the "old country." Irish-American support for the cause of home rule was of inestimable value to the Irish nationalists early in this century. Without the financial and diplomatic backing of American Jewry the state of Israel might never have become a reality and its military posture would be incalculably more precarious today.

The potential of twenty-two million plus[118] American blacks as a pressure group for their own welfare and for Africa's interests is enormous. To date their chronically depressed economic status, their fragmented leadership and general disunity, and their political powerlessness have prevented exploitation of that potential.

But a transition is in progress. As vacuums are left by whites fleeing to the suburbs, black political strength is being concentrated in urban areas. Afro-Americans, voiceless for so long, now possess articulate black political voices which are being heard. At the same time political pan-Africanism has not only

taken root, it has begun to germinate. Seemingly the color problem has been globalized although there is no worldwide black congress and none is in the offing. Postwar pan-Africanism, in no small measure, is the offspring of emergent independent Africa. It was also fathered by the despair experienced by black Americans whose hopes of achieving dignity and full equality have been cruelly dashed again and again. Like Sisyphus, the king of Corinth in Greek mythology, who was punished in Hades by having to push a boulder up a hill only to have it roll back down time after time, the Afro-American has been repeatedly disappointed in his ascent to freedom. In the African he recognizes a fellow Sisyphus. Pushing together they might just reach the hilltop, perhaps even the mountaintop of which Martin Luther King spoke so eloquently.

NOTES

1. Paul Robeson, "African Culture," *Apropos of Africa-Sentiments of Negro American Leaders on Africa from the 1800's to the 1950's,* ed. Adelaide Cromwell Hill and Martin Kilson (London: Frank Cass and Co., Ltd., 1969), p. 135.

2. *Journal of Negro History,* 22 (1937): 367.

3. *The New York Times,* February 12, 1971.

4. Stokely Carmichael, *Stokely Speaks—Black Power Back to Pan-Africanism* (New York: Vintage Books, 1971), p. 147.

5. George Breitman, ed., *Malcolm X Speaks—Selected Speeches and Statements* (New York: Grove Press, Inc., 1966), p. 169.

6. George Breitman, ed., *By any Means Necessary—Speeches, Interviews and a Letter by Malcolm X* (New York: Pathfinder Press, Inc., 1970), pp. 104-105.

7. E. U. Essien-Udom, *Black Nationalism: A Search for an Identity in America* (New York: Dell Publishing Co., 1964), pp. 217-218.

8. Era Bell Thompson, *Africa, Land of My Fathers* (Garden City, New York: Doubleday and Company, Inc., 1954), p. 16.

9. According to official figures between 1952 and 1960 sixty-eight Europeans, thirty-eight of whom were security force personnel were killed. The Mau Mau killed numbered 7,811. In addition, there were 470 African security force fatalities and 1,316 African civilian casualties.

10. *Chicago Defender,* December 1, 1956.

11. Quoted in *Freedomways,* 11, no. 1 (First Quarter 1971): 120. This was a special issue dedicated to Paul Robeson.

12. Stokely Carmichael, *Power and Racism: What We Want* (Boston: New England Free Press, 1966), p.3.

13. George Breitman, ed., *Malcolm X Speaks*, pp. 105-107. Kenyatta's policies since independence have displeased many radical Afro-Americans. Eldridge Cleaver has said that it is the "Kenyatta, in the era of the Mau Mau period" who was one of his heroes.

14. *The New York Times*, June 9, 1969.

15. *Pittsburgh Courier*, February 25, 1961.

16. James Baldwin, "East River, Downtown: Postscript to a Letter from Harlem," *Nobody Knows My Name* (New York: Dell Publishing Co. 1963), p. 67.

17. *Pittsburgh Courier*, February 25, 1961. James Forman signed a recently published letter "In brotherhood Remember Lumumba." As a tribute to the slain Congolese premier, Forman named his son James Lumumba.

18. Since the time of Du Bois the position of the NAACP has been that such semantic alterations do not ameliorate the lot of black people in America. Back in 1917 Du Bois received a letter from a teenager who bemoaned the fact that the *Crisis* commonly used the word "Negro" to denote blacks in the United States. To this Du Bois replied, "If a thing is despised, you will not alter matters by changing its name. If men despise Negroes, they will not despise them less if Negroes are called 'colored' or 'Afro-Americans.'"

19. *The New York Times*, November 20, 1967. Also see Ernest Dunbar, "The Black Revolt Hits the White Campus," *Look*, October 31, 1967.

20. "Selections From Robeson's Writings and Speeches," *Freedomways*, 11, no. 1 (First Quarter) 1971: 106. This statement was originally contained in an article in the *London Spectator*, June 15, 1934.

21. "Shindana: Black Toymakers of Watts," *Sepia*, February 1971, pp. 40-43; *The New York Times*, February 20, 1971.

22. CORE Resolution, July 1967.

23. *Amsterdam News*, August 26, 1967.

24. Alex Poinsett, "Inawapasa Watu Weusi Kusema Kiswahili," *Ebony*, December 1968; Letter to editor of *The New York Times*, January 25, 1968.

25. Poinsett, "Inawapasa," p. 164.

26. Adhama Oluwa Kijemba, "Swahili and Black Americans," *Negro Digest*, July 1969, p. 8.

27. Poinsett, "Inawapasa," p. 163.

28. *The New York Times*, November 17, 1967.

29. *Amsterdam News*, December 23, 1967.

30. Letter to editor of *The New York Times*, January 15, 1968. The author of the letter was Roy Innis, then associate national director of CORE. He later became national director.

31. Beverly Coleman, "Relevancy In Teaching and Learning Swahili," *Black World*, October 1970, p. 14.

32. *The Black Panther*, May 31, 1969. Paradoxical perhaps is the fact that Hewitt and many other Panthers have assumed African names of one type or another.

33. Lee Lockwood, *Conversation With Eldridge Cleaver-Algiers* (New York: Delta Book, 1970), p. 113. So intense has been the rivalry between the Panthers and cultural nationalists that blood was shed in 1969. Two black students at UCLA, members of the Panthers, were shot to death in a classroom building. The Panthers accused Karenga's organization of responsibility for the slayings. Karenga charged that the Panthers had become captives of white radicals but he denied the accusation.

34. *The Black Panther*, February 2, 1969. Quoted in Philip S. Foner, ed., *The Black Panthers Speak* (Philadelphia/New York: J. B. Lippincott Co., 1970), p. 151.

35. *The New York Times*, March 26, 1969. Wilkins has selectively supported certain facets of the African renaissance. He has recognized the usefulness of valid African and Afro-American studies taught by qualified faculty while simultaneously opposing "black academic separatism." See Roy Wilkins, "The Case Against Separatism: 'Black Jim Crow,'" *Newsweek*, February 10, 1969.

36. *Essence*, July 1970, pp. 14-19.

37. *The New York Times*, December 19, 1970.

38. Ibid., June 30, 1970.

39. Ibid., January 31, 1971.

40. At the same time it discouraged skin-lightening creams, hair-straighteners, and lipstick. Puritanism and a fear of western cultural forms probably explain what appears to be a paradoxical act.

41. At a 1970 luncheon in the Ivory Coast sponsored by the Union of Ivorian Women for foreign guests, many of whom were black, the sole Afro coiffure was worn by an Afro-American model.

42. *Providence Sunday Journal*, October 4, 1970.

43. William H. Grier and Price M. Cobbs, *Black Rage* (New York: Bantam Books, 1969), pp. 36-37.

44. *The New York Times*, June 26, 1971.

45. Ibid.

46. Malcolm X and Alex Haley, *The Autobiography of Malcolm X* (New York: Grove Press, Inc. 1966), p. 54.

47. *The New York Times*, March 15, 1968. In its issue dated October 25, 1971, *Time* magazine reported that the Afro's popularity was starting to ebb. One beautician was quoted as follows: "Afros are as out of date as plantation bandannas."

48. *The New York Times*, August 19, 1967.

49. *New York Post*, November 4, 1968; *San Francisco Examiner*, November 6, 1968.

50. *The New York Times*, February 16, 1969, and June 29, 1970.

51. Guyana, formerly British Guiana, is the only English-speaking nation in South America. Its two largest ethnic groups originated in Africa and India. Forbes Burnham, its prime minister, is of African extraction and depends mainly on black support. Curiously, Burnham is called the "Cabbacca" (chief) by his supporters.

52. The Foster incident was described in the *Liberator*, September 1970.
53. *The New York Times*, March 15, 1970.
54. "Stokely Takes a Bride," *Ebony*, July 1968, pp. 137-139, 142.
55. Voodoo is not the hysterical black magic it is thought to be in the white world. Actually it is an amalgam of African liturgy and religious belief which constitutes the basis for the religion followed by the Haitian masses. It is no more or less rational than European faiths. The word Voodoo is a variation of Vodun, the name used for deities in Dahomey.
56. George Goodman, "Harlem's Yorubas," *Look*, January 7, 1969.
57. Ibid.
58. Through the use of its masterful cavalry Oyo, a Yoruba kingdom, eclipsed Benin as the preeminent Nigerian forest kingdom in the seventeenth and eighteenth centuries.
59. John Henrik Clarke, "The New Afro-American Nationalism," *Freedomways*, 1, no. 3 (Fall 1961): 290-291.
60. See "Yoruba Wedding," *Ebony*, October 1968, pp. 98-101.
61. *The New York Times*, May 19, 1966.
62. Ibid., May 19, 1966, and May 20, 1966.
63. Ibid., February 23, 1967.
64. *Life*, July 15, 1966.
65. *The New York Times*, May 27, 1966.
66. David Llorens "Ameer (Leroi Jones) Baraka," *Ebony*, August 1969, pp. 75-83; *Black News*, I, 4 (n.d.). *Black News* is published in Newark.
67. *The New York Times*, April 10, 1970.
68. For a touching description of his visit to Ghana's Elmina slave castle, see Leslie Alexander Lacy, *The Rise and Fall of a Proper Negro: An Autobiography* (New York: Macmillan Co., 1970), pp. 138-144. Fort Amsterdam, a seventeenth century Ghanaian slave castle, is currently being transformed into an historical shrine. The project has been undertaken by Afro-Americans who created the African Descendants Association Foundation to do the restoration job. See "A Shrine to Slaves," *Ebony*, January 1972, pp. 88-91.
69. "African Riviera," *Ebony*, December 1970.
70. Jack Shepherd, "Who Am I," *Look*, January 7, 1969.
71. "A Cultural Safari," *Ebony*, May 1969.
72. Ted Joans, "Natural Africa," *Black World*, May 1971, pp. 4-7.
73. *The New York Times*, August 3, 1967.
74. George Shepherd, "Reflections on the Pan-African Cultural Conference in Algiers," *Africa Today*, 15, no. 4 (August-September 1969): 1-3.
75. Malcolm X and Alex Haley, *The Autobiography of Malcolm X*, p. 36. An excellent source of information about Malcolm's pan-African thinking is Ruby M. and E. U. Essien-Udom, "Malcolm X: An International Man," *Malcolm X—The Man and His Times*, ed. John Henrik Clarke (New York: Collier Books, 1969), pp. 235-267.
76. Malcolm X and Alex Haley, *Autobiography of Malcolm X*, p. 350.
77. Ibid., p. 351.

78. Ibid., p. 357.
79. Breitman, *Malcolm X Speaks,* p. 75.
80. Carmichael, *Stokely Speaks,* p. 221.
81. Ibid., p. 179.
82. Ibid., 225.
83. Imamu Amiri Baraka (LeRoi Jones), "The Pan-African Party and The Black Nation," *The Black Scholar,* 2, no. 7 (March 1971): 24-32.
84. For the entire text see James Forman, "The Black Manifesto," *The Review of Black Political Economy,* 1, no. 1 (Spring—Summer 1970): 36-44.
85. In his remarks of April 26, 1969 Forman said that African leaders in 1967 had reacted favorably to the idea of black Americans going to Africa to contribute their skills and expertise. There was some suspicion of Afro-Americans mainly because of Negroes working for the CIA and the State Department who had been sent to the continent, but "the respect for us as a people continues to mount and the day will come when we can return to our homeland as brothers and sisters" (p. 37).
On the other hand in a letter written in December 1969 and subsequently published, Forman said, "Our brothers and sisters in Africa have forgotten us, the sons and daughters of Africa, their brothers and sisters. They have a flag, a seat in the United Nations, a capitol [*sic*] city, a few French, English or American cars, coca-cola, pepsi-cola, Kodak . . . and all the other trappings of neocolonialism . . . . Our brothers and sisters have paid no attention to the experiences of those of us who have been wrenched from the shores of Africa." Forman was in Martinique collecting data for a book on Frantz Fanon when he wrote these words. See James Forman, "Ten Years Plan (Letter from Fort-de-France)," *Acoma,* I (janvier-mais 1971): 6-26.
86. On the list of projects envisioned by Forman were a Southern land bank, four major publishing houses, audio-visual networks, a strike and defense fund for black labor, a research skills center to conduct research on black problems, and a black university in the South.
87. *The New York Times,* May 10, 1970.
88. Ibid., September 4, 1970 and September 8, 1970. Jones sees the need for a worldwide organization to cope with international problems but an effective party to function on the local level is also needed. "Many times bloods [blacks] want to deal internationally or Pan-Africanistically and cannot even win a local councilmanic election. To do the large you must learn by doing the small." See Baraka, "The Pan-African Party," p. 29.
89. *New Jersey Amsterdam News,* September 11, 1971, and September 18, 1971. *The New Jersey Amsterdam News* is actually a special section of the weekly *New York Amsterdam News.*
90. Ibid., September 11, 1971. An article in *The Amsterdam News* also rebutted the Borders thesis which had inflamed black American opinion in many quarters. The article by reporter Simon Anekwe was based on interviews with

Afro-Americans who had toured Ghana the previous summer under the sponsorship of a Ghanaian-based friendship society for Africans and Afro-Americans. Interviewees found concern in Ghana for Angela Davis, indeed for the cause of racial justice. See the *New York Amsterdam News*, October 9, 1971.

91. *The New York Times*, September 12, 1970; *African Studies Newsletter*, February 14, 1971.

92. CORE Resolution (July 1967).

93. Fred C. Shapiro, "The Successor to Floyd McKissick May Not Be So Reasonable," *The New York Times Magazine* (October 1967).

94. *The New York Times*, January 23, 1969.

95. Ibid., September 7, 1970.

96. "Mzee," meaning an old person, is the name by which President Kenyatta is popularly known in Kenya.

97. *Amsterdam News*, August 21, 1971.

98. *The New York Times*, August 22, 1971.

99. *Liberator*, III, no. 2 (February 1963): 3.

100. ANLC Resolutions (November 23, 24, 25, 1962).

101. ANLC Resolutions (September 24, 25, 26, 27, 1964).

102. ANLC Resolutions (January 26, 27, 28, 1967).

103. *Crisis*, January 1966, p. 52. Afro-American troops were proffered to the United Nations for the independence struggle in Southern Africa. The offer was made in 1967 by H. Rap Brown, then the leader of SNCC.

104. Ibid., April 1970, p. 163.

105. The African name for Rhodesia is Zimbabwe.

106. Martin Luther King, Jr., *Where Do We Go From Here: Chaos or Community* (New York: Harper and Row, 1967), pp. 53, 173, 174.

107. *The New York Times*, April 26, 1968.

108. Ibid., December 1, 1970.

109. John Oliver Killens, *Black Man's Burden* (New York: Pocket Books, 1969), p. 171.

110. A few black Americans have been posted to Africa as ambassadors. Supposedly African leaders initially frowned on the practice believing that such appointments constituted a downgrading of the diplomatic stature of black countries. The fact that blacks have served as ambassadors to Finland, Sweden, and Luxembourg in the last decade may have dissolved African disapproval if it ever actually existed. One can only guess if African states are suspicious that a black appointee might be overzealous in proving that his loyalty to his country supersedes his racial loyalty. Curiously, since 1948 American ambassadors to Israel have all been Gentiles.

111. *The New York Times, The Week in Review*, December 13, 1970.

112. A copy of Diggs' speech delivered before the National Newspaper Publisher's Association in Chicago was kindly provided by the Congressman's office.

113. Senator Edward Brooke, the only Negro in the Senate, has requested

the U.S. to end its "pattern of implied complicity with the Southern African regimes." In an April 1968 speech on the floor of the Senate he asked for American sanctions against those regimes. Although Brooke used strong language, pan-Africanism did not provide the framework for the speech. Brooke was not speaking as a black man.

114. *The New York Times,* March 26, 1971.

115. *Christian Science Monitor,* August 14 and 20, 1971. In December 1971 Diggs quit his post as a "public member" of the United States delegation to the United Nations. According to the Congressman his resignation was triggered by the announcement of an American treaty with Portugal which made this country a partner in the subjugation of African peoples.

116. For a study of United States involvement in South Africa's economy see *Africa Today,* September-October 1970.

117. In a statement on the principles of African policy submitted to President Nixon on March 16, 1970, Secretary of State Rogers enumerated the various reasons why Africa is deserving of the "active attention and support" of this country. Listed last, perhaps because it is also least important in shaping government thinking, was the observation that "we are linked by the cultural fact that one out of every ten Americans has his origins in Africa."

118. Blacks have frequently asserted that they are under-enumerated in the decennial census. Statements especially those emanating from black nationalist camps often claim a black population of at least thirty million. Forman's *Black Manifesto* is a case in point: ". . . we maintain there are probably more than 30,000,000 black people in this country."

BIBLIOGRAPHY

BOOKS

Africa From The Point of View of American Negro Scholars. New York: The American Society of African Culture, 1963.

Alexander, Archibald. *A History of Colonization on the Western Coast of Africa.* Philadelphia: William S. Martien, 1846.

Azikiwe, Nnamdi. *Renascent Africa.* Accra: Published by the Author, 1937.

————————. *Zik: A Selection from the Speeches of Nnamdi Azikiwe.* Cambridge: Cambridge University Press, 1961.

Baraka, Imamu Amiri [LeRoi Jones], ed. *African Congress—A Documentary of the First Modern Pan-African Congress.* New York: William Morrow and Co., 1972.

Barbour, Floyd B., ed. *The Black Power Revolt.* Boston: Porter Sargent Publisher, 1968.

Barrett, Leonard E. *The Rastafarians—A Study in Messianic Cultism in Jamaica.* Rio Piedras: Institute of Caribbean Studies, 1968.

Bell, Howard H., ed. *Minutes of the Proceedings of the National Negro Conventions 1830-1864.* New York: Arno Press, 1969.

Bennett, George. *Kenya, A Political History: The Colonial Period.* London: Oxford University Press, 1963.

Benson, Mary. *The African Patriots—The Story of the African National Congress of South Africa.* New York: Encyclopaedia Britannica Press, 1964.

Bilbo, Theodore G. *Take Your Choice: Separation or Mongrelization.* Poplarville, Mississippi: Orleans House Publishing Co., 1947.

Bittle, William E., and Geis, Gilbert. *The Longest Way Home: Chief Alfred C. Sam's Back-To-Africa Movement.* Detroit: Wayne State University Press, 1964.

Bontemps, Arna and Conroy, Jack. *Anyplace but Here.* New York: Hill and Wang, 1966.

Bowen, J.W.E., ed. *Addresses and Proceedings of the Congress on Africa—December 13-15, 1895.* Atlanta: Gammon Theological Seminary, 1896.

Bracey, John H., Jr., Meier, August, and Rudwick, Elliott, eds. *Black Nationalism in America.* Indianapolis and New York: Bobbs-Merrill Co., Inc., 1970.

Breitman, George, ed. *By Any Means Necessary—Speeches, Interviews and a Letter by Malcolm X.* New York: Pathfinder Press, Inc., 1970.

————————. *Malcolm X Speaks—Selected Speeches and Statements.* New York: Grove Press, Inc., 1966.

Brotz, Howard. *The Black Jews of Harlem: Negro Nationalism and the Dilemmas of Negro Leadership.* New York: Schocken, 1970.

Brown, H. Rap. *Die Nigger Die.* New York: Dial Press, Inc., 1969.

Buell, Raymond Leslie. *The Native Problem in Africa.* 2d ed. Hamden, Connecticut: Archon Books, 1965.

Carmichael, Stokely. *Power and Racism: What we Want.* Boston: New England Free Press, 1966.

————————. *Stokely Speaks—Black Power Back to Pan-Africanism.* New York: Random House, Vintage Books, 1971.

Cleage, Albert B. *The Black Messiah.* New York: Sheed and Ward, 1968.

Cleaver, Eldridge. Post-Prison Writings and Speeches. Edited by Robert Scheer. New York: Random House, Vintage Books, 1969.

————————. *Soul on Ice.* New York: Dell Publishing Co., 1968.

Coker, Daniel. *Journal of Daniel Coker, A Descendant of Africa.* Baltimore: Edward J. Coale, 1820.

Coleman, James. *Nigeria: Background to Nationalism.* Berkeley and Los Angeles: University of California Press, 1965.

Conyers, John, Jr. "Portugal Invades Guinea: The Failure of U.S. Policy Toward Africa" In *What Black Politicians Are Saying.* Edited by Nathan Wright, Jr., New York: Hawthorne Books, Inc., 1972, pp. 94-109.

Cronon, Edmund. *Black Moses: The Story of Marcus Garvey and the Universal Negro Improvement Association.* Madison: University of Wisconsin Press, 1962.

Crummell, Alexander. *Africa and America—Addresses and Discourses.* Springfield, Massachusetts: Willey and Co., 1891.

————————. *The Future of Africa.* New York: Charles Scribner, 1862.

Cuffe, Paul. *A Brief Account of the Settlement and Present Situation of the Colony of Sierra Leone in Africa.* New York: Samuel Wood, 1812.

Cullen, Countee. *Color.* New York: Harper and Brothers, 1925.

Dean, Captain Harry. *The Pedro Gorino.* Boston and New York: Houghton Mifflin Co., 1929.

Delany, Martin R. *The Condition, Elevation, Emigration, and Destiny of the*

Colored People of the United States Politically Considered. Philadelphia: Published by the Author, 1852.

—————————— and Campbell, Robert. *Search For A Place—Black Separatism and Africa 1820.* Ann Arbor: The University of Michigan Press, 1969.

Drake, St. Clair. *The Redemption of Africa and Black Religion.* Chicago: Third World Press, 1970.

Du Bois, W. E. B. *Dusk of Dawn: An Essay Toward an Autobiography of a Race Concept.* New York: Schocken Books, 1968.

——————————. *The World and Africa: Inquiry into the Part Which Africa Has Played in World History.* New York: International Publishers, 1968.

Dunbar, Ernest. *The Black Expatriates—A Study of American Negroes in Exile.* New York: E. P. Dutton and Co., Inc., 1968.

Draper, Theodore. *The Rediscovery of Black Nationalism.* New York: The Viking Press, 1970.

Edwards, Adolph. *Marcus Garvey 1887-1940.* London and Port-of-Spain: Beacon Publications, 1967.

Essien-Udom, E. U. *Black Nationalism: A Search for an Identity in America.* New York: Dell Publishing Co., 1964.

Fisher, Miles Mark. *Negro Slave Songs in The United States.* New York: The Citadel Press, 1963.

Foner, Philip S., ed. *The Black Panthers Speak.* Philadelphia and New York: J. B. Lippincott Co., 1970.

Franklin, John Hope. *From Slavery to Freedom: A History of Negro Americans.* New York: Alfred A. Knopf, 1967.

Fyfe, Christopher. *A History of Sierra Leone.* London: Oxford University Press, 1962.

Garnet, Henry Highland. *The Past and the Present Condition, and the Destiny of the Colored Race: A Discourse Delivered at the Fifteenth Anniversary of the Female Benevolent Society of Troy. February 14, 1848.* Troy: J. C. Kneeland and Co., 1848.

Garrison, William Lloyd. *Thoughts on African Colonization.* New York: Arno Press, 1969.

Garvey, Marcus. *Philosophy and Opinions of Marcus Garvey or Africa for the Africans.* Edited by Amy Jacques Garvey, London: Frank Cass, 1967.

Gatheru, R. Mugo. *Child of Two Worlds—A Kikuyu's Story.* Garden City, N. Y.: Anchor Books, 1965.

Goodman, Benjamin, ed. *The End of White World Supremacy—Four Speeches by Malcolm X.* New York: Merlin House, Inc., 1971.

Grier, William H., and Cobbs, Price M. *Black Rage.* New York: Bantam Books, 1969.

Harris, Sheldon H. *Paul Cuffe—Black America and the African Return.* New York: Simon and Schuster, 1972.

Herskovits, Melville J. *The New World Negro—Selected Papers in AfroAmerican Studies.* Edited by Francis S. Herskovits. New York: Minerva Press, 1969.

Hicks, John D., Mowry, George E., and Burke, Robert E. *The Federal Union—A History of the United States to 1877.* Boston: Houghton Mifflin Co., 1964.

Hill, Adelaide Cromwell and Kilson, Martin. *Apropos of Africa: Sentiments of Negro American Leaders on Africa from the 1800's to the 1950's.* London: Frank Cass & Co., Ltd., 1969.

Himes, Chester. *Cotton Comes to Harlem.* London: Frederick Muller Ltd., 1965.

Holly, James Theodore, and Harris, J. Dennis. *Black Separatism and the Caribbean 1860.* Edited by Howard H. Bell. Ann Arbor: The University of Michigan Press, 1969.

Hooker, James R. *Black Revolutionary: George Padmore's Path from Communism to Pan-Africanism.* New York: Frederick A. Praeger, 1967.

Isaacs, Harold R. *The New World of Negro Americans.* New York: The Viking Press, 1964.

James, C. L. R. *The Black Jacobins.* New York: Random House: Vintage Books, 1963.

————————— [J. R. Johnson]. *Why Negroes Should Oppose the War.* New York: Pioneer Publishers, n.d.

Julian, Colonel Hubert (as told to John Bullock). *Black Eagle.* London: The Adventurers Club, 1965.

Killens, John Oliver. *Black Man's Burden.* New York: Pocket Books, 1969.

King, K. J., *Pan-Africanism and Education: A Study of Race, Philanthropy, and Education in the Southern States of America and East Africa.* New York: Oxford University Press, 1971.

King, Martin Luther, Jr., *Where Do We Go From Here: Chaos or Community.* New York: Harper and Row, 1967.

Lacy, Leslie Alexander. *The Rise and Fall of a Proper Negro—An Autobiography.* New York: Macmillan Co., 1970.

Legum, Colin. *Pan-Africanism—A Short Political Guide.* New York: Frederick A. Praeger, 1965.

Lockwood, Lee. *Conversation with Eldridge Cleaver—Algiers.* New York: Dell Publishing Co., 1970.

Lynch, Hollis. *Edward Wilmot Blyden: Pan Negro Patriot, 1832-1912.* London: Oxford University Press, 1967.

—————————, ed. *Black Spokesman—Selected Published Writings of Edward Wilmot Blyden.* New York: Humanities Press, 1971.

Malcolm X, and Haley, Alex. *The Autobiography of Malcolm X.* New York: Grove Press, Inc., 1966.

Manoedi, M. Mokete. *Garvey and Africa.* New York: The New York Age Press, 192?.

Marks, George P., III. *The Black Press Views American Imperialism.* New York: Arno Press, 1971.

Mason, George. *Reminiscences of Newport.* Newport, Rhode Island, 1884.

Mboya, Tom. *The Challenge of Nationhood.* New York and Washington: Frederick A. Praeger, 1970.

McKay, Claude. *Harlem: Negro Metropolis.* New York: E. P. Dutton and Co., Inc., 1940.

McKissick, Floyd B. *A Black Manifesto.* New York: National Congress of Racial Equality, 1967.

——————————. *Three-Fifths of A Man.* London: Macmillan & Co., 1969.

Meier, August. *Negro Thought in America 1880-1915—Racial Ideologies in the Age of Booker T. Washington.* Ann Arbor: The University of Michigan Press, 1966.

Mwase, George Simeon. *Strike a Blow and Die—A Narrative of Race Relations in Colonial Africa.* Edited by Robert I. Rotberg. Cambridge, Massachusetts: Harvard University Press, 1967.

Myrdal, Gunnar. *An American Dilemma.* 2 vols. New York: McGraw-Hill Book Company, 1964.

Nembhard, Len S. *Trials and Triumphs of Marcus Garvey.* Kingston: The Gleaner Co., Ltd., 1940.

Newby, I. A. *Jim Crow's Defense: Anti-Negro Thought In America, 1900-1930.* Baton Rouge: Louisiana State University Press, 1965.

Nkrumah, Kwame. *Ghana: The Autobiography of Kwame Nkrumah.* New York: Thomas Nelson and Sons, 1957.

——————————. *I Speak of Freedom.* New York: Frederick A. Praeger, 1962.

Nugent, John Peer. *The Black Eagle.* New York: Stein and Day, 1971.

Ottley, Roi. *New World A-Coming: Inside Black America.* Boston: Houghton Mifflin Co., 1943.

——————————. *The Lonely Warrior: The Life and Times of Robert Abbott.* Chicago: Henry Regnery Co., 1955.

Ovington, Mary White. *Portrait In Color.* New York: Viking Press, 1927.

Padmore, George. *Pan-Africanism or Communism: The Coming Struggle for Africa.* London: Dennis Dobson, 1956.

Patterson, Sheila. *Dark Strangers—A Study of West Indians in London.* London: Penguin, 1965.

Peaker, Charles. *Black Nationalism.* New York: African-American Publications, 1967.

Proceedings of the National Convention of the Colored Men of America Held In Washington, D. C., January 13, 14, 15, and 16, 1869. Washington, D. C., 1869.

Quarles, Benjamin J. *Black Abolitionists.* London: Oxford University Press, 1970.

Redkey, Edwin S. *Black Exodus:Black Nationalist and Back-to-Africa Move-*

ments, 1890-1910. New Haven and London: Yale University Press, 1969.

——————————, ed. *Respect Black: The Writings and Speeches of Henry McNeal Turner.* New York: Arno Press, 1971.

Rogers, J. A. *One Hundred Amazing Facts About the Negro With Complete Proof.* New York: J. A. Rogers, 1957.

——————————. *The Real Facts About Ethiopia.* New York: J. A. Rogers Publications, n.d.

Rosberg, Carl G., Jr., and Nottingham, John. *The Myth of Mau Mau: Nationalism in Kenya.* New York: Frederick A. Praeger, 1966.

Rose, Arnold. *The Negro's Morale: Group Identification and Protest.* Minneapolis: University of Minnesota Press, 1949.

Salvador, George. *Paul Cuffee, The Black Yankee.* New Bedford: Reynolds-Dewalt Printing, Inc., 1969.

Shepperson, George, and Price, Thomas. *Independent Africa: John Chilembwe and the Origins, Setting and Significance of the Nyasaland Native Rising of 1915.* Edinburgh: University Press, 1958.

Simpson, George Eaton. *Religious Cults of the Caribbean: Trinidad, Jamaica and Haiti.* Rio Piedras: Institute of Caribbean Studies, 1970.

Smith, M. G., Augier, Roy, Nettleford, Rex. *Ras Tafari Movement in Kingston, Jamaica.* Kingston: Institute of Social and Economic Research-University College of The West Indies, 1960.

Staudenraus, P. J. *The African Colonization Movement, 1816-1865.* New York: Columbia University Press, 1961.

Thirty Years of Lynching In The United States—1889-1918. New York: N.A.A.C.P., 1919.

Thompson, Era Bell. *Africa, Land of My Fathers.* Garden City, New York: Doubleday and Company, Inc., 1954.

Thorne, J. Albert. *An Appeal Addressed to the Friends of the African Race—the African Colonial Enterprise.* 1896.

Thwaite, Daniel. *The Seething African Pot—A Study of Black Nationalism 1882-1935.* London: Constable and Co., Ltd., 1956.

Tindall, George Brown. *South Carolina Negroes 1877-1900.* Baton Rouge: Louisiana State University Press, 1966.

Uya, Okon Edet, ed. *Black Brotherhood: Afro-Americans and Africa.* Lexington, Massachusetts: D. C. Heath and Company, 1971.

Vincent, Theodore G. *Black Power and the Garvey Movement.* Berkeley: Ramparts Press, 1971.

Washington, Booker T. *A New Negro for a New Century.* Miami, Florida: Mnemosyne Publishing Co., 1969.

——————————. *The Future of the American Negro.* New York: Negro Universities Press, 1969.

Webster, J. B., Boahen, A. A., with H.O. Idowu. *History of West Africa—The Revolutionary Years—1815 to Today.* New York and Washington: Praeger Publishers, 1967.

Weisbord, Robert G. *African Zion: The Attempt to Establish a Jewish Colony in the East Africa Protectorate 1903-1905*. Philadelphia: Jewish Publication Society, 1968.

Welbourn, F. B. *East African Rebels—A Study of Some Independent Churches*. London: SCM Press Ltd., 1961.

Wright, Richard. *Black Power—A Record of Reactions in a Land of Pathos*. New York: Harper and Brothers, 1954.

ARTICLES

Abiola, Irele. "Negritude or Black Cultural Nationalism," *The Journal of Modern African Studies*, 3, no. 3 (1965): 321-348.

"A Cultural Safari." *Ebony*, May 1969, p. 123 ff.

Adebo, Chief S. O. "The Black Revolution: An African View." *Rights and Reviews* (Winter 1966-1967): pp. 32-34.

"African Riviera." *Ebony*, December 1970, pp. 83-87.

Akiwowo, Akinsola. "Song in a Strange Land." *Phylon*, 12, no. 1 (First Quarter 1951): pp. 36-38.

"A Shrine to Slaves." *Ebony*, January 1972, pp. 88-91.

Baldwin, James. "East River, Downtown: Postscript to a Letter from Harlem." In *Nobody Knows My Name*. New York: Dell Publishing Co., 1963: pp. 67-74.

Baraka, Imamu Amiri (LeRoi Jones). "The Pan-African Party and the Black Nation." *The Black Scholar*, 2, no. 7 (March 1971): 24-32.

Bell, Howard H. "The Negro Emigration Movement 1849-1854: A Phase of Negro Nationalism." *Phylon*, 20, no. 2 (1959): 132-142.

Bennett, Lerone, Jr. "The Ghost of Marcus Garvey: Interviews with Crusader's Two Wives." *Ebony*, March 1960, p. 53.

"Black Hands Across the Sea." *Ebony*, March 1972, p. 88 *ff*.

Bond, Horace Mann. "Howe and Isaacs in the Bush: The Ram in the Thicket." *Negro History Bulletin*, December 1961, pp. 72 *ff*.

Boyd, Willis Dolmond. "Negro Colonization in the Reconstruction Era 1865-1870." *The Georgia Historical Quarterly*, 15 (December 1956): 370-382.

Brewer, William M. "Henry Highland Garnet." *Journal of Negro History*, 8, no. 1 (January 1928): 50-51.

——————————. "John B. Russwurm." *Journal of Negro History*, 8 (October 1928): 413-422.

Bryce-Laporte, Roy S. "The Rastas." *Caribbean Review* (Summer 1970): pp. 3-4.

Carmichael, Stokely. "Pan-Africanism—Land and Power." Reprinted from *The Black Scholar* (November 1969).

——————————. "We Are All Africans." *The Black Scholar*, May 1970, pp. 15-19.

Clarke, John Henrik. "The New Afro-American Nationalism" *Freedomways*. 1, no. 3 (Fall 1961): 285-295.

Cleaver, Eldridge. "Culture and Revolution: Their Synthesis in Africa." *The Black Scholar*, 3, no. 2 (October 1971): 33-39.

Cohen, Robert D. "African Students and the Negro-American: Past Relationships and a Recent Program." *International Educational and Cultural Exchange*, 5, no. 2 (Fall 1969): pp. 76-85.

Coleman, Beverly. "Relevancy in Teaching and Learning Swahili." *Black World*, October 1970, pp. 11-24.

Contee, Clarence G. "Afro-Americans and Early Pan-Africanism." *Negro Digest*, February 1970, pp. 24-30.

——————————. "Ethiopia and the Pan-African Movement Before 1945." *Black World*, February 1972, pp. 41 *ff.*

Coombs, Orde. "On Being West Indian in New York." In *The Black Seventies.* Edited by Floyd B. Barbour. Boston: Porter Sargent Publisher, 1970, pp. 183-195.

Cruse, Harold. "Black and White: Outlines of the Next Stage." *Black World* May 1971, pp. 9-40.

Drake, St. Clair. "Hide My Face? On Pan-Africanism and Negritude." In *Soon, One Morning—New Writing By American Negroes 1940-1962.* Edited by Herbert Hill. New York: Alfred A. Knopf, 1969, pp. 78-105.

——————————. "Negro Americans and the Africa Interest." In *The American Negro Reference Book.* Edited by John P. Davis. Englewood Cliffs, New Jersey: Prentice-Hall, Inc., 1966, pp. 662-705.

Drimmer, Melvin. "Review Article—Black Exodus." *American Studies*, 4, no. 2, 249-256.

Du Bois, David Graham. "Problems and Responsibilities — Afro-American Militants In Africa." *Black World*, February 1972, pp. 4-11.

Du Bois, W. E. Burghardt. "Back to Africa." *The Century Magazine*, 105, no. 4 (February 1923): 539-548.

Dunbar, Ernest. "The Black Revolt Hits The White Campus." *Look*, October 31, 1967, pp. 27-31.

Edmonson, Locksley. "The Internationalization of Black Power." *Mawazo*, 1, no. 14 (December 1968): 16-30.

Elkins, W. F. " 'Unrest Among the Negroes': A British Document of 1919." *Science and Society*, 32, no. 1 (Winter 1968): 66-79.

Essien-Udom, E. U., and Essien-Udom, Ruby M. "Malcolm X: An International Man." In *Malcolm X—The Man and His Times.* Edited by John Henrik Clarke. New York: Collier Books, 1969, pp. 235-267.

"Ethiopia '33 " *Crisis*, November 1933, pp. 250 *ff.*

"Exchange of Persons." *Intercultural Education*, 1, no. 10 (November 1970): 17-18.

Farmer, James. "An American Negro Leader's View of African Unity." *African Forum*, 1, no. 1 (Summer 1965): 69-89.

Fishel, Leslie H., Jr. "The Negro in the New Deal Era." In *The Negro in Depression and War—Prelude to Revolution.* Edited by Bernard Sternsher. Chicago: Quadrangle Books, 1969, pp. 7-28.

Fleming, Walter L. " 'Pap' Singleton, The Moses of the Colored Exodus." *American Journal of Sociology,* 15 (July 1909): 61-82.

Forman, James. "Ten Years Plan—Letter from Fort-de-France." *Acoma,* 1 (janvier-mais 1971): 6-26.

——————————. "The Black Manifesto." *The Review of Black Political Economy,* 1, no. 1 (Spring/Summer 1970): 36-44.

Fox, Richard W. "Black Panthers in Africa." *Commonweal,* October 3, 1969, pp. 6-7.

Garland, Phyl. "Soul to Soul." *Ebony,* June 1971, pp. 79 *ff.*

Garvey, Amy Jacques. "Marcus Garvey and Pan-Africanism." *Black World,* December 1971, pp. 15-18.

Garvin, Roy. "Benjamin or 'Pap' Singleton and His Followers." *Journal of Negro History,* 33, no. 1 (1948): 7-23.

Gibson, Lee Richard. "South African Toms Denounce Stokely." *Liberator,* 7, no. 12 (December 1967): 10-11.

Goodman, George. "Harlem's Yorubas." *Look,* January 7, 1969, pp. 32-33.

Harlan, Louis. "Booker T. Washington and the White Man's Burden." *American Historical Review,* 71, no. 2 (January 1966): 441-467.

Harris, Joseph E. "Introduction to the African Diaspora." In *Emerging Themes of African History.* Edited By T. O. Ranger. London: Heinemann Educational Books Ltd., 1968, pp. 147-151.

Hart, Richard. "The Life and Resurrection of Marcus Garvey." *Race* (London), 9, no. 2 (1967): 217-237.

Hill, Mozell C. "The All-Negro Communities of Oklahoma—The Natural History of A Social Movement." *Journal of Negro History,* 31, no. 3 (July 1946): 254-268.

Howe, Russell Warren. "Strangers in Africa." *The Reporter,* June 22, 1961, pp. 34-35.

——————————. "A Reply to Horace Mann Bond." *Negro History Bulletin,* February 1962, pp. 102, 104.

——————————. "On the Curious 2-Way Afro-American Influence." *Baltimore Sunday Sun,* March 19, 1972.

Isaacs, Harold R. "A Reporter At Large—Back to Africa." *The New Yorker,* May 13, 1961, pp. 105 ff.

"James Forman of S.N.C.C. Addresses the United Nations." *Liberator,* 7, no. 12 (December 1967): 8-9.

Joans, Ted. "Natural Africa." *Black World,* May 1971, pp. 4-7.

Kijembe, Adhama Oluwa. "Swahili and Black Americans." *Negro Digest,* July 1969, pp. 4-8.

King, Kenneth. "Early Pan-African Politicians in East Africa." *Mawazo,* 2, no. 1 (1968): 2-10.

——————————. "James E. K. Aggrey: Collaborator, Nationalist, Pan-African." *Canadian Journal of African Studies,* 3, no. 3 (Fall 1970): 511-530.

Kinyatti, Maina. "African Students Take Charge." *African Opinion*, January-February 1971, pp. 2-3.

Langley, Jabez Ayodele. "Garveyism and African Nationalism." *Race* (London) 11, no. 2 (1969): 157-172.

—————————. "Pan-Africanism in Paris, 1924-36." *Journal of Modern African Studies*, 7, no. 1 (1969): 69-94.

Leopold, James. "Mboya Shown Like It Is." *African Opinion*, May-June 1969, p. 5.

Llorens, David. "Ameer (Leroi Jones) Baraka." *Ebony*, August 1969, pp. 75-83.

Lowenthal, David. "Race and Color in the West Indies." *Daedelus* 96, no. 2. (Spring 1967): 580-626.

Lynch, Hollis R. "Pan-Negro Nationalism in the New World Before 1862." *Boston University Papers on Africa*, 2, *African History*. Edited by Jeffrey Butler. Boston: Boston University Press, 1966, 149-179.

Martin, Kingsley. "The Jamaican Volcano." *New Statesman*, March 17, 1961, pp. 416-418.

Mboya, Tom. "Mboya's Rebuttal." *Ebony*, August 1969, pp. 90-91, 94.

—————————. "The American Negro Cannot Look to Africa for an Escape." *The New York Times Magazine*, July 13, 1969, p. 30 *ff.*

Mehlinger, Louis R. "The Attitude of the Free Negro Toward African Colonization." *Journal of Negro History*, 1, no. 3 (July 1916): 271-301.

Meier, August, and Rudwick, Elliot. "The Boycott Movement Against Jim Crow Streetcars in the South 1900-1906." *Journal of American History*, 55, no. 4 (March 1969): 756-775.

Mphahlele, Ezekiel. "The Blacks." *Africa Today*, 14, no. 4 (August 1967): 22-25.

Nagenda, John. "Pride or Prejudice? Relationships Between Africans and American Negroes." *Race* (London) 9, no. 2 (1967): 157-171.

Norton, Graham. "The West Indies as Centres for Migration—Black British Adventurers." *The Round Table*, no. 242 (April 1971): 273-281.

Obadele, Brother Imari Abubakar I. "The Republic of New Africa—An Independent Black Nation." *Black World*, May 1971, pp. 81-89.

Obatala, J. K. "Exodus: Black Zionism." *Liberator*, October 1969, pp. 14-17.

Ofari, Earl. "The Emergence of Black National Consciousness in America." *Black World*, February 1971, pp. 75-86.

Okoye, Felix. "The Afro-American and Africa." In *Topics in Afro-American Studies*. Edited by Henry J. Richards. Buffalo: Black Academy Press, 1971, pp. 37-58.

Padmore, George. "Ethiopia and World Politics." *Crisis*, 42, no. 5 (May 1935): 138 *ff.*

Pease, William H., and Pease, Jane H. "The Negro Convention Movement." In *Key Issues in the Afro-American Experience*. Vol. 1. Edited by Nathan I. Huggins, Martin Kilson, Daniel M. Fox. New York: Harcourt Brace Jovanovich Inc., 1971, pp. 191-205.

Poinsett, Alex. "Inawapasa Watu Weusi Kusema Kiswahili." *Ebony,* December 1968, p. 163.
——————————. "It's Nation Time." *Ebony,* December 1970, p. 98.
Preece, Harold. "War and the Negro." *Crisis,* November 1935, pp. 329,338.
Quarles, Benjamin. "Black History's Early Advocates." *Negro Digest,* February 1970, pp. 4-9.
Redkey, Edwin S. "Bishop Turner's African Dream." *Journal of American History,* 54, no. 2 (September 1967): 271-290.
Reed, Beverley. "Amy Jacques Garvey: Black, Beautiful and Free." *Ebony,* June 1971, p. 45.
Rippey, J. Fred. "A Negro Colonization Project in Mexico 1895." *Journal of Negro History* 6, no. 1 (January 1921): 66-73.
Robeson, Paul. "African Culture." In *Apropos of Africa-Sentiments of Negro American Leaders on Africa from the 1800's to the 1950's.* Edited by Adelaide Cromwell Hill and Martin Kilson. London: Frank Cass and Co., Ltd., 1969, pp. 132-135.
Rowan, Carl T. "Has Paul Robeson Betrayed the Negro?" *Ebony,* October 1957, pp. 31-42.
Rudwick, Elliott M. "DuBois Versus Garvey: Race Propagandists at War." *Journal of Negro Education,* 38 (Fall 1959): 421-429.
Sale, J. Kirk. "Wasema Kiswahili Bwana?" *The New York Times Magazine,* February 4, 1968, p. 28.
Salmond, John A. "The Civilian Conservation Corps and the Negro." In *The Negro In Depression and War—Prelude to Revolution,* Edited by Bernard Sternsher. Chicago: Quadrangle Books, 1969, pp. 78-92.
"Selections from Robeson's Writings and Speeches." *Freedomways,* 2, 1 (First Quarter 1971): 105-124.
Shapiro, Fred C. "The Successor to Floyd McKissick May Not Be So Reasonable." *The New York Times Magazine,* October 1, 1967, p. 33.
Shepherd, George. "Reflections on the Pan-African Cultural Conference in Algiers." *Africa Today,* 15, no. 4 (August-September 1969): 1-3.
Shepherd, Jack. "Who Am I." *Look,* January 7, 1969, p. 30.
Shepperson, George. "Ethiopianism and African Nationalism." *Phylon,* 14 (1953): 9-18.
——————————. "Notes On Negro American Influences On the Emergence of African Nationalism."*Journal of African History,* 1, no. 2 (1960):299-312.
——————————. "Nyasaland and the Millennium." In *Black Africa—Its Peoples and Their Cultures Today.* Edited by John Middleton. London: Macmillan & Co., 1970, pp. 234-247.
——————————. "The African Abroad or the African Diaspora." In *Emerging Themes of African History.* Edited by T. O. Ranger. London: Heinemann Educational Books Ltd., 1968, pp. 152-176.
Sherwood, Henry Noble. "Paul Cuffe." *Journal of Negro History,* 8 (April 1923): 153-229.

_____. "Paul Cuffe and His Contribution to the American Colonization Society." *Proceedings of the Mississippi Valley Historical Association for the Year 1912-1913,* 6 (1913): 371-402.
"Shindana: Black Toymakers of Watts." *Sepia,* February 1971, pp. 40-43.
"Stokely Takes a Bride." *Ebony,* July 1968: p. 137.
Strong, John. "Emerging Ideological Patterns Among Southern African Students." *Africa Today,* 14, no. 4 (August 1967): 14-17.
"The Irrepressible Envoy from Ghana." *Ebony,* November 1970, p. 68.
"The Smell of Mussolini." *Black Man,* July-August 1936.
Thompson, Era Bell. "Africa's Problems—The Other Side of the Story." *Ebony,* July 1969, p. 116.
_____. "Are Black Americans Welcome in Africa." *Ebony,* January 1969, p. 44.
Van Deusen, John G. "The Exodus of 1879." *Journal of Negro History,* 21, no. 2 (1936): 111-129.
Wachuku, Jaja A. "The Relation of AMSAC and the American Negro to Africa and Pan-Africanism." In *Pan-Africanism Reconsidered.* Edited by the American Society of African Culture. Berkeley and Los Angeles: University of California Press, 1962, pp. 361-376.
White, Gavin. "Patriarch McGuire and The Episcopal Church." *Historical Magazine of the Protestant Episcopal Church,* 38, no. 2 (June 1969): 109-141.
Wilkins, Roy. "The Case Against Separatism: 'Black Jim Crow.' " *Newsweek,* February 10, 1969, p. 57.
"Yoruba Wedding." *Ebony,* October 1968, pp. 98-101.

NEWSPAPERS AND PERIODICALS

Specific Articles are cited under "Articles."

Africa Today. 1965-1972.
African Methodist Episcopal Church Review. 20, no. 3 (January 1904).
African News and Views (New York). May 1962; July 1, 1969.
African Opinion. June-July 1961; August-September 1968; March-April 1970; January-February 1971.
African Studies Newsletter. February 14, 1971.
Afro-American (Baltimore). September 28, 1935; September 21, 1935; October 5, 1935; October 12, 1935; October 19, 1935.
A.M.S.A.C. Newsletter (American Society of African Culture). September 1962.
Barbados Advocate. October 12, 1935; October 22, 1935; November 12, 1935; December 7, 1935.

Black Man. Late October 1935; July-August 1936.
Black News (Newark). 1, no. 4 (n.d.).
The Black Panther. February 2, 1969; May 31, 1969.
Black Scholar. 1970-1972.
Black World (Previously *Negro Digest*). 1965-1972.
Chicago Defender. May 14, 1921; June 29, 1935; July 3, 1935; October 5, 1935; December 14, 1935; June 6, 1953; December 1, 1956.
Christian Science Monitor (Boston). August 14 and 20, 1971.
Crisis. February 1914; February 1919; March 1920; January 1921; February 1922; May 1924; February 1935; November 1935; January 1966.
Daily Gleaner. (Kingston, Jamaica), October 7, 1935; October 14, 1935; October 23, 1935; October 15, 1935; November 8, 1935; July 12, 1964.
Daily Telegraph (London). August 15, 1930.
Ebony. 1965-1972.
Essence. July 1970.
Freedomways. 1965-1972.
Illustrated Missionary News. May 15, 1897.
Jamaica Star. July 9, 1965.
Jamaica Times. November 10, 1956.
Jerusalem Post. February 10, 1971.
Journal of Negro History 22 (1937).
Lagos Weekly Record. February 7, 1920.
Liberator. February 1963, 1965-1972.
The Liberian Star. November 4, 1969.
Life. July 15, 1966.
New Crusader. February 27, 1960.
New Jersey Amsterdam News. September 11, 1971.
New York Age. August 12, 1922; May 12, 1923.
New York Amsterdam News. September 10, 1924; October 12, 1935; October 5, 1935; November 28, 1964; August 26, 1967; December 23, 1967; March 29, 1969; August 21, 1971; October 9, 1971; October 16, 1971.
New York Post. August 3, 1958; November 4, 1968.
The New York Times. February 23, 1892; June 25, 1904; July 17, 1904; February 26, 1914; April 17, 1922; August 6, 1924; May 19, 1963; May 24, 1964; 1965-1972.
New York World. July 29, 1922.
The North Star. November 16, 1849.
Opportunity 2, no. 21 (September 1924).
Pittsburgh Courier. October 12, 1935; November 2, 1935; November 9, 1935; February 25, 1961.
Providence Evening Bulletin. October 7, 1971.
Providence Sunday Journal. October 4, 1970.
San Francisco Examiner. November 6, 1968.
Savannah Tribune. March 21, 1896.

REPORTS AND PUBLIC DOCUMENTS

Chicago Commission on Race Relations. *The Negro In Chicago—A Study of Race Relations and a Race Riot.* Chicago: The University of Chicago Press, 1922.
Historical Survey of the Origins and Growth of the Mau Mau. Cmnd. 1030. London: H.M.S.O., 1960.
Kenya National Assembly, Senate. *Official Report.* Vol. 16, 1968.
The Congressional Record. January 7, 1890; January 16, 1890.

MANUSCRIPTS

Cuffe Manuscripts. New Bedford Public Library, New Bedford, Massachusetts.
Public Record Office. Colonial Office. 267/600; 536/119; 536/277; 884/13.
Public Record Office. Foreign Office. 267/607; 395/389; 371/4567; 371/5684; 371/5708; 371/7236; 371/7286; 371/8153; 371/8513; 371/9553; 371/7316; 371/9633; 371/10632; 371/16618; 371/17585; 371/19175; 371/19176; 371/20154; 371/20155.

OTHER UNPUBLISHED SOURCES

Bunche, Ralph. The Programs, Ideologies, Tactics and Achievements of Negro Betterment and Interracial Organizations—A Research Memorandum. Unpublished Study Conducted for the Carnegie-Myrdal Project. Vol. 2.
The Case For Repatriation. Philadelphia: African-American Repatriation Association, n.d.
Chalk, Frank. "DuBois and Garvey Confront Liberia: Two Incidents of the Coolidge Years." Paper delivered at the 52nd annual meeting of the Association for the Study of Negro Life and History. Greensboro, North Carolina, October 1967.
Scott, William R. "Going to the Promised Land. Afro-American Immigrants in Ethiopia 1930-1935." Paper delivered at the 14th annual meeting of the African Studies Association. Denver, Colorado, November 1971.

PERSONAL INTERVIEWS

Bryan, Arden. Personal interview with the author. New York City. April 5, 1965.
Julian, Colonel Hubert F. Personal interview with the author. New York City. January 3, 1970.
Whitehurst, Stan. Personal interview with the author. Kingston, Rhode Island. December 16, 1970.

INDEX

Abbott, Robert S., 98
Abernathy, Rev. Ralph David, 139
Abeta Israel Hebrew Center, 133
Abidjan, University of, 203
Abyssinia, black repatriation to, 90
   see also Ethiopia
"Abyssinian," rejection of term, 100
Abyssinian Baptist Church, 197
Abyssinianism, rise of, 91
Addis Ababa, conference at (1963), 171
Adebo, S. O., 172
Adefunmi, Ofuntola Oseijeman, 199-200
Aduwa, Ethiopia, Italian defeat at, 108
Africa
   Afro-American settlements in, 40
   Afro hairdo banned in, 195
   Agnew and, 5
   American Negro universities in, 212
   Black Americans in, 6, 169, 203
   colonization schemes for, 13
   Congo rebellion and, 187
   cosmopolitan atmosphere of, 157
   Du Bois rejection of migrations to, 71
   Empire of, 53-54

as "foreign country," 137-138
   history of, 6
   ideas about Americans in, 165
   Kenyatta and, 5, 77, 109, 157
   oppressive climate of, 71
   pride in, 9
   racism in, 157, 174, 213-214
   reasons for emigration to, 32
   transportation of slaves to, 13
   vs. United States as home for blacks, 5
   see also Afro-Americans; East Africa; South Africa; West Africa
Africa for the Africans (Booth), 39-40
African-American Repatriation Association, 10, 130-132
African-American Teachers Association, 189, 210
African ancestry, pride in, 6, 9, 56
African Colonial Enterprise, 41, 44
African Colonization Association, 45, 117
   see also Nationalist-Negro Movement
African dream, Turner and, 32
African fashions and clothing, 193
African Free School, 202

241